COMHAIRLE CHONTAE ÁTHA CLIATH THEAS
SOUTH DUBLIN COUNTY LIBRARIES

MOBILE LIBRARIES
TO RENEW ANY ITEM TEL: 459 7834

Items should be returned on or before the last date below. Fines,
as displayed in the Library, will be charged on overdue items.

The GAA

A History
Second Edition

The GAA

A History

Second Edition

MARCUS DE BÚRCA

Gill & Macmillan

Gill & Macmillan Ltd
Goldenbridge
Dublin 8
with associated companies throughout the world
www.gillmacmillan.ie
© Marcus de Búrca 1980, 1999
0 7171 2914 4

Index compiled by Helen Litton
Print origination by Carole Lynch
Printed by ColourBooks Ltd, Dublin

This book is typeset in Berkeley 10.5/12.

A CIP catalogue record for this book is available from the British Library.

1 3 5 4 2

Contents

PREFACE

In the early 1970s the GAA decided, as part of the advance preparations for its centenary in 1984, to commission a history of the Association. Its History Committee invited me to undertake the task, and in 1980 *The GAA: A History* was published in hard cover, with a paperback edition in 1981.

I am grateful to Gill & Macmillan for the opportunity to revise and update the earlier edition, and to include two specially written chapters covering the years 1980 to 1999. This second edition also contains both a new Index and a new Bibliography.

My original brief was to give an account of the GAA from its foundation, and to assess its role in the community over the past century, including in particular its influence on the national movement of the pre-1922 era. Because their inclusion would have unduly prolonged both the research and the text, some topics (such as Gaelic games overseas and the games of handball and camogie) received only marginal treatment.

My thanks are due to the Director General, Liam Ó Maolmhichíl, for permission to use his annual reports to Congress as the main source material of Chapters Nine and Ten, and to Fergal Tobin, publishing director of Gill & Macmillan, for his interest in this second edition, which brings the story of the GAA right to the edge of the Millennium.

Marcus de Búrca
September 1999

INTRODUCTION

This book is an attempt to record the revival 115 years ago of native Irish games and pastimes, and to trace the growth of the body responsible for that revival. It also tries to show the role of that body in the cultural and political events that led to the establishment in 1922 of an independent Irish State, and to assess the influence of that body on the life of the country since then. However, since hurling and football flourished on this island for centuries before the foundation of the GAA, this introduction attempts to sketch the historical and social background against which the rise of the GAA should be seen.

Ball games have been played by man from the earliest stages of civilised society. The Old Testament, the poet Homer and ancient Egyptian monuments all show that ball games were known in biblical times, in pre-Christian Greece and in pagan Egypt.[1] Imperial Rome, Arthurian England and Viking Scandinavia all had their own types of ball game.[2] So had the ancient Persians, the Indians, the Aztecs and the Celts.

The early Europeans played three kinds of ball games. In one, the ancestor of modern hurling and hockey, the ball was driven by a partly-curved stick. In another, the ancestor of soccer, the ball was propelled by foot only. In the third type, from which modern Gaelic football, rugby and Australian rules all derive, the ball was partly thrown by hand and partly kicked. A version of this last game, popular in these islands up to the mid-1800s, was played across the open countryside by hundreds of participants.

The national game of hurling has been a distinctively Irish pastime for at least two thousand years. The earliest references to it come from the very dawn of civilisation in this country.[3] Until the late 1840s hurling had been played all over this island from at least the early Christian period. As a sporting spectacle it has attracted the admiration of foreign visitors here for centuries. As the uniquely Celtic brand of the ball game played with sticks it has survived invasions, wars, internal strife, famine and numerous official and semi-official attempts at its suppression.

Hurling features widely in rural folklore — played by moonlight, by fairy folk, on the surface of lakes and even under their waters.[4] Much more real than any legend or folk-tale is the evidence supplied by the Brehon Laws of the place of hurling in the social life of pre-Christian Ireland.[5] These laws contained elaborate provisions for compensation to a person injured or killed by a hurley or hurling-ball. Widely known is the story of the visit to the Ulster royal palace paid by Cúchulainn, who died about AD 40.[6] On his way to Ulster he practised with his bronze hurley and silver ball; on reaching the palace grounds he found a hurling game in progress and joined in, outplaying the participants.

From the Norman invasion in the twelfth century attempts were made to persuade or force the Irish to shed their racial distinctiveness. The parliament sitting in Kilkenny in 1367, arguing that too much game-playing led to neglect of military service, prohibited 'the plays . . . men call horlings with great sticks upon the ground'.[7] Shortly after this Archbishop Colton of Armagh threatened excommunication for Catholics who played hurling, which led to 'mortal sins, beatings and . . . homicides'.[8] In 1527 the Statute of Galway ordered loyal subjects 'at no time to use . . . the hurling of the little ball with hockey sticks or staves'.[9]

None of these attempts to kill hurling succeeded. Instead, the invaders themselves eventually took to the game. A ballad published in 1789 describes a hurling match, probably played in the 1400s, in south Wexford by Welsh settlers close to where the Normans had first landed.[10] In this account can be found local forms of Irish sporting terms still used today — camán, cúil and báire. In the 1600s many Gaelic chieftains had their own teams of paid or hired hurlers.[11]

Recent research has shown the existence until modern times of two distinct styles or games of hurling.[12] Camánacht (or 'commoning' in English), played in the northern half of the island in winter-time with a slender stick and a hard ball, was a form of ground hurling in which the ball was not lifted into the hand. Hurling (or iománaíocht in Irish), confined largely to the modern province of Leinster and played only in summer-time, used a soft ball and a broad stick and allowed the ball to be lifted into the hand. Occasionally the summer game was played in a cross-country version (scuaibín in Munster); the winter game was confined to a restricted area such as a field.

By the time the GAA began 115 years ago winter hurling was practically extinct in Ireland, though it was still played in the Larne region and in parts of Derry by men of planter or Scots origin up to the end of the 1800s, and even into the present century. As shinty it still flourishes in Scotland. Although it is the summer or Leinster game that the GAA has taken over, the Association has in a sense managed to fuse both styles, ground hurling and the lift-and-strike style, each still being associated with different counties.

Both hurling and commoning on Sundays were banned by the Sunday Observance Act of 1695.[13] This law also proved ineffective; in the next 150 years accounts of or references to the game continue to occur. Hurling was played all through the eighteenth century in many places — Sligo and Roscommon (early 1700s),[14] Wexford (1720 and 1779),[15] Meath (1745 and 1790),[16] Dublin and Mayo (1756),[17] Tipperary (1750, 1768, 1776),[18] Kilkenny and Laois (1768),[19] Cork (1763, 1776, 1780),[20] Limerick (1776),[21] Waterford (1779),[22] Wicklow and Carlow (1780),[23] Louth (1790),[24] Galway (1791)[25] and Clare, Donegal, Down, Tyrone and Antrim (late 1700s).[26]

Particularly in those Munster and Leinster counties now regarded as producing the best players, hurling survived well into the first half of the nineteenth century. It is known to have been played then in Tipperary, Kerry, Limerick, Cork, Clare, Galway, Kilkenny, Dublin and Wicklow.[27] Like so much else in rural Ireland, however, the game was seriously disrupted by the famines of the 1840s.

Although much less widely recorded, football in various forms has been played in this island since the Middle Ages, though references to Irish football are practically non-existent before the 1600s. In Oxford in 1303 a student died while playing football with Irish students. In 1338 when the river Liffey froze hard the men of Dublin footballed on the ice, a feat their descendants repeated in 1740.[28]

Notwithstanding the banning in 1695 of Sunday football by the Sunday Observance Act (already mentioned), the seventeenth and eighteenth centuries provide several detailed accounts of Irish football. The English traveller John Dunton saw the footballers of Fingal (in north Dublin) in action.[29] The blind Louth poet Séamas Dall Mac Cuarta described a football match played near Slane in the late 1600s between teams from the districts bordering the rivers Boyne and Nanny.[30] A poem published in Dublin in 1722 tells of 'a match at foot-ball' played about 1720 at Oxmantown Green near Phoenix Park between teams from Swords and Lusk.[31] Omeath in Louth was the venue about 1750 of another football match recorded in poetry; the teams were of sixteen-a-side.[32]

Between 1758 and 1766 Dublin newspapers reported football games at Finglas, Milltown and Drumcondra.[33] Twenty years later the game was drawing crowds at New Ross, and in the 1790s it was popular in Kildare, but had declined in Laois.[34] In the 1780s football was discouraged among boys at Trinity College in Dublin. In Kildare in 1797 a magistrate was dismissed for accepting an invitation to start a football match.[35] Football flourished in many areas in the first forty years of the nineteenth century. Dublin, Wexford, Wicklow, Monaghan, Armagh and Louth are counties from where accounts of football matches have survived. In Kerry the cross-country version known as *caid* was then popular, as it continued to be all through the century.[36]

The famines of the late 1840s weakened the entire rural social system. Among the major casualties of the famines were the field games and other traditional pastimes of rural Ireland, which in many areas suffered an irreversible decline. Yet, while the forty-year period from the famines to the rise of the GAA probably saw them nearer than ever to extinction, native games did not die. Dublin Castle itself admitted that by the late 1850s hurling was being played all over Munster.[37] Other sources establish hurling in the 1860s and 1870s in Cork, Limerick, Kerry, Tipperary and even Dublin city.[38]

Michael Cusack, the founder of the GAA, saw hurling in Clare in the 1850s. In east Galway the game was still being played at the foundation of the GAA in 1884.[39] In Donegal and Down hurling survived the famines, and was also being played in Kilkenny and Longford in the years just before 1884.[40]

Much the same story can be told of Irish football in the period between the 1840s and 1884. In the early 1860s, according to evidence given at the Fenian State trials, football was being played regularly in Tipperary. Around the same time it was being widely played in Kerry,[41] and by the mid-1870s was being played all over Cork and in Limerick.[42]

Famine was not the only obstacle Irish games had to contend with in the nineteenth century. All over the country hurling and football were either discreetly discouraged or openly prohibited by government officials such as policemen and magistrates, as well as by some Catholic clergy and many landlords. The reasons given for such action varied from fear of violence and insobriety to suspicion of games being used as cover for meetings of various nationalist bodies.[43]

From the middle of the nineteenth century cricket began to rival Irish games in many areas. By the late 1860s nearly every town had its own cricket club, patronised by members of the local loyalist community — government officials, bank clerks, policemen — and supported by the local garrison. By the 1870s cricket had even spread to rural areas like north Tipperary and north Galway traditionally associated with hurling. This appalled Cusack when he came to assess the decadent state of Irish sport generally.

Taking all these adverse circumstances into account, it would have been surprising if nobody ever thought of forming a single body to control them. At least one person did. Denis Holland, a Cork journalist who edited the weekly nationalist paper *Irishman* from 1858 to 1867, advocated the revival of Irish games and the setting up of a network of parish clubs in 1858.[44] However, Holland emigrated to America and his idea was forgotten until the arrival in Dublin sixteen years later of Michael Cusack.

Chapter 1

1874–1884

To understand how and why the GAA was founded it is essential to know something of the personality of its founder, Michael Cusack. To Cusack must go all the credit for starting the GAA; without him there would have been no GAA, certainly not in the 1880s. He it was who supplied the inspiration and the driving force that led to its foundation. Although he and the other leaders of the GAA parted company after less than two years, Cusack's place in modern Irish history is secure and rests almost entirely on his role in founding the GAA.

Born of Irish-speaking parents in a humble cottage in the remote Burren area of Clare in 1847, Cusack became a national teacher. After teaching in various parts of Ireland he became in 1874 a professor in Blackrock College (then known as the French College) near Dublin.[1] Three years later he set up his own Civil Service Academy — Cusack's Academy it was called — near the centre of the city, and for ten years his pupils had a remarkable run of successes in public examinations, mainly for the civil service.[2] At the height of his career Cusack was reputed to have an income of £1,500 a year, an astonishingly high figure for that time.

From his writings a clear portrait of Cusack can be drawn. Immortalised as the citizen in Joyce's *Ulysses*, he became a colourful and often controversial figure in Dublin. A man of wide learning, he was a forceful and frequently intemperate speaker. Nevertheless, he was not long in Dublin before he had made a wide circle of acquaintances, embracing both nationalists and unionists. They included university professors, parliamentarians, prominent journalists, government officials and humble workingmen. Politically Cusack was an orthodox Home Ruler, although he sometimes gave the impression that he was an advanced nationalist of the physical force school. However, all his life his first allegiance was to Irish culture, rather than to political ideals. Like many other nationalists of his day, Cusack seems not to have fully thought out his political philosophy, regarding Ireland primarily as a cultural entity.

A man of boundless energy, Cusack gave what was practically individual tuition to his students, with the result that soon after its foundation Cusack's Academy became the most successful grinding establishment in the country — a remarkable achievement for a man who was unknown when he arrived in Dublin. Not content with directing their studies, Cusack also regularly encouraged his pupils to engage in physical exercise in their spare time, and frequently he joined them himself in athletic pursuits. As a young man Cusack had been a leading athlete in the provinces, but on his marriage had reluctantly given up athletics. Now in his mid-thirties he found himself back in the athletic arena, and drawn into the management and politics of athletics in Victorian Dublin, with results that were to be far-reaching for Irish sport.

Cusack's arrival in Dublin coincided roughly with the revival of amateur athletics in Ireland, which had begun in the mid-1860s in Dublin with the Civil Service and Dublin University clubs. It was from rural Ireland, however, and especially Munster, that the first real impetus came, with several consecutive seasons of sports meetings from 1868 onwards.[3] By the early 1870s hardly a summer or autumn weekend passed without meetings in every county in the South. At these informal events, usually patronised by the gentry, all classes and creeds mixed in an atmosphere hitherto unknown in nineteenth-century Ireland. To Cusack, however, it was also an anglicised atmosphere where the average nationalist rarely made his presence felt. It was a state of affairs that a man of Cusack's temperament could not be expected to tolerate indefinitely.

In Munster Tipperary and Clare soon produced some outstanding athletes.[4] In Connacht athletics quickly became popular in south Galway and north Mayo. In the north-east the North of Ireland Cricket Club (in Belfast) and the Lurgan Athletic Club were prominent; so was Dundalk Football Club. From the start too the universities of Cork and Galway sponsored athletics. In Cork city the Harbour Rowing Club was to the fore before the arrival of the progressive Cork Amateur Athletic Club. From the autumn of 1872, with the formation of the Dublin Amateur Athletic Club, the capital more than made up for its slow start in the revival of athletics that had begun in that city.

With the founding in 1873 of the Irish Champion Athletic Club came the first of several attempts to put athletics on an organised basis. The ICAC took a lease of the grounds beside Lansdowne Road railway station that later became the headquarters of the Irish Rugby Football Union, which itself grew out of the ICAC. Soon athletics were more popular in Dublin than anywhere else in Ireland. However, the rigid social conventions of the city, and the failure of nationalists there to assert themselves in the management of sports before the arrival of Cusack, between them ensured that athletics in Dublin remained the preserve of the well-to-do and of the small class of white-collar workers. Both groups were predominantly unionist in outlook.

Into this elite social atmosphere in the autumn of 1874 came Michael Cusack, who at different times in his life had been an athlete, hurler, footballer, handballer, cricketer and oarsman. From competing at sports meetings he soon moved to participation in the management of athletics in Dublin, both as club official and judge. Athletics now became for some years one of his main interests in life. For the sake of athletics he was prepared to modify strongly-held political views; for the sake of athletics too he was to give up a lucrative profession and to live precariously for the rest of his life.

The first public reference to Cusack is to his playing in a handball tournament organised late in 1874 by Trinity College rowing club. On his arrival in Blackrock College he took charge of the type of football (not yet rugby) then played there; with the students and other teachers he drew up rules for the game.[5] The following summer (1875) he competed for the first time in athletics in Dublin, winning the 16 lb and 42 lb shot events at a meeting sponsored by the Dublin Amateur Athletic Club.

For the next four or five years there is no record of Cusack's actually competing at sports meetings in Dublin. But in 1876 he held two teaching posts outside Dublin, which would have necessitated residence out of the city. Then for some time after October 1877, when he opened his own academy, he would have had little time for athletics. In addition, he was now devoting much of his spare time to advancing the cause of the Irish language. However, he continued to attend meetings regularly, acting as judge. He also accepted an invitation to a seat on the council of the ICAC.[6] By 1878 or so Cusack had become a familiar and respected figure at Dublin sports-grounds with his rotund broad-shouldered profile, his bushy black beard, open frock coat, broad-rimmed hat and blackthorn stick.

However, by late 1879 Cusack had become disillusioned with Dublin athletics. Standards had fallen and abuses had crept in. A riot at Trinity races in 1878 had led to this important meeting's suspension for two years. Money prizes were being commonly given to amateurs; betting was being widely tolerated; handicaps were being framed to favour popular athletes, to the discouragement of younger men. Much of the adult male population, including manual workers, policemen and soldiers, was debarred from competing simply because its members were not 'gentlemen amateurs'. Traditional events involving weights and jumping were often omitted from programmes in favour of ordinary running races, which urban athletes had a better chance of winning.

In these circumstances Cusack decided to change his pupils to football. Irish football was then hardly known in Dublin, and soccer had only begun to spread southwards from Belfast. So Cusack turned to rugby, a logical decision in view of the close links between the ICAC, of which he was now a leading member, and the recently established rugby association. For two seasons from October 1879 Cusack's Academy XV played in Dublin rugby competitions, with the future founder of the GAA as one of its best forwards.[7]

Around this time Cusack, increasingly concerned at both the falling standards and the growth in professionalism, began to campaign for a revival of what he called pure athletics. In correspondence and discussions he argued trenchantly for the restoration to programmes of weight and jumping events, the lifting of the class barrier preventing the man-in-the-street from taking part in sports and the achievement of unity in the management of Irish athletics. For inspiring this last part of Cusack's campaign, which was to lead eventually to the foundation of the GAA, P. W. Nally seems to have been largely responsible.

Pat Nally of Balla in Mayo, the eldest son of a prosperous farmer of advanced nationalist views, was born in 1857 and had been a Fenian from boyhood. By the late 1870s he was a leading organiser of the Irish Republican Brotherhood, the Fenian body; by 1880 he was on its supreme council. At the foundation meeting in August 1879 of the Land League of Mayo (precursor of the Land League) he was elected a joint secretary.[8] From 1876 onwards Nally was also one of the country's most promising athletes, becoming probably the most successful competitor outside Dublin. The most talented of six brothers, he often competed at every event at a meeting.

To Nally, as to many nationalists and unionists at the time, politics and sports were inseparable. For some years Fenianism and the cause of the small tenant-farmer had been closely allied in Connacht; hence Nally had become a bitter opponent of landlordism, the class then patronising rural athletics. It was natural for him to advocate that, instead of remaining under landlord control, athletics should be organised by nationalists. In November 1877 Nally had supported an attempt to set up an Irish National Athletics Committee. His ideas were identical with Cusack's; so when the two met in 1879 it was athletics, rather than Irish games, that they discussed.

Twenty years later when Nally was dead Cusack recalled how they had strolled through the Phoenix Park in Dublin, to find only a handful of people engaged in sport in this fine park. The sight so depressed Nally and Cusack that they agreed it was time to 'make an effort to preserve the physical strength of our race'.[9] Nally went home to Mayo, where in September he organised the first National Athletic Sports of Mayo, held on his father's estate, under the patronage of Parnell and a local Home Rule MP, a novel idea at the time. The event was repeated in October 1880.

In April 1880 Cusack organised a similar event in Dublin, the National Athletic Meeting, to which 'artisans' were invited, and in May 1881 he held his own Cusack's Academy sports in the Phoenix Park. That summer too Cusack, now almost thirty-four, made a remarkable come-back to athletics. At the championship meeting in Dublin in July he became the Irish champion weight-thrower. By then Nally, wanted by the police for his political activities, was living under an assumed name among Irish emigrants in England.

Over a six-month period in 1881 Cusack contributed anonymously three articles to the *Irish Sportsman*, then the leading Irish sporting publication, which (in spite of a predominantly unionist bias) had shown some leanings towards what it called Home Rule in Irish athletics. These articles illustrate the development of Cusack's ideas on athletic unity, and explain his dissatisfaction at the existing situation. The articles reveal a moderate and balanced view of the need for a controlling body for athletics in this country. They underline Cusack's insistence on the inclusion of nationalists in any such body if it was to be genuinely representative of all Irish athletes.

In his first article Cusack deplored the recent decline in what he called the athletic spirit, arguing that if this should continue it would lead to a fall in the standard of public morals. He called for the creation of a public opinion favourable to athletics, and for the subsequent formation of clubs in every town and village to organise regular local meetings. He suggested that the athletic year should always start with a big national meeting, and pleaded for the restoration to programmes of the traditional tests of jumping and weight-throwing. The tone generally was mild and conciliatory, in comparison with what followed a few months later.

The second article expanded on a point briefly mentioned in the first. In a country like ours, where political differences were fundamental, sport (Cusack pointed out) could be a bond of unity in the community. As one of those 'trying to keep the platform of sport clear of the party spirit', he was saddened to observe that whenever a new political crisis broke sport suffered. In England, he pointed out, 'the lord of the manor, the middle man, the mechanic and the artisan are all Englishmen in sport'.

The third article bluntly pointed out what Cusack felt was wrong with Irish athletics and how he thought it should be remedied. Those now controlling sports must appreciate that the events of the previous two years heralded a new social revolution in Ireland; Gaelic democracy was pushing against the doors of Dublin Castle. Outside of Ulster the ruling class in Ireland were not the proper people to organise sports. They must 'make room for a strip of green across their colours and their ground'.

The year 1882 was to prove particularly rewarding for Cusack. In his work for the Irish language he achieved a major success with the publication in November of the bilingual *Gaelic Journal*, sponsored by the Gaelic Union for the Preservation and Cultivation of the Irish Language, of which he was treasurer. This modest magazine, a founder of the Gaelic League asserted years later, marked the real start of the language revival movement.[10] In athletics 1882 was memorable for Cusack because he was one of the founders of the Dublin Athletic Club, which opened its competitions to artisans and that summer held the first open sports meeting in Ireland.[11]

The most significant achievement by Cusack in 1882 was the foundation in December of the Dublin Hurling Club, the direct successor of which, the Metropolitan Hurling Club, was the seed out of which the GAA grew in 1884. Why he suddenly switched his efforts from athletics to hurling is not difficult to guess. Ireland's national game had not been seen in Dublin for over fifty years; what was being played there for some years before Cusack's arrival was a genteel or debased form known as hurley, which later became the Irish version of hockey. Confined largely to the Protestant colleges and rugby clubs, hurley had originated in Trinity College, where the University Hurley Club had drawn up rules as early as 1870.[12] After a lapse of four years the Trinity club (one of whose members was Edward Carson) was revived in 1877. This led in December 1881 to the Dublin Hurley Union, and early in 1882 to the Irish Hurley Union.

A glance at the 1877 rules of hurley shows why Cusack would not have thought much of this version of the robust game he had seen played in his native Clare thirty years before. Kicking the ball, 'swiping' (not defined) and pushing an opponent were all forbidden; only the goalkeeper and 'the half-back' were permitted to puck the ball. The goalkeeper could save and clear without hindrance; 'crooking' an opponent's stick was 'discountenanced as being dangerous'; the stick could only be touched if he were off-side.[13] Clearly hurley was much closer to hockey (then gaining popularity in England) than to the ancient Irish game. Already an attempt had been made to bring the rules of hurley closer to those of English hockey, with a view to arranging matches with English hockey clubs — precisely the sort of subservient attitude that would have incensed Cusack.

In these circumstances Cusack decided 'to take steps to re-establish the national game of hurling', lest hurley should be passed off as the genuine article. In an effort to keep politics out of sport he obtained the co-operation of some prominent hurley players, so that the attendance at the foundation meeting of the DHC was evenly balanced between nationalists and unionists. At Cusack's suggestion the chair was taken by Dr. H. A. Auchinleck of the College of Surgeons, in whose lecture-room the meeting was held; F. A. Potterton of the Omega Hurley Club was appointed secretary. A committee directed to draft rules and to arrange the transition from hurley to hurling included Auchinleck, Potterton and Cusack. They were instructed to make the transition from hurley to hurling 'as easy as the superiority of the latter game permits', and it was agreed that the DHC should not be 'antagonistic to any outdoor sports and athletics already in existence'.[14]

After some weeks' delay because nobody in Dublin knew how to make either hurleys or balls, Saturday afternoon practice began in the Phoenix Park. The polo authorities loaned their ground and the Board of Works provided a shed for dressing-rooms.[15] The venture was not, however, a success. Although some well-known hurley players managed to play both games through the spring of 1883, most hurley players were opposed to what they regarded as an attempt to kill their game; the hurlers for their part became increasingly hostile to hurley.[16] Perhaps the tense political atmosphere did not help either; 1882 had been the year of the Phoenix Park assassinations and of the subsequent trials and executions.

In the summer of 1883, when it must have become apparent to him that the DHC would not resume in the autumn when the athletic season ended, Cusack decided in effect to combine his two campaigns for the reorganisation of athletics on a democratic basis and for the revival of hurling. To this end he attended many rural sports meetings, especially in Munster, where he argued the case for Home Rule in athletics and for the inclusion of hurling in any new scheme. At the annual Cork city sports in May Cusack was involved in a scene on the track over the weight-throwing event. More significant than the episode itself is the fact that in the subsequent press controversy he implicitly admitted an allegation by a leading Cork official that Cusack had come to Cork solely 'on the Gaelic mission'. At the same time he used his position as editor of an educational column in the weekly Home Rule magazine *Shamrock* to appeal to the young readers to help revive hurling and to take part in athletics.[17]

Late in September 1883 Cusack resumed practice at the Phoenix Park polo ground, where six months earlier the shortlived DHC had played. With him on the first Saturday were four of his own pupils; two spectators joined in the play.[18] Each week the group grew in size; each Saturday more spectators joined in. This time too, with no hurley-players to appease, the game played was the full-blooded hurling played in Clare in Cusack's boyhood — hurling, to quote Cusack himself, 'in all its glorious simplicity and freedom from restraining rules'. Soon the outsiders joining Cusack included some experienced hurlers from hurling areas; he then realised he had sufficient to form two teams. In October he formed Cusack's Academy Hurling Club;[19] then in December at a meeting in his school in Gardiner Place he founded the Metropolitan Hurling Club.[20]

The rise of the Metropolitans encouraged Cusack to consider the possibility of a revival of hurling on a countrywide scale, and directed his attention to both the need for rural support and the necessity for an organisation that included rural Ireland. Soon there was a promising move that must have delighted him. From south Galway, where hurling was widely played, there came early in 1884 an invitation to the Metropolitans from Killimor club to a game on the fair-green in Ballinasloe on Easter Monday, the winners to get a silver cup donated by two local businessmen.

Augmented by several of Cusack's hurlers (including himself), the Dublin team arrived by train to find a large and boisterous crowd. The event was only a quali-fied success.[21] Soon after the start of the game spectators encroached on the pitch and, although play was resumed, it became impossible to clear the field fully.

Instead, in the spaces cleared of spectators impromptu athletic contests were held. Since it was probably the clash of styles and of interpretation of rules that caused the local crowd's exuberance, this incident must have impressed on Cusack the need to standardise rules of play.

Once again (as in the previous summer) the opening of the 1884 athletics season found Cusack attending many rural meetings, mostly in Munster, seeking support for his ideas. He was now convinced that a body such as he planned was more urgent than ever, because in many places officials were accepting only entries from athletes recognising the Amateur Athletic Association (of England) as the governing body for Irish sport. Yet he must have been encouraged by evidence of growing support for him now appearing in various parts of the country, particularly areas like south Galway and north Cork where hurling had survived.[22]

Possibly because of the strength of his opponents in Dublin, Cusack considered basing his proposed body elsewhere. His first choice was Cork; but soon he abandoned it in favour of Loughrea, a town in the centre of the Galway hurling area. In or near it lived others as anxious as he to revive Irish games, among them John Sweeney, local Land League leader, Willie Duffy, later a Home Rule MP, and Peter Kelly and John McCarthy, local IRB leaders, all associates of the absent P. W. Nally. There too lived Bishop Duggan of Clonfert, friend of the advanced nationalists, a hurler and notable athlete in his youth.[23] Cusack probably realised how useful clerical patronage would be for a venture such as he was planning.

At a meeting in Loughrea in August 1884 Cusack outlined his plans to the local men; it was decided to approach Bishop Duggan for support.[24] The bishop, now seventy-one, declined because of ill-health. But he was strongly in favour of Cusack's plans and advised an approach to Archbishop Croke in Thurles, who (he pointed out) was a younger man and also a supporter of Irish culture. Curiously, Cusack made no approach to Croke until after the GAA was founded, although it seems likely that the two were known to each other.

The only apparent result of the Loughrea meeting was to start Cusack thinking of Cork again. This renewed preference for Cork was to last nearly to the end of October, just before the invitations to the foundation meeting were posted. Early in October Cusack was arguing for 'the formation of a society for the preservation and cultivation of our national pastimes . . . based in Cork, because most of our champion athletes are from Munster'.[25] Another source close to a founder of the GAA has suggested that a name had been decided on — the Munster Athletic Club.[26] Probably geographical convenience was the determining factor that prompted the choice of Thurles as the site for the first meeting of the new body.

In an effort to reach a wider audience Cusack had in the early summer of 1884 approached the nationalist press for support. With two of the most widely read papers, the Home Rule organ *United Ireland* edited by William O'Brien MP, and the more extreme *Irishman*, edited by Richard Pigott (the future forger of the so-called Parnell Letters) he was successful. As a result for several months Cusack anonymously argued his case and surveyed the Irish athletic scene from these influential platforms. It was through the medium of these two papers that events moved to a climax in October 1884, after Maurice Davin had publicly declared his support for Cusack's plans.

Davin, whose name was soon to be linked for ever with those of Cusack and Croke through the GAA, was one of three Tipperary brothers who had dominated Irish athletics for over a decade.[27] He possessed two attributes decisive in the formative period of the new body which Cusack lacked. Through a series of major victories over leading British athletes in the 1870s he had achieved international fame, and as a moderate nationalist he would be acceptable to all shades of opinion.

Recently retired from athletics to manage the family farm, Davin, now forty-two, had supported earlier attempts to form a governing body for athletics. Like Cusack and Nally he was an all-rounder, his interests extending to rowing, boxing and even coursing.[28] He had taken no part in Cusack's recent controversies, having been out of athletics since 1883 because of his mother's death.[29] By openly supporting Cusack he was about to bring his immense personal prestige to the aid of the new organisation.

On 11 October 1884 both *United Ireland* and the *Irishman* carried identical articles headed 'A Word on Irish Athletics'. Clearly from Cusack's pen,[30] they succinctly put the case once again for a body such as that formed in Thurles a few weeks later. No movement aiming at the social and political development of a nation was complete, he wrote, unless it also provided for the cultivation and preservation of the nation's games. Because the recent athletic revival was sponsored by people of anti-Irish outlook, the ordinary citizen was largely excluded from sport. Yet, although the management of sport was in non-national hands, most of the best athletes were nationalists; they should now take control of their own affairs.

The next issue of both papers contained a letter from Davin closely associating himself with the views in this article.[31] Irish football and hurling deserved public support, and he would support any move to revive both games under new rules. A week later again Cusack in a signed letter announced that a meeting would be held in Thurles on 1 November. Finally in another letter to both papers on 1 November, Cusack announced that Davin and himself had issued invitations to all interested to meet that afternoon in Miss Hayes's Commercial Hotel, Thurles. This circular had been drafted in Dublin by Cusack in consultation with a group of associates there.[32]

At three o'clock on Saturday afternoon, 1 November 1884 Cusack opened the meeting in the hotel billiard room. Probably not more than thirteen people, and possibly only seven, were present. The accepted number of founder-members is seven. Soon afterwards Cusack put the number at a dozen; twice later, in uncontradicted statements made publicly when all concerned were still alive, he changed to nine.[33] In addition to the seven accepted founders — Cusack, Davin, John Wyse Power, John McKay, J. K. Bracken, Joseph O'Ryan and Thomas St George McCarthy — the following were reported in reliable papers as having attended: William Foley of Carrick-on-Suir, T. K. Dwyer, C. Culhane, William Delahunty, John Butler and M. Cantwell, all of Thurles itself.[34] The absence of anybody from Galway is surprising; but illness prevented John Sweeney of Loughrea from travelling.[35]

The proceedings were brief. Davin took the chair and Cusack read the convening letter. Davin in a short statement pointed out the incongruity of Irishmen permitting Englishmen to organise Irish sport, emphasised that this had led to the decline of native pastimes and called for a body to draft rules to aid in their revival and to open athletics to the poor. Cusack followed with a longer speech, censuring the press for not reporting Irish sport and reading sixty messages of support; McKay also spoke. On the proposal of Cusack with Wyse Power seconding, Davin was then elected president of what was initially called the Gaelic Athletic Association for the Preservation and Cultivation of National Pastimes; Cusack, Wyse Power and McKay were elected secretaries. After agreeing to ask Archbishop Croke, Charles Stewart Parnell and Michael Davitt (the founder of the Land League) to become patrons, the meeting adjourned.[36] In many respects it was an unpromising, even a shaky, start; neither date nor venue for a further meeting was fixed.

Chapter 2

1884–1888

'The Association swept the country like a prairie fire', wrote Cusack years later regarding the first two years of the GAA.[1] He did not exaggerate. Few movements in modern Ireland have taken root so rapidly and so firmly as the GAA. Inside a few months the nationalist community everywhere except in Ulster had answered the call that went out from the first few meetings of the new body. In the North too some areas, including Derry city and Cavan county, Monaghan and Belfast, were in the vanguard of the GAA. All over the country, but especially in Munster, adjoining areas of Leinster, the midlands and the Dublin region, influential nationalists (and in a few cases even some unionists) got together to organise athletics meetings or to form hurling or football clubs.

The Association was only ten days old when on 11 November 1884 the first GAA athletics meeting was held near Macroom in Cork.[2] From the start the Dublin Metropolitans regarded themselves as affiliated; Clara in Offaly, which joined in mid-December, seems to have been the first club outside Dublin.[3] The year 1885 was only six days old when a hurling match under GAA rules was played in Tynagh in Galway between two local parishes before 6,000 spectators.[4] Five days later a GAA sports meeting was held in Tulla in Clare, and in mid-February the first football game under GAA rules was played at Callan between two Kilkenny teams.[5] A week earlier Belfast had seen its first-ever hurling match; early in March Wallsend near Newcastle-on-Tyne became the first GAA club in Britain. So it continued until the late autumn of 1885, with hurling, football, but mostly athletics, contests being held in towns and villages all over Munster and Leinster, the greatest activity of all being in the Dublin area.

Many supporters of the Association today will be surprised to learn that for the first few years of its life the GAA was much more concerned with athletics than with games. To Cusack the need for nationalists to control Irish athletics and the desire to open athletics to every social class were at this stage more important than the revival of hurling and Irish football. Until 1887 or so hurling and football games were usually subsidiary events at athletics meetings; often they did not figure on the programme at all. Similarly handball, neglected by the GAA for many decades, although revived in many places and known to be the favourite game of Archbishop Croke, was crowded out by athletics.

This early emphasis on athletics goes far in explaining the initial success of the GAA in 1885 and 1886. Although hurling and football rules were adopted early in 1885, in practice athletic contests were less likely to give rise to differences in styles. For sports meetings all that was needed in addition was efficient advance preparation; this the tireless Cusack always provided or ensured. Sometimes he arrived himself beforehand to supervise the work of organisation for the last few days; often all the management was done locally, with the Home Rule machine co-operating with what many of its officials regarded as a promising new recruit to the nationalist movement. The leading role played by Davin at this stage also goes far in accounting for the strong athletics bias of the infant GAA. For a man who, one suspects, Cusack had intended would play a passive role in the Association, Davin must have surprised many of his associates by his energy and enthusiasm in 1885 and 1886.

The GAA's first big sports meeting was held in Clonmel near Davin's native area late in February 1885.[6] It was followed three months later by another meeting in Blarney, and a month later again by one in Cork city on 3 June. A fortnight later Tralee was the venue of a still bigger meeting, which drew a crowd of between 15,000 and 20,000 and gave a vital impetus to the new Association in that part of Munster. In mid-July New Ross held a successful sports meeting; in October 1885 Tramore was the venue for the first GAA national athletic championships. At all of these, as well as at hundreds of smaller meetings, the standards were remarkably high, particularly considering that many of the competitors were previously unknown to the public. They had either been barred on social grounds from competing under pre-GAA rules or had deliberately refrained from competing at meetings controlled by the non-nationalist community.

In striking comparison with all these athletics meetings is the almost complete absence in the Association's first full year of hurling or football games at anything above a local or parish level. This is not to underestimate the importance of these local matches. Had the GAA not been founded, most of them would never have been played.

The hurling and Irish football being played before 1885 was mostly on an unorganised basis, hampered by the lack of influential encouragement and authoritative rules. The arrival of the GAA had a rejuvenating effect in many areas. It encouraged existing clubs and led to new clubs, adding to the competitive element. Players in places like south Galway, Cork city and north Tipperary, previously playing games in isolation, now knew that the new body would mean the spread of the game and the end of their isolation. The rapid growth of the GAA also brought to a halt the spread of cricket in rural areas where the game had gained a foothold.

Not until 1886 were games between clubs in different counties, or between teams drawn from clubs in different counties, first played on any scale. In February of that year Cusack refereed a hurling match in Dublin between south Galway and north Tipperary, the first hurling match between county teams seen in the capital for at least seventy-four years. Two months later on Easter Sunday, Thurles and Athlone were the venues for more inter-county tournaments in both hurling and football, each attracting many thousands. Kilkenny, Dublin and Cork city all held inter-county tournaments in both codes later that summer, with smaller contests between clubs from different counties taking place at Birdhill and Portumna, as well as in the Dublin region between clubs from the city and various parts of Wicklow. However, by the time the Association was two years old in November 1886 the number of major inter-county matches played was still only about a half-dozen.

'The Association', commented one of its abler early officials, 'began with an éclat and enthusiasm unique in athletic annals'.[7] Its initial growth and success were a complete vindication of Cusack for his three-year campaign culminating in the Thurles meeting of November 1884. From his intimate knowledge of rural Ireland in the 1880s he had sensed that conditions were just right for a popularly-run body catering for athletics and national games for the nationalist community. The country-wide revival of athletics, hurling and Irish football in 1885 and 1886 proved him dramatically right, as nationalist Ireland in both town and country flocked to the newly-unfurled banner of the GAA.

Apart from Davin's role in October 1884, there is no evidence that any of the other founders (apart from Cusack) played an active part in starting the GAA. J. K. Bracken, a Tipperary stonemason and father of the future British politician Viscount Bracken, had apparently been active in local athletics for some years. However, like John Wyse Power, a Waterford journalist then on the *Leinster Leader* in Naas, Bracken was a Fenian; both probably came to ensure an IRB foothold in the new body. Of John McKay, a Belfast journalist then on the *Cork Examiner*, it seems likely that it was also athletics that drew him into the GAA. Joseph O'Ryan, a Tipperary solicitor, later emigrated to the United States.[8] The remaining founder, McCarthy, a Kerryman then in the RIC, almost certainly attended because he had been a pupil of Cusack. Like O'Ryan he never came near the GAA again — except as a spectator at Croke Park in his old age, when unknown to everybody in the GAA he achieved the distinction of being the only founder alive at its golden jubilee in 1934.[9]

'In less than two years', wrote Cusack later, 'Ireland south of a line from Dundalk to Sligo was overwhelmingly Gaelic'.[10] Indeed, in rural Ireland the found-ing of the GAA caused something approaching a social revolution. Many sports meetings were held in places that had not seen such contests for half-a-century; they drew crowds of sizes that had not been seen since O'Connell's repeal meetings of the 1840s. In conjunction with many of these meetings hurling and (to a lesser extent initially) football games were organised, mostly in places where one or both games had survived the Famine. As a result hurling was saved from almost certain extinction. Its position where it was still played was greatly strengthened, and often a revival of the game in adjoining areas occurred.

Looked at against the social conditions in rural Ireland at that time, the achievement of Cusack and the other early GAA officials was remarkable. Apart from the railways, which were admittedly fully availed of by these early GAA players (but not yet by spectators), travel in the 1880s was still slow and in many cases almost primitive. Roads were poor, and such modern facilities as dressing-rooms and other now accepted pavilion conveniences almost unknown. Above all, the long working-day of the small farmer, the shop assistant and farm labourer — the occupations from which most early GAA players came — not only ruled out practice in advance of games or sports meetings, but also taxed the physical endurance of athlete and player alike.

Another now forgotten achievement of the early GAA was the extent of unionist and Protestant support it got. Cusack later acknowledged the assistance he got in founding the Association from colleagues in the Gaelic Union, some of them Protestants or unionists or both; they included Douglas Hyde and Rev. Maxwell Close.[11] Among the leading members of the Metropolitan club, the backbone of the early GAA in Dublin, were several Ulster Protestants, including Rev. Samuel Holmes of Down, L. C. Slevin of Armagh, Trueman Cross of Tyrone and the brothers Frank and Robert Patterson of Newry.[12] Several of the Dublin clubs in 1885 contained Protestants or unionists, all of whom were to leave in 1887 when the Association acquired an extreme nationalist character. Another fact to Cusack's credit often overlooked is that in point of time the modern Gaelic cultural revival, which led ultimately to the rise of Sinn Féin, began with the GAA. The Association was nine years old when the Gaelic League was founded in 1893.

Within seven weeks of the Thurles meeting Archbishop Croke of Cashel, who resided in Thurles and was then a leading nationalist member of the Catholic hierarchy, gave the GAA his unqualified approval. A long letter of 18 December 1884, accepting Cusack's offer to become the Association's first patron, put the case for the revival of Irish pastimes so forcibly that it has ever since been justifiably regarded as the *de facto* charter of the GAA.[13] From London and Dublin too about the same time came shorter, but equally approving, letters from the two other original patrons of the Association, Charles Stewart Parnell, the Home Rule leader, and Michael Davitt, the founder of the Land League.[14] With such influential backing from both cleric and layman, the support of nationalist Ireland was assured from the start — which was just as well, since Cusack soon found the future of his new organisation seriously threatened.

❖

For some ten years after its foundation the GAA, despite its initial impact and some later successes in that period, had to struggle to remain alive, its existence threatened intermittently either by internal dissension or by external opponents. From the start Cusack encountered apathy and lack of support from people on whom he had reason to depend. In spite of his own public statements, one may surmise from his switching from Cork to south Galway and back again to Cork in 1884 that his plans had not met with unqualified support. Even allowing for the remoteness of the venue for many, the attendance at the Thurles meeting must have disappointed Cusack. Some of those present, particularly O'Ryan and McCarthy, had no commitment to native games. Between 1 November and 27 December, the date of the second meeting (arranged for Cork) an organised but unsuccessful attempt was made by athletics officials in that city to kill the GAA.[15] Around this time too one of the founders, Wyse Power, took such a gloomy view of the GAA's survival prospects that Cusack had difficulty in dissuading him from backing out altogether.[16]

A much more serious threat to the continued existence of the GAA came in the form of a series of determined assaults on it during the first half of 1885 by a vocal group of anti-nationalist athletics officials based in Dublin. To a large extent this group, the counterpart of one in Cork which had tried to sabotage the December 1884 meeting, consisted of leading members of the rugby section of the now defunct Irish Champion Athletic Club, with whom Cusack had broken four years earlier. Apparently annoyed to find that his new body now looked like succeeding, they first concentrated their attacks on Cusack himself. At a series of meetings in Dublin in the spring of 1885 a self-appointed committee, representing existing clubs controlled by non-nationalists, declared its intention first of 'quashing the Gaelic Union', then of refusing recognition to the GAA and finally of denying Cusack's right to speak for the athletes of Ireland.

However, the athletes of Ireland, especially (but not exclusively) those in rural areas and of nationalist outlook, showed in greater numbers every month that they were happy to allow the GAA not only to speak for them but also to manage their contests. Cusack's opponents then found that they had to fall back on the allegation that the new body was a political organisation rather than a sports body, raising an issue that has often been a live one in the history of the GAA. The relationship between sports and politics has become the subject of much controversy again in recent years, and it is at least arguable that the belief that the two could be, or ought to be, kept apart was an illusion of the Victorian era, from which so untypical a Victorian as Cusack at times suffered. Given the circumstances of the foundation of the GAA, it was inevitable that this allegation should have been made; the struggle for legislative independence had become so intense that it was almost impossible to keep politics out of any but the most insignificant movement.

So far as Cusack was concerned, his opponents' allegation in 1885 that the GAA was begun as a political organisation simply did not stand up. At the foundation meeting he emphasised that no politicians had received invitations and that William O'Brien had advised him not to make the movement 'political' in any sense. On several occasions, including one when under oath in court, Cusack asserted that his dual object in starting the GAA was to open athletics to the ordinary citizen and to halt and reverse the decline in Irish games.[17] While frankly admitting that 'every social movement in Ireland is to a certain extent necessarily political', he swore that the GAA was 'not in any way connected with politics'. This view was strongly supported by his joint Secretary McKay, who once told a hostile audience in Dublin that the GAA 'was not begun on political lines'. According to Michael Davitt, the only one of the original patrons consulted in advance about the foundation of the GAA by Cusack, 'the idea was national, not political'.[18]

It is clear from his writings that Cusack envisaged all along that in sporting activities the GAA would cross political and sectarian boundaries, as the Gaelic Union had already done in its work for the Irish language.[19] Since his arrival in Dublin ten years earlier he had striven, in the face of bigoted opposition, to co-operate with well-disposed non-nationalists in his work for both athletics and the language. His non-partisan approach had, however, met with only limited success. As the idea of the GAA gradually took shape in his mind in 1883 and 1884 he sought advice from associates in the Gaelic Union, including in particular Douglas Hyde and Rev. Maxwell Close, the one a moderate nationalist and the other a con-firmed unionist.

At the same time Cusack also prudently canvassed the support of several prominent Home Rule leaders of his acquaintance, principally Davitt, O'Brien, Justin McCarthy MP and Tim Harrington MP. McCarthy, although he had publicly encouraged Irish games, never did anything to help Cusack or the GAA.[20] As for Harrington, he became a critic of the Association within a short time of its foun-dation. O'Brien on the other hand gave Cusack a valuable column in the influential weekly Home Rule organ United Ireland, until he and Cusack parted company in mid-1886. Davitt, although pessimistic at the start about the GAA's prospects, a few years later gave a vital loan to the Association and also publicised its activities in a socialist paper he edited from London.[21]

Unfortunately for Cusack, a tactical blunder was made shortly after the foun-dation of the GAA which supported the argument that the Association had political undertones. The second meeting, held in Cork in December 1884, was attended by a local group which consisted largely of prominent Home Rulers, including the

Lord Mayor-elect (Alderman Paul Madden) and some other members of Cork Corporation, among them 'Long' John O'Connor, later a leading Irish figure at Westminster. This group was instrumental in having a resolution adopted drafting on to the GAA executive committee two nominees of every athletic club in Ireland and the entire organising committee of the National League.[22] Happily this decision, which would have brought in nominees from clubs like Dundalk Football Club which had refused the Thurles invitation, was never acted on. Some months later the National League officially denied the existence of any formal link between it and the GAA.[23]

Although it ought to have been clear to them that once influential nationalists supported Cusack in large numbers their campaign to kill the GAA was doomed, his opponents continued it into the summer of 1885. In the early months of that year it caused much bitterness on both sides. Almost weekly Cusack replied in abusive terms in *United Ireland* to the latest attack on him in the *Irish Sportsman* by former associates; he was successful in a libel action he brought in the High Court against that paper's editor.[24] Characteristically, he also brought the attack into the enemy camp when on several occasions he attended meetings of his opponents; once even the usually mild Davin accompanied him, gallantly supporting every noisy interruption by Cusack. Probably the most lasting effect of this controversy was the foundation in the spring of 1885 of the Irish Amateur Athletic Association, which until its dissolution nearly forty years later remained non-nationalist in membership and outlook.

Meanwhile in Munster, then a decisive area in any contest for control of Irish athletics, Cusack taught his critics a lesson in consistency by his handling of the Tralee sports of mid-June 1885. In a challenge to the anti-GAA lobby in an area where there was considerable co-operation between nationalists and unionists in sports, he fixed the GAA sports for the same date as those of the County Kerry Amateur Athletic and Cricket Club. Arriving some days in advance, he pushed ahead with his plans even after learning that his rivals had the backing of the local National League branch led by Edward Harrington (brother of Tim) of the Irish Party. Cusack promptly enlisted local Catholic clerical support, and on the day of the rival meetings over ten thousand people packed the GAA field while the Kerry AACC venue was almost deserted.

For Cusack the Tralee episode was much more than a local victory; he regarded it as the turning-point in the GAA's first struggle to stay alive. Not only did it pre-vent the IAAA from gaining a foothold in the South; it also convinced his opponents in Dublin that the GAA was not intended by Cusack to have political undertones.[25] One suspects too that on Cusack himself the bitterness of his clash in Tralee with the National League had the effect of souring his relations with the Home Rule leaders, especially Tim Harrington, who issued a blunt statement on behalf of the

League denying any link between Cusack's movement and the party machine.[26] From about this time one may date the beginning of Cusack's apparent subsequent disillusionment with the parliamentary movement, and by the end of his life he had become a Sinn Féin supporter.

On the playing-field and in the athletic arena the GAA continued to make steady progress in both 1886 and 1887, when its achievements were hardly less spectacular than in 1885. Two months after the big hurling game in Dublin in February 1886 a six-team hurling tournament between Dublin and Tipperary clubs was held in Thurles. On the same day Athlone was the venue for another hurling tournament between teams from Connacht and Leinster; a month later a six-team football tournament took place in Kilkenny between teams from Kilkenny, Waterford, Dublin and Tipperary. On Whit Monday Dublin saw the biggest GAA event (a hurling, football and athletics tournament) so far; in September the GAA athletic championships were held in the city's RDS grounds. Cork city had a hurling and football tournament between ten clubs from Cork and Tipperary in August. At least forty-four major sports meetings were held in three provinces in 1886, two-thirds of them in Munster and nearly all the others in one of the eastern counties of Leinster.

Although this was not appreciated at the time, of much greater significance for the future growth of the GAA was the inauguration in 1887 of inter-county championship competitions in both hurling and football. Twelve counties entered, six from Leinster, five from Munster, and Galway; but for different reasons — inability to field teams, local dissensions in particular counties or refusal to agree to venues — only nine counties took part in football and only five in hurling. The hurling championship ultimately consisted of only four matches, in three of which Tipperary figured; in football Limerick played in four of the seven games. Neither final was played until April, 1888, when Tipperary (the Thurles club) became the first All-Ireland football champions.

In the number of successful sports meetings held and games played 1887 was not far behind 1886. In many places that had seen major events in 1886 new clubs appeared; Dublin now boasted almost forty, many based on suburbs or villages, each with its own group of supporters. In February Kilkenny city had its first hurling game for twenty years; three months later Nenagh staged a four-county athletic contest. In Thurles and Dublin the Easter and Whit tournaments of 1886 were successfully repeated, the Thurles event drawing 25,000 spectators.[27] Among major new events in 1887 were a tournament in the grounds of Parnell's home at Avondale, a sports meeting in Clonmel that attracted 20,000 and an eleven-match football tournament in Tipperary.[28] In July the Craughwell horse-race meeting in Galway was revived under GAA auspices, one race being confined to horses owned by members of a Gaelic club. Prominent GAA figures officiated and betting was allowed in the enclosures. Near the end of the athletic season the GAA held its third annual athletic championships in Tralee, where two years before Cusack had scored a decisive win over the IAAA.

Cusack was not, however, at the Tralee sports of 1887 because in July 1886, only twenty months after he had founded the GAA, he had been removed from his post as Secretary. From the start he had been a difficult and dictatorial man to work with. Early in 1886, when the initial wave of enthusiasm had subsided and the routine of administration had to be tackled, his shortcomings as chief officer became apparent. His abrupt manner was ill-suited to the task of gaining support for a young association; by April 1886 there was friction between him and other officers, notably McKay and Wyse Power. That month a tactlessly-worded letter by Cusack unintentionally included Archbishop Croke among the targets of his abuse. At a meeting of the executive he made a complete retraction and a motion to dismiss him was lost by thirty-eight votes to thirteen. However, a decision was made that future major statements by the GAA should carry the signatures of at least two officers.

To anybody more prudent than Cusack this episode would have served as a warning. Instead, smarting under the admonition, he began to behave even more irresponsibly. He quarrelled with more and more local officials and permitted correspondence to pile up by a too strict interpretation of the two-signature rule of April. Finally the matter came to a head at a special general meeting — the best attended GAA meeting so far — in Thurles on 4 July 1886. A strong case was built up against Cusack by several of his colleagues, especially McKay, Wyse Power and the influential John Clancy (later an MP) of Dublin. Cusack was accused of being negligent in answering letters, of having failed to keep accounts and of having been violent and offensive to anybody who had dared disagree with him. After a heated discussion, in which Dublin delegates gallantly defended him and in which Cusack evaded the main allegations but dwelt at length on his aims in founding the Association, a motion dismissing him was this time carried by forty-seven votes to thirteen. A few weeks later, following understandable representations from the executive, he lost his post as Gaelic games correspondent of *United Ireland*. No comparable case exists in modern Irish history of a national movement dismissing its founder within such a short time.

If the GAA thought it had seen the last of Cusack it was mistaken. His dismissal merely added to the difficulties now building up into a formidable obstacle to the continued growth of the Association. For most of the nineteenth century nationalist Ireland was divided into two clearly recognisable groups, those who believed in constitutional agitation and those who favoured physical force to achieve political independence. A struggle for control of the GAA now developed between representatives of the two, which was not only to weaken the GAA but more than once to threaten its very existence. That it survived such a prolonged and occasionally bitter power struggle is striking evidence of the resilience of the Association.

Precisely when the Home Rule movement, led by the parliamentary party at Westminster and controlled at home by the National League, began to take an interest in the GAA cannot be stated. The extent of support for the Association by Home Rule leaders became blurred in the intense verbal cross-fire between Cusack and his opponents at the time of the Tralee sports of June 1885. However, although none of the original GAA leaders was apparently in the League, at local level there was no mistaking the support of Home Rulers everywhere for the GAA from its foundation. But for the active intervention of the party machine before the second meeting of the Association in Cork in December 1884 the GAA might have been stillborn, largely because of the boycott by local athletic officials. Moreover, the enthusiastic participation of prominent Home Rulers all over the country in the spate of sports meetings in 1885 and 1886 did much to put the Association on its feet.

The physical force camp, led by the secret oath-bound Irish Republican Brotherhood, had for its part supplied at least two of the seven founders, Bracken and Wyse Power, and it later became obvious that many other IRB members had also joined the GAA soon after its foundation. In several areas local IRB officers were elected to prominent posts in the GAA in 1885 and 1886. Bracken and Wyse Power took a leading part from the start in GAA affairs, Wyse Power becoming chairman of the Dublin county committee when he took up a post in the city in 1886. Two decisions made at a general meeting of the Association in September 1886 clearly showed the strength of the Fenian element and might be regarded as the beginning of the IRB take-over. P. T. Hoctor, a well-known IRB man from Tipperary who had built up the GAA in Clare, was elected vice-president, and an invitation was extended to the Fenian leader John O'Leary, recently home after fourteen years' political exile in Paris, to become the fourth patron. The following month at a GAA meeting in Athenry Hoctor made the revealing admission that 'every party now had a fair representation among the patrons'. Events of the next year were to show that among the rank-and-file GAA membership the IRB had more than a fair share of representation.

The year 1887, which was to prove a critical one for the GAA, began with the publication in January of a new weekly paper, *The Celtic Times,* edited by Cusack, the first publication ever to cater almost exclusively for Irish games.[29] This historic paper lasted for over a year, and there is clear evidence of its popularity with members later in 1887. Cusack claimed that its circulation had risen by mid-May to 20,000.

For Cusack the main purpose of *The Celtic Times* was to act as a vehicle from which to mount a sustained attack on the whole leadership and administration of the GAA since his dismissal in mid-1886. Understandably embittered by his rejection by a body he had founded and no longer subject to the editorial restraint imposed on his *United Ireland* writings, Cusack's tone became intemperate in his own paper. Yet his criticism was so keenly felt that inside three weeks calls were made for a rival journal to act as the organ of the GAA. Following unanimous resolutions early in 1887 at the annual conventions of the Limerick, Kilkenny and Galway county committees, *The Gael*, claiming to be the official organ of the central executive, first appeared in April 1887.[30]

About *The Gael* nearly as little can be said as of its rival; only one complete issue has survived. Edited by Hoctor, the GAA's newest vice-president and by now an influential figure on the executive, *The Gael* lasted over nine months. Like Cusack, Hoctor seems to have been unable to castigate opponents in mild language; like Cusack too, he even included Archbishop Croke among his targets. *The Gael* has, however, earned a place in the early history of the literary revival because in its literary columns, edited by John O'Leary, were published some of the earlier poems by the then almost unknown W. B. Yeats, as well as contributions by others with no GAA connections such as Douglas Hyde and T. W. Rolleston.

The publication of *The Gael* was the latest of a series of events which resulted in the IRB tightening its grip on the GAA. Meetings of the executive towards the end of 1886 and at the start of 1887 revealed serious friction, ostensibly on how the Association should be run, between the president Maurice Davin and an IRB group consisting of Hoctor (its spokesman), J. K. Bracken, Frank R. Moloney and Robert Frewen, all of Tipperary, and Frank Dineen, Anthony Mackey and Patrick Hassett, all of Limerick. Some others on the executive, especially the two Secretaries John B. O'Reilly and Tim O'Riordan, acquiesced in the decisions of the IRB men; but early in 1887 Wyse Power resigned from the executive. In February 1887 the IRB group was instrumental in pushing through, at an executive meeting held in Dublin without Davin's knowledge, major revisions of the rules which under the GAA's constitution required a general convention of club delegates (the equivalent of a special congress today) to effect.

Equally unwisely, Hoctor and his allies insisted on enforcing strictly another rule which required every 'large' GAA meeting that included athletics to have an official handicapper in charge. This development provoked immediate and widespread resentment in the provinces, as the rule had been frequently disregarded up to then and had also been the subject of genuine disagreement as to its interpretation. The main point at issue was whether or not a meeting was a large one; the rules gave no indication of what constituted such a meeting. Suspensions of meetings or of sponsoring clubs now began to be imposed by the executive for breaches of this rule, and members were warned by press notices that participation in suspended events suspended participants. In August the entire Dublin committee, and consequently all GAA activities in that county, were suspended because the committee had supported the Grocers Assistants Athletics Club in its refusal to permit its annual sports to have an official handicapper.

Meanwhile in April 1887 Davin, understandably concluding that he could play no further useful role in the GAA, resigned from the presidency. By mid-summer the executive had lost three of its most important members — Davin, Wyse Power and James Butler of Thurles, the record secretary, who had left with Davin. Even allowing for the hopeless position in which Davin had found himself on the executive, it is doubtful if his resignation was a wise move. It left the GAA without a titular head for a vital eight-month period; it also left the moderates without a voice on the executive. Above all, it put the IRB group led by Hoctor in complete control while the power struggle was at its height, with the important tactical advantage of a monopoly of press statements. In addition, a self-imposed silence by Davin between Easter and Christmas deprived moderates throughout the country of his support during that eventful period.

Not only did nationalist politics invade the committee rooms of the GAA, but it became impossible from 1887 onwards to consider the progress (or lack of progress) of the Association in isolation from the current political situation. By the summer of that year the Irish political temperature had risen sharply as the nationalist movement fought back against what it regarded as the oppressive policy of the British Government, as enforced by Dublin Castle. As the Plan of Campaign, the organised refusal begun in 1886 to pay exorbitant rents, began to hurt, the Castle drive to defeat the Plan was intensified. Prosecutions and imprisonment of leading Home Rule figures, including some prominent Catholic clergymen, were followed in turn by the dramatic resignation of the Chief Secretary, his replacement by the hard-line Arthur Balfour and the suppression in July of the National League.

Notwithstanding the defeat in 1886 of the Home Rule Bill, many nationalists continued to believe that self-government was still just around the corner. To at least some leaders of the IRB the GAA must have seemed an ideal means of gaining by stealth the power they could not hope to win through the ballot box. The Castle police were fully alive to such a possibility; to them, no less than to their political masters across the Irish Sea, the growing split in the GAA must have given increasing satisfaction in the second half of 1887. Any weak link must, in the eyes of the Castle, necessarily damage the whole nationalist chain of power — and if the dissension was in a body sponsored by Croke, the champion of the tenant-farmers, so much the better.

By mid-summer the GAA presented a picture of growing disunity, with the two leading counties of Dublin and Tipperary in open revolt against what they regarded as the dictatorial regime of the Hoctor-dominated central executive, and with athletes in several areas considering transferring their allegiance to the rival IAAA. In August the breach with the Dublin county committee became wider when a new handicapping dispute broke out over a sports meeting to be sponsored by the *Freeman's Journal* club. The previous month two special conventions of Dublin clubs had decided not to submit to the executive's ruling in the Grocers club dispute; now for the first time Hoctor found himself opposed by the powerful *Freeman's Journal* itself, which entered the arena in support of its employees' club. Events of the next few months were to suggest that this intervention was as unwise as Davin's resignation; in retrospect, it looks as if the action of Davin and that of the paper produced an effect directly contrary to that desired by each.

If the GAA executive was angered by the intervention in its affairs by the *Freeman*, its anger was understandable. From the start Cusack had been justifiably critical of the lukewarm attitude of this leading organ of nationalist opinion to his new body. Even before 1884 he had been dismayed by the general lack of support for native games shown by most of the nationalist journals. He never forgave the *Freeman's Journal* for its initial lukewarm attitude to the Association, and he continued for many months to attack the paper for not publishing, either in its daily issue or in the weekly subsidiary *Sport*, regular reports of the meetings and games sponsored by the GAA. That the proprietor of the *Freeman's Journal*, Edmund Dwyer Gray MP, keenly felt Cusack's accusations need not be doubted; it is possible that there was some substance in a story Cusack used to relate years later, to the effect that a blatant attempt to stifle his criticism was made by offering him a post on the editorial staff.

The files of the paper itself show that it gave scant publicity to GAA activities before 1886 and little encouragement to the GAA before 1887. In the first six months of 1887 this nationalist organ found ample space for laudatory leading articles on rugby and cricket internationals, the Trinity College sports and the French Grand Prix; it also reported a fashionable Dublin tennis tournament on its main news-page. Not until 21 July 1887, when the GAA was nearly three years in existence, did the *Freeman's Journal* first refer to the Association in its editorial column, and then only because of the impending dispute between the executive of the GAA and the paper's employees' athletic club. Between then and the end of 1887 it published no fewer than sixteen leading articles on the affairs of the Association, all but a few of them critical of the executive — and those few published after the executive had been overthrown. It is impossible to acquit the *Freeman's Journal* of the charge of taking an interest in the GAA only when control of that body seemed to be passing from Home Rule hands, which the paper supported, into the hands of the physical force camp, to which it was opposed. As for the *Freeman's Journal* Athletic Club, before 1886 it was affiliated to the IAAA; its belated accession to the GAA that year was, one of its leading members admitted, dictated mainly by a desire simply to follow the lead of others.

Not all the influence of the *Freeman's Journal* or the power of the Home Rule and National League machines could match the determination of Hoctor, who was now backed by Patrick Neville Fitzgerald of Cork. Fitzgerald, a native of Midleton and a member of the IRB from boyhood, had since the death of Charles Kickham in 1882 risen to the top of that body; he combined the occupation of a traveller in wine with that of full-time roving organiser for the IRB. A sincere advocate of native games, he would probably have been at the GAA foundation meeting in 1884 had he not then been in jail awaiting trial for treason for his nationalist activities; on his acquittal soon afterwards P. N. Fitzgerald took a leading part in the affairs of the GAA. Now in the autumn of 1887 he planned with Hoctor and other IRB leaders to thwart the expected attempt at the coming annual meeting of the GAA in Thurles in November to wrest control of the GAA from the IRB group on its central executive.

Early in September a convention was held of Clare clubs, and another of North Tipperary and Laois clubs jointly. Both came out strongly in support of the executive and were critical of the *Freeman's Journal*. At the second meeting it was claimed that the Limerick county committee had also come out in support of the executive. The anti-Hoctor wing then took its turn in holding conventions in preparation for the Thurles meeting. A conference of delegates from south Tipperary clubs decided — with only one dissentient, R. J. Frewen of the central executive — to oppose the re-election of Bracken and Moloney to the executive. A month later a bigger meeting in Clonmel of clubs from Tipperary, south Kilkenny and Waterford went a step further by calling for the return of Maurice Davin to head the GAA. Early in November conventions in Waterford, Cork and Wicklow repeated this call.

Since most of the preparations for the Thurles convention were made secretly, evidence of them is hard to find. However, rigging or packing of county conventions, by such an obvious step as appointing delegates from non-existing clubs, seems to have been resorted to by the Hoctor-Fitzgerald party. A critic of the Clare meeting claimed that the county could not muster fifty-five genuine clubs, although the meeting had delegates from this number; at the Thurles meeting two months later only thirty-three Clare clubs sent delegates! There are also indications that attempts were made to obstruct, or even to prevent the holding of, meetings in places known to support Davin. On the other hand, the Thurles meeting itself showed that in Tipperary the clergy had indulged in much successful anti-Hoctor lobbying, probably on Croke's orders. In the last few weeks before Thurles Cusack added his probably still influential voice to those campaigning for the defeat of Hoctor and the return of Davin, although at the same time he made it clear that he resented the power which the Home Rule party had gained in the GAA.

When the afternoon of Sunday, 9 November 1887 arrived, the size of the attendance in the old court-house of Thurles showed that the IRB had done its work well. The scene in the town that morning suggested the imminence of a major political event. The handful of hopeful men who three years before had sat around the billiard-table in Hayes's Hotel had now grown to 1,000 excited, determined and well-drilled delegates from twelve counties. Long before the hour of the meeting the IRB section had occupied every available seat in the court-room; outside anxious, angry and bewildered Home Rule men and priests, as well as the whole of the suspended Dublin delegation, tried to gain access. Along the streets of this small town, which had not known such tension since the rising of 1848, a large force of armed police, together with picked detectives from many parts of Ireland, patrolled and watched, as the court-house door was guarded by IRB scrutineers who examined each delegate's credentials. Some 1,600 tickets had been issued in advance, and a special train had brought delegates from Kerry, Limerick and south Tipperary. About eight hundred delegates attended; they included neither of the two principal founders, Cusack having returned to Dublin the previous night and Davin having remained at home in Carrick-on-Suir.

The meeting itself proved to be the noisiest and most violent in the history of the GAA. The choice of P. N. Fitzgerald as chairman pending the election of a new president was at once disputed by a group of Tipperary delegates, whose spokesman, Father John Scanlan of Nenagh, engaged Fitzgerald in a long wrangle. Despite the priest's warning to the meeting that Fitzgerald's selection would give the GAA an undesirable and unwarranted political tinge, the Corkman twice defeated a Tipperary candidate for the chair on a show of hands. The Fitzgerald-Scanlan argument was punctuated by frequent interruptions, the longest and most emotional coming from Hoctor; as the verbal battle continued, fist fights broke out in parts of the court-room. Wrongly believing that Fitzgerald would be the presidential choice of the outgoing executive, the Scanlan group, led by the priest himself, tried to storm the platform but was repulsed by stewards and only succeeded in wrecking the press stand. Finally Scanlan with his supporters withdrew from the room, and the meeting resumed with the election as president of the comparatively unknown E. M. Bennett of Ennis, the IRB candidate, who defeated Maurice Davin by 316 votes to 210.

Meanwhile in the yard outside Father Scanlan announced his intention of forming a rival athletic association that would pledge its support to the National League. Followed by the excluded Dublin delegation and by a substantial number of delegates (mostly from Kilkenny and Wexford) who had remained inside at the meeting to vote for Davin, Father Scanlan then led the way to Hayes's Hotel; from a brake outside the entrance he chaired a rival meeting which predictably called on Archbishop Croke for support. Two of the outgoing vice-presidents, J. K. Bracken and J. E. Kennedy, neither of whom had been re-elected (presumably because of their defection) addressed the gathering.

With the hindsight of over a century it is obvious that most of the blame for the only serious split in the GAA must rest with the IRB group led by Hoctor and Fitzgerald. However, it is equally clear that responsibility for the formal breach must lie with Father Scanlan, whose impetuous and intemperate behaviour showed him to be devoid of any sense of tactics. To propose in opposition to P. N. Fitzgerald a retired British army officer, Major John O'Kelly of Moycarkey in Tipperary, was incredibly insensitive and imprudent. Moreover, had the seceding group, which claimed to be 200 strong, remained inside at the meeting and helped to vote Davin back into office, the subsequent capture of the other offices by IRB men would almost certainly have been prevented.

It soon became clear that in provoking the Scanlan secession the IRB had overplayed its hand. Delegates had barely reached home when meetings of clubs all over the country began to be held, which showed feeling to be against the group that had dominated the Thurles meeting. Croke dissociated himself from the new executive and, as the list of anti-Bennett clubs daily grew longer, it became evident that unless some agreement between the two groups could be reached the GAA (whether as a controlling body for Irish sport or a wing of the nationalist movement) was finished. By Christmas the anti-Bennett clubs numbered several hundred; the *Gael* could only find two supporting the new executive. In the press, controversy over the Thurles meeting continued daily, with supporters of the executive always in the minority, although not without able spokesmen like Kendal O'Brien, MP for Tipperary.

In November the clerical lobby took the initiative in a move to avert the breakup of the GAA. A proposal by Davin for a provisional committee equally representative of both sides was publicly suggested by a Tipperary priest as a basis for talks; following a private meeting the executive issued a statement showing readiness to compromise. Croke and Davitt now conferred in the archbishop's residence, Croke having taken over leadership of the clerical wing and Davitt conveying the views of P. N. Fitzgerald. At another meeting in Thurles early in December, Davin joined the two patrons; here the membership of the provisional committee was settled — Davin and Wyse Power for the anti-Bennett wing, O'Riordan and Frewen for the executive. A special general convention was fixed for Thurles for 4 January 1888; it became clear that a proposal by Croke, to replace the old-style central executive by a new central council with defined powers, would be adopted.

The proceedings at the eighteen county conventions held before the second Thurles convention of January 1888 give a fair idea of the extent of the swing back to what might now be called the Davin wing. Disputes about club credentials and allegations of election-rigging were almost entirely absent this time. In many cases priests attended; at some conventions (notably Clare, where Bennett was displaced) a priest presided; at others a priest was included among the delegation for Thurles. Understandably, the IRB lost heavily in the elections for delegates, although in several counties they showed that they had not yet lost all their influence. In Cork P. N. Fitzgerald won a place on the delegation, and in Galway four of the five-man delegation were known physical force advocates, among them a future president,

Peter Kelly. To suggest clerical dominance of rank-and-file members would be un-justified; events in Irish public life at this time proved that in vital matters affecting the Home Rule movement even nationalist leaders were not prepared to be subservient to the Church. It would be fairer to assume that the backlash in December 1887 in favour of Davin was an authentic reflection of feeling in the GAA as a whole.

In striking contrast to the November meeting the reconstruction convention, as it was called, in Thurles on 4 January 1888 was orderly, if not without some excitement. The claims of rival delegations from Limerick, Kilkenny and Waterford were all settled by compromise. Nineteen counties were represented by eighty-three delegates, of whom only four were from the executive elected in November. As expected, Davin was elected president; William Prendergast of Clonmel decisively defeated Tim O'Riordan (an outgoing Secretary) to become new Secretary. Of the Bennett executive only Frewen (elected treasurer) and O'Riordan (elected to the new post of central council secretary) obtained places on the new executive. Like Cusack, Hoctor was present only as a journalist. A new constitution drafted by Davin and restoring control to county committees was approved, and an invitation (accepted in April) extended to William O'Brien MP, now second only in popularity to Parnell, to become the GAA's fifth patron.[31]

With the ending of the six-week split tempers suddenly cooled in the GAA. Neither side can have been completely satisfied with the result of the mediation begun by Croke and supported by Davitt. However, presumably because of the prestige of the two patrons, everybody accepted the settlement. Almost overnight the controversy that had so disrupted the Association for nearly a year subsided, and the two rival papers of Hoctor and Cusack ceased publication permanently. Orderly administration of the Association resumed, and the year 1888 later came to be regarded as the most successful so far experienced by the GAA — as, indeed, in many respects it was. However, it was also the year in which it suffered its most serious set-back so far.

When in the autumn of 1884 Cusack had put his plan for a Gaelic athletic association to Michael Davitt, the two had enthusiastically discussed another associated proposal, the revival on a quinquennial basis of the ancient Tailteann Games. Davitt claimed the idea as his; but the details sound as if they originated with Cusack, and Davitt on several occasions in his public career claimed credit for ideas that were almost certainly first put forward by associates who later loyally remained silent. For a body like the GAA, just recovering from such a serious split, the plan sounds naively ambitious and impractical even today. Every five years a great Celtic cultural festival would be held, with the aim of strengthening Ireland's claim to separate nationhood. Not only field games but also athletic contests, as well as an industrial exhibition and literary and musical competitions, would be included. The occasion would, it was optimistically hoped, be availed of by people of Irish birth or descent in the United States to visit their motherland; entries for all contests would be accepted from Wales, Scotland and the Isle of Man.

To run such an event in Dublin in the summer of 1889 as he envisaged, Davitt estimated that a minimum prize fund of £5,000 would be needed. To find this sum it was proposed that a team of hurlers and athletes, some fifty strong, would tour Irish centres of the United States. The first public reference to this project was made early in March 1888; Davin had warmly adopted the idea as his own the following month, when he first put the plan to the new central council. One suspects that the financial side of the venture caused continuous concern. By early June a proposal that expenses be guaranteed in advance by clubs became transformed into a campaign, sponsored by the council, to build up a fund out of individual subscriptions and a voluntary levy on clubs.

Despite widespread promises of support from county committees, clubs and individual members, the fund-raising campaign proved a failure. No list of subscriptions was ever published. The Dublin county committee contributed only £5, and even the support of Archbishop Croke for the projected tour produced no reaction in the form of cash. As a result, the original departure date of the party was put back from mid-August to mid-September; the central council only finally gave the scheme its blessing on 6 August. Eventually John Cullinane of the council (later MP for Tipperary) went out in advance to make arrangements; even his trip did not augur well for the tour's success, for he found himself caught up in a major internal athletic dispute in America. He sided with the secessionist National Amateur Athletics Association, only to meet with boycott threats from the rival and more powerful American Amateur Athletic Union. Meanwhile back in this country a series of exhibition contests by the teams selected, which took place in Wexford, Dundalk, Tullamore, Kilkenny, Thurles, Dublin and Dun Laoire, drew small crowds and low receipts.[32]

Finally on 16 September the GAA's American Invasion, as it came to be called, began when a party of over fifty — hurlers, athletes and officials — sailed from Cork. Tipperary with nine representatives, Cork (eight), Limerick (six) and Dublin (five) accounted for the greater part of the contingent. Offaly sent four, Clare and Kilkenny three each and Wexford, Laois, Waterford and Kildare one each. In several cases, including that of Davin's brother Pat, one 'invader' travelled both as an athlete and a hurler; William Prendergast of Clonmel sailed both as an official and a hurler; P. P. Sutton of Dublin went both as a journalist and a hurler. Davin led the party, which also had a Catholic chaplain, Father Concannon of Offaly.

In New York the Irish party was given a tumultuous welcome by public and athletic officials and by prominent Irish-American personalities. Davin confirmed Cullinane's decision to accept the patronage of the Manhattan Athletic Club, the most powerful member of the NAAA, and a series of exhibition hurling games and athletic contests was staged. In addition to several venues in the New York area, the Irish also played or competed in Boston, Philadelphia, Trenton, Newark, Patterson, Providence and Lowell. At several of the athletics meetings Irishmen defeated American champions and set up new records. From the social viewpoint, and in laying the foundations of the GAA in the United States, the five-week visit was undeniably successful.[33]

In every other respect the GAA's American Invasion of 1888 was a failure. In the first place, far from building up a surplus fund of £5,000, it incurred so many debts that only a grant of over £400 from Michael Davitt from a fund under his control enabled the party to purchase tickets for the trip home.[34] Everywhere except in Boston, where there were already four flourishing hurling clubs, attendances were poor and receipts proportionately low. Continuous bad weather and the rival distraction of a presidential election campaign kept crowds from going to the GAA meetings; in some cases events took place in torrential rain, and in others with a major political meeting in progress nearby. A plan to extend the tour to take in Canadian cities had to be abandoned when snow and exceptionally cold weather set in there, and Cullinane's initial hostility towards the AAAU made visits to cities in the mid-West and West of the United States by the Irish party out of the question.

Finally, the American Invasion cost Ireland the cream of her athletes, because at least seventeen, and probably several more, of the forty-five hurlers and athletes settled permanently in America. These included the new Secretary of the Association, Prendergast, one of the two Molohan brothers who had been in the pre-GAA hurling revival with Cusack, and the world champion weight-thrower, J. S. Mitchell of Tipperary.[35] The Tailteann Games project died a sudden death, and was not resurrected for another thirty-five years.

Chapter 3

1889–1897

Less than three months after the unhappy end to the American Invasion the GAA was plunged into yet another crisis even more serious than any it had so far faced. This time the dissolution of the Association was actually mooted; once again there was a presidential resignation; it in turn was followed by the capture of the main executive posts by members of a particular faction of the nationalist movement. Although not in any way connected with the trip to the United States, this new crisis nevertheless came to a head as an indirect result of that event. While the real root of the trouble lay in renewed efforts by the IRB to dominate the GAA, the ostensible and more immediate cause of the crisis was the worsening financial position of the Association, which had naturally become more acute through the loss incurred on the American Invasion. Once again Davin was to find himself at loggerheads with other leading members; this time he and the Association he had helped to found were to part company permanently.

That the GAA had hitherto paid little attention to finance is perhaps understandable. Since Cusack had, with considerable success, tried to ensure that none of the elements of professionalism which he had deplored in Irish athletics was carried into the GAA, money was of little importance in the early years of the Association. With the single exception of the accusations against Hoctor when editor of *The Gael* there was never a suggestion that any of the early GAA leaders profited privately out of the Association; any such possibility can be discounted. It can be safely assumed that such income as the young Association received went entirely on such basic essentials as rent for playing-fields, the purchase of medals and other prizes and — to a much smaller extent — travelling expenses of leading officers.

Apart from a brief comment by Cusack in his report as Secretary that only sixty-eight clubs had paid him affiliation fees, there was no reference to finance at the first annual meeting of the GAA, held in Thurles in October 1885 and adjourned to February 1886. The smallness of the Association's income — probably as low as £34, since the annual affiliation fee per club is believed to have been only ten shillings (50p) — may be attributed largely to Cusack's failure to look after the administrative side of things, a factor that was mainly responsible for his dismissal in July 1886. Oddly, in view of the accusations against Cusack, the second annual meeting (held in Thurles in November 1886) concluded without any financial statement from an officer of the executive. However, it approved of a revised constitution for the Association fixing ten shillings per club as the annual affiliation fee. At the stormy convention in Thurles in November 1887 the Secretary reported an income of £413 for the previous fourteen months, corresponding roughly with the minimum of 500 clubs believed to have sent delegates.[1]

The following summer (1888) Davin reported to the central council on the Association's financial position, having had a special investigation carried out after his re-election as president earlier that year. Unpaid debts incurred from the start in 1884 amounted to £211, to which had to be added another £230 for medals and prizes in 1887. He explained that, since it was estimated that £400 would be received in fees and entrance charges for 1888, it was hoped to be able to clear off all liabilities that year. This optimistic forecast proved wrong. By the end of that same year Davin had to report that the Association's total indebtedness had risen to almost £500, a figure clearly exclusive of the debt of £400 owed to Michael Davitt over the American trip.

Instead of an income of £400 for 1888 only £260 came in, and new debts turned up from the previous summer of which Davin had to admit he had been unaware. While Davitt did not press for repayment, other creditors did; in Dublin legal proceedings were commenced against the former Secretary, John Wyse Power, who found himself threatened with bankruptcy. Little wonder that shortly before Christmas 1888 the central council made it clear that a firm line would be taken on the obligation of county committees to pay annual affiliation fees. Against this gloomy background the annual meeting for 1888 opened in Thurles at the end of January 1889.

Predictably discussion at the meeting centred on finance. Most delegates blamed Davin for the heavy debt, although Cusack for the Dublin delegation firmly supported him. Eventually Father Eugene Sheehy led out the Limerick delegation in a move that must have reminded some of the secession from the Thurles convention fourteen months before. Disorder then broke out and Davin left. At a meeting of the Limerick delegates in an adjoining room which Davin attended a resolution was passed calling for the abolition of the central council. Davin and Sheehy, possibly with a view to paying off the debts, now proposed to wind up the GAA, leaving each county to run its own competitions. Meanwhile, back at the main meeting Davin's departure was interpreted as a resignation from office, and delegates from the sixteen counties left elected Peter Kelly of Loughrea as president. Davin, who lived for another thirty-six years, never again actively participated in the GAA.

Davin's second resignation was the result of an organised movement inside the GAA by the IRB to regain control of the Association, which had begun soon after the reconstruction convention of January 1888. With the departure of Davin in January 1889 must be linked the defeat, at the resumed annual meeting held immediately after his walk-out, of the other officers of the Association who had been elected at the reconstruction convention. The January 1889 meeting replaced the Davin executive by a new council headed by the IRB man Peter Kelly, and dominated by members of the IRB. In short, despite the reverses suffered by the IRB after the Thurles convention of November 1887, by January 1889 control of the GAA was back in Fenian hands, where it was to remain for many years.

Although it may seem astonishing that the IRB was able to regain control so quickly of a body in the affairs of which leading parliamentarians and churchmen had taken an active part, on reflection it will be seen that this was almost inevitable. All that Croke, Davitt and the reconstruction convention between then had done early in 1888 was to alter the personnel of the GAA leadership. But, without ensuring that the majority of the rank-and-file membership (which elected the county delegates, who in turn elected the executive's officers annually) were not members of the IRB, neither the two principal patrons nor the executive elected in 1888 could prevent a return to power by IRB men on the next executive — precisely what happened in January 1889. Not only did many more Fenians join the Association in 1888, but it must be inferred from subsequent events that that year also saw at least some Home Rule supporters leave the GAA. In addition, the small number of Protestants and unionists who had stayed on in the GAA after the 1887 crisis now left permanently.

Despite the apparent settlement put into effect at the reconstruction convention in 1888, dissension continued in several of the more active counties for most of the year. Within a few weeks of the convention Limerick had two rival county committees, representing respectively the IRB and the National League clubs in the county. This split lasted at least until October, when mediation by the central council, which had sponsored a joint convention in June, ended it for the time being. By then Cork found itself also with two rival county committees; in this case the gap widened the following year. In both these and in other less serious instances the cleavage was along easily-distinguishable party lines, with either Home Rule or National League supporters on one side and IRB members on the other. In Limerick, for example, one county committee was dominated by the militant tenant-farmer spokesman Father Sheehy, and the other by Frank Dineen and Anthony Mackey.

When towards the end of 1888 the central council made clear its determination to insist on the punctual payment of affiliation fees, even to the extent of suspending defecting counties, the old issue of the independence of county committees was added to the rivalry between the IRB and its opponents. As a result, not only was

1889 remarkable for the number of counties severing their connections with the central council; it also became impossible to state of a given county whether the cause of its dissidence was its disinclination to pay affiliation fees or its refusal to accept a governing body dominated by Fenians. On the whole, it seems more likely that it was opposition to P. J. Kelly and his IRB-controlled central council that provoked previously submissive or co-operative county committees into open revolt. As early as January 1889 those of Tipperary, Dublin and Galway had announced their intention of defying the council; the following month Wexford and Kildare joined them, with Louth and Laois contemplating defiant action too. Although both Tipperary and Dublin later recognised the council, and Louth and Laois remained loyal to it, the authority of the council was gradually weakened during 1889 by more and more defections. By December the alarming position had been reached in which nine counties of Leinster (all but Dublin, Laois and Louth), together with Mayo, Waterford, Cavan and Monaghan, had seceded.

Ranged against these thirteen dissident counties were thirteen others still loyal to the central council — Antrim, Galway, Sligo, Leitrim, Roscommon, Cork, Kerry, Limerick, Clare and Tipperary, together with the three Leinster counties just named. A closer look suggests that much of the support for the central council was shaky. While some counties, such as Clare, Kerry, Laois and Leitrim, which had not been represented at the reconstruction convention of January 1888, could now muster an impressive number of affiliated clubs, the position was different elsewhere. Dublin and Tipperary, hitherto two of the most active counties, experienced falls of around fifty per cent in the number of clubs in 1889; in Louth there was a falling-off of seventy-five per cent that year. If Limerick's troubles had ended, Cork's had not; it now had no fewer than three rival boards. Even some counties like Mayo and Cavan, where the IRB was well organised, no longer supported the central council. In the case of other IRB-dominated county committees, such as Sligo and Kerry, the apparently sudden steep rise in the number of clubs makes one doubt the cause of the increase. The best clue to the crisis now confronting the GAA lay in the astonishing disappearance of some sixty clubs in Tipperary.

It was for the emergence of a new and powerful critic of the Association, the Catholic hierarchy and clergy, that the year 1889 was notable in GAA affairs. Although the strength of this new opposition may have surprised the IRB, it can hardly have expected the Church to acquiesce in the taking-over by the Fenians of a body like the GAA to which nationally-minded youths and men had flocked. Because of the support given to the GAA by the National League, in which priests were everywhere prominent, and also doubtless with a view to counteracting the influence in the GAA of the IRB, the clergy had up to now been among the most enthusiastic supporters and members of the Association. Suddenly after the 1889 convention this position was reversed. As if fearing that the new IRB control of the

GAA would exclude them from a voice in its councils, priests left the Association in large numbers. Led by most of the bishops, they mounted a determined verbal attack on the GAA that was clearly designed to kill it. That the GAA survived at all, when to the effect of this clerical onslaught was added the impact on the Association of the disaster that overtook the whole nationalist movement in 1891, was astonishing.

The first serious clerical criticism of the GAA came from no less a person than the Primate, Archbishop (later Cardinal) Logue of Armagh, who from the pulpit in that city four days after the Thurles convention of January 1889 condemned the working of the Association and its 'demoralising effects' on its members.[2] Several further clerical denunciations from various places in the North followed in the next few months — in Clones later in February, in Newry late in April and in Enniskillen in mid-May, to give only three samples.[3] The Bishop of Dromore directed his clergy to order their parishioners not to become involved in the GAA; the Bishop of Clogher ordered pulpit denunciations of the GAA and alleged that even Croke was now heartily sick of the Association.[4] At the other end of the country successful litigation brought by three members (including the chairman) of the IRB-controlled Cork county committee against a priest who had described them as 'Dublin Castle spies' showed that the clergy there too were opposed to the GAA because of their conviction that it had been infiltrated by the Fenians.[5] In Meath Bishop Nulty and his clergy were particularly hostile to the Association.[6]

There were some notable exceptions to this otherwise concerted opposition to the GAA by the hierarchy. Archbishop Croke not only refrained from public denunciation but even continued to encourage and assist the Association. On several occasions in 1889 and 1890 he went out of his way to offer his influential services in the protracted efforts to reduce the heavy debts of the GAA. In July 1889 Archbishop Walsh of Dublin, a committed if moderate nationalist, gave a press interview on the Association which was more important for what it omitted than for what it stated. Although he admitted that he was well aware of attempts to 'graft on the GAA a secret society of a political character', he declined to utter a word of condemnation of the Association and ridiculed a rumour that had been published in the London *Times* newspaper that the bishops had banned the playing of football.

In many areas individual priests continued to work in the GAA after 1888, even in places where episcopal censures had been issued; such exceptions were apparently permitted if they kept a club or county out of IRB control. As late as May 1890 nearly half of the thirty clubs left in Tipperary were under clerical control.[7] Around the same time all but four of Wexford's thirty-three clubs were controlled by priests; the corresponding figures in Kilkenny and Waterford were eleven and six 'clerical clubs' respectively, out of forty-eight and twelve.[8] At the end of 1890 priests still remained on the executives of seven of Cavan's thirty-eight clubs; in Kildare the figure was six out of thirty-eight.[9] In Laois priests were firmly in control, three being

on the county board.[10] Elsewhere the position was less satisfactory for the Church —
only twenty-five clerical clubs in Cork in 1890 as against ninety-seven 'IRB clubs',
only two priests still in the GAA in Longford and only one in Leitrim'.[11] The presence in 1890 of one priest in a Fermanagh club, of another in Monaghan and of a
third in Tyrone were all regarded as unusual by the police; in Dublin the election of
a priest as president of a Lucan club merited special mention in the press.

It was in 1889 that the GAA first came under serious notice from the police force
of Dublin Castle, the RIC. This paramilitary body, which served as the model for police
forces in other parts of the English-speaking world, acted effectively for nearly a
century as the eyes and ears of the British administrative machine in Ireland. For most
of the nineteenth century the RIC was the principal source of official information
on the strength and disposition of all nationalist activity. It may seem surprising that
the GAA was over four years in existence before its potential as a new recruit to the
nationalist cause was realised. However, apart from the presence at the foundation
meeting of the GAA of an RIC officer, Thomas St George McCarthy, it may be
assumed that the police authorities in Dublin Castle were well aware of the growth
of the early GAA. That they took little notice of it until shortly before the convention of November 1887 further supports the view that under Cusack's leadership
the Association was non-political. When the RIC did wake up to the political implications of the GAA, they more than made up for their earlier neglect.

For some months before the convention of November 1887 the IRB infiltration
and the reaction to it by non-IRB members had been under study by the RIC in various parts of the country, presumably on orders from the Special Branch of the
Crime Department in Dublin Castle. As already mentioned, plain-clothes RIC men
attended in Thurles from many counties; it seems at least possible from their
subsequent reports that a few actually gained access to the court-house where the
GAA delegates were meeting. Although they can hardly have gathered much
information there, it seems that the strength and success of the IRB at the meeting
so impressed the Castle that a special report on the political aspect of the GAA was
commissioned. This first of many such surveys over the next thirty-five years somehow found its way to the Colonial Office in London, and has survived.[12]

The main interest in this report lies in its introductory section, which, though
occasionally factually incorrect, accurately summarises the political implications of
the GAA as seen by Dublin Castle. Having explained the circumstances of the
Association's foundation, it comments that 'without doubt Cusack was quite honest
in his original idea . . . to initiate a purely non-political association of athletes to compete with and, if possible, overshadow the Irish Amateur Athletic Association . . .
which was too aristocratic and conservative in its constitution to suit . . . Cusack and
his followers'. The report continues: 'the two parties in the Nationalist camp from
the first took possession of it. Archbishop Croke and Mr Parnell . . . encouraged the

priests to keep the local branches in their hands and to hold the clubs loyal to the Parliamentary Party, while the Fenians worked steadily in a stealthy . . . way . . . to gain . . . as large a section as possible . . . This party cleverly succeeded in getting hold of the executive. The success of the Fenians alarmed the Parliamentary Party and dissensions arose which culminated in the Thurles convention of 9 November 1887. The proceedings at this convention themselves amply prove the dangerous political character of the Association . . .'.

From the time of the 1887 convention the GAA, in the eyes of Dublin Castle, was a fully-fledged member of the nationalist movement, and as such came under the monthly notice of the Special Branch of the RIC. Since the policy of the Castle administration was obviously to ensure a continuation of the political union of Britain and Ireland, the GAA now joined the list of bodies whose aims and activities were regarded as subversive, if not treasonable, because their success would have involved at least the erosion of British rule in Ireland and possibly the establishment of a politically free Ireland. To this list then belonged not only the IRB and the National League, but also less obviously political bodies like the Ancient Order of Hibernians, the Irish National Foresters and the intermittent and mostly agrarian groups conveniently labelled Ribbonmen by the RIC.

To the historian of the GAA the real value of the increased attention paid to the Association by the RIC from 1888 onwards lies in the statistical material concerning the strength and membership of the Association to which it gave rise. Revealing some of the apparatus of a police State with which later generations became familiar, the police records relating to the GAA provide useful data at a stage in the Association's history when both press reports and minutes of meetings are either deficient or non-existent. In each town the RIC man with political duties was obliged to compile periodical lists of local GAA clubs and officers, which were duly passed on to divisional headquarters and thence to Dublin Castle, often acquiring informative comments from officers along the way. Although the extent of these records varies from town to town and the accuracy of the details may occasionally be open to question, there is no reason to doubt the authenticity of the overall picture of the growth or decline of the GAA.

The earliest statistics relating to the GAA come from Cusack himself. In a statement made in the late 1890s he recalled that in 1884 he estimated that inside three years the Association would have 300,000 members, and that eighteen months after its foundation it had 50,000.[13] In another statement a year later he claimed that at some unspecified stage in the early years, probably 1888, the GAA had 500 clubs in Munster, 450 in Leinster, 200 in Connacht and 120 in Ulster.[14] A membership of

50,000 spread over about 1,250 clubs would give an average club membership of forty, a reasonable figure for the time. It seems that the sixty-eight clubs recorded in Cusack's report of March 1886 as having paid affiliation fees were only a tiny proportion of the total; in any event this report covers the period when Cusack was not properly carrying out his duties as Secretary, of which the collection of fees would have been a major one.

The first statistics showing the strength of the GAA in individual counties are in O'Riordan's report to the Thurles convention of November 1887. As the details in col. 1 of the following Table show, they claim a total of 635 clubs in eleven counties, a figure that is close to the 600 mentioned by Cusack nine years later as having sent delegates. Column 2 of the Table records the attendance at the reconstruction convention of January 1888, as reported in the jubilant *Freeman*; this time sixteen counties are included, and if allowance is made for some spurious representation at the November meeting, the total of 506 is near enough to O'Riordan's 635 to strike one as authentic. Both the 1887 and 1888 totals are comparable with an estimate of 400 clubs by the well-informed P. P. Sutton in November 1886, after which it is clear that the total grew rapidly during 1887.

TABLE OF GAA CLUBS 1887–1890				
(1) 1887	(2) 1888	(3) 1889	(4) 1890	(5) 1890
LEINSTER 175	214	297	323	271
Carlow		20	25	28
Dublin 40	47	28		60
Kildare	8	38	38	33
Kilkenny 40	17	24	48	18
Laois		41	40	40
Longford		13	23	18
Louth 55	45	10	38	16
Meath 40	50	36	15	19
Offaly	11	22	23	3
Westmeath		5	6	6
Wexford		33	33	18
Wicklow	36	27	34	12
MUNSTER 380	255	289	258	152
Cork 70	70	76	97	50
Clare 60		30	39	16
Kerry		36	31	35
Limerick 90	64	73	49	30
Tipperary 130	106	46	30	15
Waterford 30	15	28	12	6

TABLE OF GAA CLUBS 1887–1890 *continued*				
(1) 1887	(2) 1888	(3) 1889	(4) 1890	(5) 1890
CONNACHT 80	31	74	206	87
Galway 70	26		59	63
Leitrim		19	27	6
Mayo 10	1	30	37	18
Roscommon			49	
Sligo	4	25	34	
ULSTER 0	6	37	88	47
Antrim			5	6
Armagh			5	10
Cavan	1	37	37	
Derry			8	16
Donegal			3	
Down			4	
Fermanagh			14	9
Monaghan	5		12	3
Tyrone			0	3
TOTALS 635	506	697	875	557

Sources
Col. (1): See p. 41 & *FJ*, 10.11.1887 & 12.11.1887.
Col. (2): *FJ*, 27.12.1887 to 31.12.1887.
Col. (3): *Sport*, 26.10.1889 & 2.11.1889 (Dublin); do., 26.10.1889 (Leitrim); do., 7.12.1889 (Munster); also SPO (Dublin), Spec. Crimes branch, files 2562, 2964 & 4467.
Col. (4): *Sport*, 6.12.1890; SPO, SC branch, file 501–296.
Col. (5): *Sport*, 14.6.1890; 6.12.1890; also O'Sullivan, p. 89.

The statistics for 1889 (col. 3 of the Table) show the value of the RIC records. Of the twenty-two counties for which club-totals are available, these records are the only source for no fewer than thirteen. Without them and one other source, figures of clubs in 1889 would be available for only two counties, Dublin and Leitrim. That the police figures are on the whole reliable is suggested by a comparison with the figures in col. 5 for 1890, nearly all of which come from Sutton. In several cases, including five of the twelve Leinster counties, the RIC figure and Sutton's are identical or nearly so. In others, such as Wexford, dissension during 1889 was such as to make it likely that a sharp fall in the number of clubs — somewhat of the size indicated by deducting a figure in col. 3 from the corresponding figure in col. 5 — occurred.

The surprisingly high figures for 1889 are a reflection of a feature of the GAA at different times in its history. No matter how serious divisions at top level might be, no matter how deeply split the Association was at any level, no matter how disrupted social and sporting life was by political events, games continued to be played in many areas and clubs survived to re-affiliate in more settled times. Particularly interesting in this respect are the figures (in col. 4 of the Table) for May 1890, which (because they come entirely from RIC sources) are not concerned with affiliation to the GAA. They show that in many counties — Louth, Cork, Clare and Leitrim are notable examples — far more clubs were then operating outside the Association than were affiliated. In some counties such as Cork the creation of rival boards resulted in an even greater number of clubs than before.

The figures for 1889 and 1890 are surprisingly high for another reason; they suggest that the Church's attack had not so far weakened the GAA to any great extent. In some cases this is known to have happened — Galway, where Bishop Duggan's co-adjutor, Bishop Healy, was particularly hostile to the IRB, and Meath, where Bishop Nulty organised strong clerical opposition to the GAA.[15] But the figures show that these were exceptions. The known total number of clubs in Ulster, despite Cavan's defection, increased substantially; the apparent fall in club-numbers in Munster was caused largely by dissensions in Cork and Limerick that led to a refusal by many clubs to affiliate, rather than to a fall in club-numbers. In Leinster, although seven counties had by December 1890 recorded a drop in the number of clubs as compared to 1889, in half these cases the fall was slight; Dublin then had far more clubs than it ever had.

So far from wilting under the clerical onslaught of 1889, it looks as if both that year and 1890 saw a determined effort by the central council to continue the normal activities of the Association to the extent permitted by widely varying local conditions. It is probable that the remarkable revival in Dublin in 1890 after the slump of 1889 may be traceable to a concerted effort to exploit the neutral, if not benevolent, attitude of Archbishop Walsh. Moreover, despite all its troubles in 1889, the GAA managed to complete its current inter-county championships in both codes — an unusual achievement in those unsettled early years — although only eight counties (all from Leinster or Munster) entered in each code. Many special tournaments were played that year, mostly for funds for patriotic purposes — Tone's grave, national (mostly Fenian) monuments, and various groups of evicted tenants. It is arguable that the vigorous support the GAA gave to the nationalist movement in 1889 had a beneficial effect on the Association itself and accounts for the surprising vitality it displayed in both 1889 and 1890.

However, the GAA could not flourish indefinitely without clerical support, and even in 1889 there were ominous signs of what lay ahead. At the annual convention held in Thurles in November 1889 only forty-four delegates from nine counties attended. That same month at least ten counties refused to accept the central council's authority; this figure rose to thirteen the next month. In addition, the president told the convention that in another six counties insufficient clubs existed to form a county committee. Four of these — Monaghan, Derry, Antrim and Down — were in Ulster; of three other Ulster counties (Donegal, Fermanagh and Tyrone) there is no record of any activity at this stage. When to them is added dissident Cavan an alarming picture of the GAA's decline in the North emerges. In three Munster counties (Cork, Limerick and Waterford) almost one hundred unaffiliated clubs were operating. In Leinster six county boards had seceded by November 1889, a figure that rose to nine before the end of that year.

A year later when the 1890 convention came to be held (again in Thurles in November) only twenty-six delegates from seven counties attended. Although the president could claim that twenty-six counties were affiliated compared to about thirteen the previous year, col. 5 of the Table on pp. 41–2 shows that eight of these could not muster ten affiliated clubs each. The total number of known clubs (affiliated or otherwise) fell by nearly two hundred that year. In Tipperary only fifteen clubs affiliated, and the county sent no delegate to the convention. Comparison of the figures in cols. 4 and 5 shows a downward trend in many counties. For every Munster county, for six Leinster counties and for the most important Connacht counties a sharp fall in club-numbers occurred between the summer and winter of 1890. Although both hurling and football championships were undertaken, the football final for 1890 was not played until June 1892 and, of the fourteen counties that entered in football (double the hurling entry), not one was from Ulster or Connacht.

Complete statistics of GAA clubs for 1891 have not survived; however, other information makes it clear that the year saw another steep decline by the Association. The annual convention did not take place until January 1892; it was attended by only eighteen delegates from six counties, together with five officers. They heard their president admit that only 200 clubs were now affiliated, with perhaps another 100 scattered through the country. Once again, however, the council managed to complete its championships, although only on an even more reduced scale than in 1890. Seven counties (none from Ulster or Connacht) entered in hurling; only five played, and the final did not take place until February 1892. In football there was an entry of eleven counties, five from Leinster and three each from Munster and Ulster, the final being played also in February 1892. The seventh annual GAA athletic championships in Tralee in August 1891 were a fiasco. Among counties with no board were Tipperary, Cavan and Westmeath; counties where the RIC could not find a single club at the end of the year included Louth, Monaghan and Tyrone; Mayo had three clubs and Clare one.[16]

To find the explanation of the almost total eclipse of the GAA in 1891 one has to return to the political arena. Ironically, where neither the Fenians with their intriguing and domineering nor the clergy with their boycotting and verbal onslaughts managed between them to kill the Association, the Home Rule party nearly succeeded in doing so, when early in 1891 it broke into two bitterly opposed sections. With the Parnell Split disaster overtook the whole nationalist movement; after the parliamentary party itself probably the biggest casualty was the GAA, which (like the party) was to take a decade to recover. That the Association, already weakened by clerical opposition, managed to survive in view of its isolated stand in this unprecedented national controversy, is little short of a miracle. It is doubtful if it would have survived but for three factors — its surprising readiness to adapt to changing circumstances, and even to compromise what had hitherto been regarded as unchangeable principles, the tenacity and loyalty of a handful of its leaders (mostly IRB men), and its part in the cultural revival that began to gather momentum just before the turn of the century.

When in mid-December 1890 the previously monolithic Irish Party met in Committee Room 15 at Westminster to decide the political fate of its leader, the closeness of the links between the Home Rule movement and the GAA became at once apparent. The only outsiders allowed to attend this historic conference were five journalists from the *Freeman's Journal*; they included Tim O'Riordan of Cork, a former secretary to the executive committee of the GAA. More important was the discovery that, when the voting lists for the vital motion on Parnell's leadership were published, well-known GAA officials or figures found themselves on opposite sides — to give some examples at random, J. J. Clancy voting with the 26-strong pro-Parnell group, but Justin McCarthy and William Martin Murphy with the forty-five MPs who had effectively deposed Parnell. Clancy some days later accompanied Parnell to the editorial offices in Dublin of *United Ireland*, where they literally retook possession of the newspaper premises; McCarthy went on to lead the larger (anti-Parnellite) section of the Party at Westminster for nine years.

This was only the beginning of the GAA's involvement in the historic Split. When two months later, with the collapse of talks in France between Parnell and his opponents, the Split was confirmed leading figures in the GAA were among prominent IRB men all over the country who came out openly on the Parnellite side.[17] They played major parts on the Parnell Leadership Committees set up in nearly every large town. On the Dublin committee were John Wyse Power, a founder of the GAA, and Fred Allan, a leading figure in the Dublin GAA from the start. The former president E. M. Bennett was on the Clare committee; Maurice Moynihan, soon to be Secretary of the GAA, was on the Kerry committee; Anthony

Mackey was on the Limerick committee and Robert Frewen on the Tipperary committee. Michael Cusack supported the pro-Parnell Dublin board; in Cork P. N. Fitzgerald organised support for Parnell. Even the GAA patrons were divided by the Split, with the Fenian John O'Leary heading the Dublin pro-Parnellite movement and Michael Davitt and William O'Brien equally prominent on the opposite side.

As the Split widened and the struggle for control of the nationalist movement grew in intensity, the GAA as a body lined up solidly behind Parnell. The first meeting of the new central council in April 1891 decided to hold a special general meeting of the Association, partly to try to halt the decline in activities, but also 'to take such action as may be deemed advisable . . . in support of the integrity of the national cause'. At this meeting, held in the Rotunda in Dublin in July and attended by delegates from sixty-three clubs (one-third of them from Dublin), a resolution was passed pledging the GAA's support for the leadership of Parnell. Clearly the national cause was now regarded as more important than the re-organisation of the GAA. Nor was this support confined to the leaders of the Association. As early as February, two months before the decision to hold the July meeting, the Dublin board had sponsored a successful demonstration by the Gaelic players and athletes of the city and county. At this Parnell himself spoke to a packed hall of delegates from twenty-seven clubs in the National Club and to an overflow crowd in the street outside. To a huge Parnellite convention held in Dublin just after the GAA's July meeting eleven counties sent special GAA delegations.

As students of modern Irish history know, Parnell suffered one major defeat after another in the last eight months of his life. Rejected by a majority of the parliamentary party which he had controlled for ten years, and opposed by the bishops and priests who had once been his most powerful allies, he lost vital by-elections to anti-Parnellite candidates and forfeited the support of the influential *Freeman's Journal*. The reaction of the deposed Irish leader was startling, unpredictable and even irresponsible. Defiantly Parnell tried to reach over the heads of cleric and politician alike to appeal directly and desperately to the fighting instincts of the average nationalist. It was in this last gamble, in which all his constitutional principles were thrown overboard, that Parnell obtained the enthusiastic aid of the IRB and of a big section of the GAA. Unfortunately, neither he nor the GAA stopped to consider the price the Association, from then on completely alienated from Home Ruler, lay and clerical, would have to pay for Parnell's recklessness, when his death in 1891 removed the principal justification for the Parnellite cause but only widened the gap and increased the bitterness between the two groups of Home Rulers.

How deeply committed to both the cause of Fenianism and that of Parnellism the GAA had become was never more obvious than at two notable public funerals which took place in Dublin late in 1891. The first, early in October, of Parnell himself, was described even by neutral observers as one of the biggest political demonstrations ever seen in Dublin. Occupying a prominent place in the vast cortege were the men of the GAA — said by some to number as many as 2,000 — who walked each carrying a hurley draped in black and held in reverse to resemble a rifle, through the city to Glasnevin cemetery. A few weeks later came the mysterious and tragic death in Mountjoy jail, shortly before his expected release after a ten-year sentence for treason, of the great Mayo athlete Pat Nally. This time the funeral was a joint GAA-IRB affair, with long lines of silent marching men in military formation following the coffin, on which lay the same green flag that a month before had covered Parnell's coffin; directly behind came the entire central council of the GAA.

Whatever hopes the GAA had up to the end of 1891 of halting the decline of the previous few years were dashed with the death of Parnell. As the divisions in the Home Rule movement became deeper than ever, the GAA stood out as the one national body that had defied the more substantial volume of nationalist opinion by supporting Parnell to the end. The price had now to be paid; how high it was to be is painfully obvious from the state of the GAA's affairs during the next ten years. Members left the Association in large numbers; clubs went out of existence; organised competitions and tournaments lapsed; in whole counties the GAA simply died. To give only two examples, from 1890 to 1896 Monaghan had no county board; for three years in the 1890s not a single Wexford club affiliated to the central council. Admittedly much of this decline was merely part of the general apathy that all sections of the nationalist movement experienced in the '90s; but for the GAA the position was aggravated by its stand for Parnell in 1891.

The annual convention for 1892 was not held until April 1893; it was attended by only fifteen delegates from three counties (Dublin, Cork and Kerry), and by five officers of the Association; J. K. Bracken, one of the founders, was present in a personal capacity and not representing Tipperary. Only the three counties represented at this convention played in the hurling championship, and only six — the same three, together with Waterford, Kildare and Roscommon — in the football championship; neither competition concluded until March 1893. Rural emigration was at a high level and attendances at games, even in the Dublin area, were unusually low. Despite occasional signs of renewed activity on the playing-field — in Monaghan, Laois, Down, Sligo, Meath, Leitrim and Tipperary — only four county boards held annual meetings. Apart from the six counties that participated in the football championship, the Association was in a semi-moribund condition everywhere.

Nor did 1893 bring any noticeable worthwhile improvement. Once again the annual convention was deferred to the following year; to it in Thurles in April, 1894, came a total of fourteen members, consisting of the Association's officers and delegates from six counties — Dublin, Cork, Kerry, Tipperary, Louth and Limerick. If attendance at the annual meeting of a voluntary body such as the GAA be accepted as a measure of its strength, this convention found the Association at its weakest. Emigration continued to drain many rural clubs of members; there was evidence of mismanagement at all levels of administration; many fixtures had to be abandoned because of the failure of one team to attend. At no time during that year could the central council claim to control more than eight counties — Dublin, Cork, Kerry, Louth, Waterford, Laois, Kildare and Tipperary. Cork was now reduced to only fifteen affiliated clubs; Connacht and Ulster were lost to the Association, with even Galway, from where the president hailed, unaffiliated for the first time since 1884. Little wonder that the possibility of a change of emphasis from the two field games to athletics was urged by a leading official early in 1893. Even this remedy was out of the question, for the simple reason that in all provinces the GAA was now for the first time in almost ten years losing control of athletics to the IAAA.

Nothing indicated the seriousness of the GAA's position at this stage better than the decision of the convention held in April 1893 to revoke the police rule. This rule, which denied membership of the Association to members of the RIC, was first introduced in February 1887 by the executive shortly after the IRB had gained control. Eleven months later, when a new constitution for the GAA was approved by the reconstruction convention of January 1888, the rule was restated in terms that also excluded the Dublin Metropolitan Police. The police had incurred the understandable enmity of most nationalists, who rightly regarded them as the force which — often all too willingly, not to say brutally — enforced the coercive policies of Dublin Castle against the nationalist population. That a body of now wholly nationalist athletes should not be prepared to admit policemen was not only reasonable but even defensible, given the high political temperature of the time. When that body was controlled by Fenians, such a rule was almost inevitable. That the GAA had a case for revoking the rule in 1893, when the dissensions caused by the Parnell Split had been followed by an easing-off of pressure by the Castle and when a Home Rule Bill was again being mooted, is undeniable. But the decision still suggests a greatly weakened GAA.

Associated with the police rule — certainly in the eyes of critics and opponents of the GAA — were two other rules, the boycott rule and the foreign games rule, one of which had long before 1893 been revoked because the circumstances justifying its existence no longer existed. This was the boycott rule, which had its origin in events preceding the foundation of the GAA, and was also the earliest of the three rules. Always conscious of the decline of native athletics in the years before 1884, and having for years tried to co-operate with unionist athletes in Dublin to halt this decline, Cusack never forgave his opponents for a move they made in the summer of 1884. Realising that his campaign for Home Rule in athletics was rapidly gaining in support, entries were refused from clubs or athletes not prepared to accept the Amateur Athletic Association (of England) as the governing body for Irish sport.[18] This deliberate and clearly concerted action Cusack justifiably regarded as a boycott of nationalist athletes; he would not have been human if he did not resolve to retaliate if given an opportunity.

With the foundation of the GAA Cusack's chance came. The second meeting of the Association (held in Cork in December 1884) decided that anybody competing at an athletics meeting held under the laws of another body would be ineligible to compete at sports meetings held under GAA laws. A rule to this effect, which became known as the boycott rule, was unanimously adopted at the next meeting of the GAA, held in Thurles in mid-January 1885.[19] With the other rules passed that day it came into operation on 17 March 1885, and could not be altered before the following November. Meanwhile in February 1885, as part of the campaign to kill the GAA already mentioned, the Irish Amateur Athletic Association, catering mostly for unionist athletes, had been founded. It now retaliated by passing a corresponding rule barring GAA athletes from participation at IAAA meetings from 1 September 1885.[20] According to Cusack, the GAA's boycott rule was merely a temporary expedient to help the Association to survive its critical early period when its existence was threatened by the anti-GAA campaign of 1885. Accordingly, when in November of that year its principal patron Archbishop Croke declared his opposition to both boycott rules, the GAA agreed to rescind its rule. The IAAA soon followed suit.

Equally defensible in the circumstances of the 1880s, and probably for years afterwards, was the foreign games rule, which later became known as the Ban and was to last to 1971. This began innocuously. At the GAA's first annual meeting in October 1885 Davin for the executive ruled that, while a man might play any type of football without losing his status as a GAA athlete, if he played non-Gaelic football his club (presumably his athletic club) could not join the GAA.[21] The adjourned meeting in February 1886 sent out a request to clubs not to play hurling or football with non-affiliated clubs — meaning in this case any hurling, football or athletic club. In September 1886 the executive extended the ineligibility to persons (as well as clubs) playing football or hurling under non-GAA rules. Finally in November 1886 the element of compulsion was introduced at the second annual meeting, which incorporated this ruling into the GAA's rules by declaring members of 'any other athletic association in Ireland' ineligible for membership of the GAA.

These three rules when taken together represented a deliberate stand by the early GAA which soon crystallised into what might fairly be called the Ban policy. Each rule, especially that on foreign games, represented a positive application in amateur sport of the boycott idea, which had proved so effective in the agrarian campaign of the Land League. However, simply to equate the rules with a boycott is not to do justice to the early leaders of the GAA, all of whom were much more conscious of its positive and protective element than of any negative or divisive aspect or impact. As Cusack had found, politics and sport could not be kept in separate compartments in nineteenth-century Ireland; sport was controlled by the anti-nationalist minority, which hoped to kill native pastimes. The GAA was begun largely as a bulwark against the rising tide of anglicisation that threatened to submerge Irish culture; and the Ban policy became for the GAA a means towards the end of preserving and extending native games.

For the GAA to revoke the police rule in 1893 was to admit that the fortunes of the Association were at an extremely low level, because to drop this rule was to compromise on one aspect of what it had regarded since 1887 as a fundamental and unalterable policy. That this should have happened in 1893 is surprising, because signs of a change in the GAA's fortunes were then beginning to appear. Attempts to diagnose the cause of the decline and to recommend remedies were being made by members and supporters, showing a widespread determination not to allow the Association to die. The possibility of revising the rules so as to reduce rough play and so improve the standard of play was debated in the press, where a measure of agreement emerged on the need to reduce the numbers of teams. In addition, the annual convention decided to appoint a special committee to attempt revivals in counties no longer affiliated to the central council. The need to increase income was generally recognised; from Kerry came a suggestion that two enclosed pitches be acquired in each province. Attempts at reorganisation were begun in several counties of Leinster and Munster; in November the central council issued a realistic appeal for a general revival of activities.

The promising position reached in 1893 was noticeably improved on in several respects in 1894. The first quarter of the year saw hopeful signs of revival, mostly in the form of conventions which produced provisional county committees, in Wexford, Tipperary, Kildare, Louth and Meath. In November a county committee reappeared in Limerick; Kerry also held a convention during the year; in Cork and Kilkenny there was a noticeable increase of activity by clubs over the previous few years. Once again the Association met with set-backs, probably the most serious being its failure to hold any annual convention for 1894. There was still no organised activity in Connacht or Ulster; even in mid-summer major games arranged for Dublin, Cork and Kilkenny fell through. That the Dublin board had to make important fixtures in April for the Phoenix Park was regarded as a bad omen; worse still, two All-Ireland finals had to be played at the same venue two months later.

Perhaps the most encouraging development for the central council in 1894 was the resumption by Dublin of its influential role in the GAA after a nine-month period of non-affiliation. The trouble had begun with the election in March 1893 of Michael Cusack as county secretary at a convention which revealed strong opposition to him. There followed withdrawals by many clubs from the county board, protests by some of them to the central council, a ruling in July by that body that Cusack's election was invalid, and a demand in August from council to board to replace him. The board rejected this demand and seceded. Two months later the position changed; two meetings of Dublin clubs reaffirmed loyalty to the Association. By February 1894 a new board without Cusack was affiliated. This prolonged dispute naturally weakened the GAA in Dublin; the number of clubs fell from thirty-four to thirteen in six months and it took a couple of years for the county to regain its pre-1893 strength.

From both the playing-field and the athletic arena the GAA was able to report further improvement in 1895. In some counties which had been seriously weakened by the Parnell Split — particularly Limerick, Kildare, Meath and Antrim — the number of clubs rose substantially. The attendance of 10,000 at a major fixture in Thurles in April was the highest so far recorded. The extent of activity in Dublin showed that the county was fast recovering from the 1893 split. Leinster and Munster both experienced a revival of athletics under GAA rules; the Secretary reported that thirty-two meetings had been registered with him by early August, and another thirty-eight by mid-November. A welcome move was the take-over from the IAAA of the all-round athletics championships, which that body had had to abandon for lack of support. In the championship eight counties (three from Leinster and all Munster except Cork) contested in hurling, and eleven (five each from Munster and Leinster, with Cavan) in football; neither final was played until March 1896.

That so marked an improvement in the GAA's fortunes in 1894 and 1895 should so quickly follow the revocation of the police rule in 1893 suggests that the lifting of the rule was the cause of the improvement. This was in fact the case. The 1893 decision was the beginning of a shift in policy by the Association designed to halt the decline in the years immediately after Parnell's death in 1891. Faced with a real danger of extinction within ten years of its foundation, the GAA now soft-pedalled on its hitherto inflexible support of the extreme nationalist philosophy. With a view to regaining that mass support it had enjoyed before 1891, it gradually shed and ultimately reversed its previous policy of shunning all opponents. It also adopted a new positive policy of co-operation with its main rival in the athletic arena, the IAAA.

Calls, all from inside the Association, for the GAA to keep out of politics began as early as the spring of 1893, nearly two months before the police rule was revoked. One of the more outspoken advocates of this policy was William Field MP of Dublin, who was treasurer to the central council from 1891 to 1893. A butcher by trade and a semi-professional politician of the anti-Parnellite majority, Field remained an influential figure in the GAA all during the nineties. In February 1893 a letter from him to the central council urging the GAA to steer clear of party politics received unanimous support. The following October, when the council was discussing reorganisation, Field repeated his views. In the intervening eight months there had been evidence of support for this line from the rank-and-file members, and the council's call in November (already mentioned) for a revival of activities frankly admitted the damage suffered through political involvement.

It was not until the rise to prominence of Dick Blake of Meath that the campaign for a non-political GAA really got off the ground. Blake, a native of Navan and of well-to-do farming stock noted neither for its support of extreme nationalism nor for its sympathy with Irish culture, first became prominent early in 1893 when he called for an overhaul of the rules of Gaelic football. Urging more detailed rules of play, he also advocated reforms such as the reduction of teams from seventeen- to fourteen-a-side, the abolition of special point-posts and the adoption of a standard size of ball. At a time when the foreign games rule was still unquestionably accepted, he openly admitted to a partiality for rugby and cricket and also suggested the borrowing of the best features of both rugby and soccer to make Gaelic football more attractive as a game to play and to watch.

With P. P. Sutton and Patrick Tobin of Dublin, a former Secretary of the Association, Blake spent much of 1894 reorganising the GAA in Meath and elsewhere, especially Tipperary and Wexford. Between them these three contacted 500 clubs that had lapsed after 1891. Later events suggest that Blake also that year widely canvassed members throughout the country for support for his ideas on a new-look GAA. He played a prominent part in the revival of Gaelic football in Meath and was one of the county's delegates to the April 1894 convention, which lifted the police rule. Towards the close of 1894 he found fault publicly with the administration of the Association, attributing much of its trouble to the dominant influence of the IRB, to which he was opposed, as well as to the Ban policy, to which he was also opposed.

By early January 1895 the Meath county board, of which he was chairman, had agreed to adopt and advance Blake's views on the reorganisation of the GAA at the next annual convention of the Association. Two remarkable letters which he wrote to the press a few weeks later give a clear picture of these views. Recalling the circumstances of the foundation of the GAA ten years before and praising the founders for their achievement, he argued convincingly for the proposition that, after the initial tidal wave of emotional success had subsided, no permanent basis had been built for the practical control and spread of the Association. This was demonstrated, Blake suggested, by the fact that Gaelic football, unknown in a codified form before 1885, had now surpassed hurling in popular appeal. In a scathing analysis of the looseness of the football laws based on personal experience of having played all three codes, he pleaded for new and more detailed rules; the game in its existing form, he believed, was 'crude and imperfect and unworthy of the GAA'. Finally, he alleged that from the start the GAA suffered from excessive personal wrangling based on political animosities and was too preoccupied with political topics.

Two months after publication of these views Blake found himself, as occupant of the chief post in the GAA, in a position to initiate the reforms he had been urging for two years. At the convention in Thurles in April 1895 a major re-shuffle of the Association's officers occurred. Peter Kelly, president since the second IRB take-over of January 1889, was succeeded by Frank Dineen of Limerick, vice-president since 1891. Dineen's place as vice-president went to Tobin, Secretary in 1891 and 1892. Field, after three years as treasurer, withdrew in favour of David Walsh of Cork, Tobin's successor as Secretary in 1892. Walsh's switch from Secretary to treasurer left the way open for the election of Blake as Secretary, a post he was to hold until 1898.

Blake lost no time in putting his mark on the Association now that he had become its leading administrative official; with Dineen and Tobin he formed an influential triumvirate committed to reform. Within a month of his election the central council announced a revision of the constitution and rules. The old rule permitting political discussions at the annual convention was replaced. In its place came an explicit declaration that the GAA was non-political and non-sectarian, a prohibition on the raising of political issues at GAA meetings at any level, a ban on the participation by clubs in any political movement and a recommendation for the avoidance of party names for clubs. In future the central council was to meet at least once monthly, alternately in Dublin and Thurles. Major changes in football laws were also made by the council. A standard size of ball was fixed; sideline linesmen with flags were introduced to assist referees; substitutes were prohibited. A player ordered off would not in future be allowed to return during the same game, and clubs were to be responsible for the conduct of both players and officials.

Nor was this all. Conscious of the emphasis placed on Irish athletics by the founders of the GAA, Blake concentrated on this field of activity too. At a central council meeting early in May 1895 he had himself, Dineen, Tobin and Sutton appointed as a special sub-committee to examine the laws of athletics. They reported back to the next meeting of the council, which made amendments to the rules and added several new events to the Association's athletic programme. Particularly since the Parnell Split, the grip of the GAA on rural athletics had been gradually weakening; by the mid-1890s the IAAA had penetrated to places where it had never before held meetings. This was especially the case in Connacht; towns like Galway and Claremorris no longer supported GAA meetings. To repair this damage Blake visited many places where GAA clubs had died out; realising that the revival of football and hurling clubs would help athletics, he issued a special circular appeal to such clubs in June 1895. All the time he continued to referee major games weekly all over Leinster and Munster.

The hand of Blake is also evident in several other new departures by the GAA in 1895. As if recognising that it was inevitable that nationalists and unionists would each remain in their own athletic organisations, the Association that year responded, if rather cautiously, to the latest overtures from the IAAA for co-ordination of suspensions and of records. The first move came from E. J. Walsh, Blake's opposite number, early in June; the following month Dineen, Tobin and Blake were authorised by the central council to meet the IAAA, but on reciprocity of records only. For a reason not now clear the two delegations did not meet until early in December; after only some hours' discussion, agreement was reached on a joint GAA-IAAA records committee. The central council at once ratified this and appointed the three GAA delegates as its members on the joint committee. It was apparently the IAAA also which first mentioned the possibility of an Irish team participating in the first revived Olympic Games fixed for March 1896. This idea was discussed by the central council and a decision taken to canvass clubs on the chances of forming a team; but by December the project had been abandoned.

Another welcome development for the GAA in 1895 for which Blake, as the main architect of a politically neutral Association, is entitled to most of the credit was the renewal by Archbishop Croke of active support after several years' aloofness. No longer politically active since the Parnell Split, Croke's return was all the more surprising because it involved a direct clash with Bishop Coffey of Kerry. Coffey had refused to support the GAA in Kerry because of what he regarded as its Fenian associations; his refusal was stated in terms so strong as to suggest his intention to cover GAA activities outside his own diocese. Shortly after Coffey's speech Croke showed his support by attending a major fixture at Thurles; he also assured the central council both of his disagreement with Coffey and of his intention to remain a patron of the GAA.

It was not until 1896 that, with the lifting of the foreign games rule, Blake made the principal change in the GAA with which his regime as Secretary is associated. It was inevitable that in his efforts to shift the GAA on to non-political lines he should sooner or later tackle this issue. In June 1895, shortly after his election as Secretary, Blake wrote to the Cork and Limerick boards pointing out that, because the foreign games rule had been abolished, there was now nothing to prevent a rugby or soccer player from also playing under GAA rules. Since there had been no central council decision to this effect, this communication was received with hostility in Cork and pointedly marked 'read' in Limerick. But Blake was not to be rebuffed so easily, least of all by two boards with strong IRB connections, and one may assume that he kept up the pressure to revoke the rule. Inside a year he was to succeed.

The exact circumstances of the revocation of the foreign games rule in 1896 are a mystery. At the annual convention in Thurles in May (attended by thirty-four delegates from eleven counties) the only relevant reference was a remark by Dineen in his presidential address that he would be asking for 'power to deal with members who play under rugby rules', suggesting the central council's opposition to such a practice[22]. No decision on this matter is reported, although the meeting lasted five hours. Two months later an appeal to the council by Thomas Irwin, a prominent player and later a well-known official, against his expulsion by the Cork board for having played rugby, was reversed by the council in terms implying that the rules did not now bar members from playing rugby. Cork was told that it could not make rules 'at variance with the rules of the Association'.

Cork did not let the matter rest there. To the August meeting of the central council it sent its chairman Michael Deering, who had been absent from the July meeting. When he asked when the rule barring rugby players from joining the GAA had been altered, Dineen told him that this had been done at the adjourned meeting of the recent convention. If Deering was puzzled by this explanation he had good reason to be, because the annual convention of 10 May 1896 had ended that day without any adjournment. However, it was the practice for annual conventions of this period to empower the incoming central council to conclude unfinished convention business. Although there is at least one recorded instance of a dissenting delegate successfully challenging this custom, in general county boards accepted it — as Cork did on this occasion.

At the same meeting in July 1896 at which it effectively killed the foreign games rule, the central council made another decision that demonstrated its determination to apply with rigid consistency to all political groups the new no-politics ruling. An invitation to send delegates to a Convention of the Irish Race, a gathering of some 2,000 Home Rule supporters from all parts of the English-speaking world, especially the United States, planned for Dublin for September 1896, was brusquely rejected. A warning was issued to all members of the GAA that attendance except in a personal capacity would lead to expulsion from the Association.[23] Because this Convention was largely anti-Parnellite, one may suspect the motives of some of the GAA leaders in imposing this ban. It provoked a characteristically irate comment from Michael Cusack, who was scathing on the incongruity of a body claiming to further the interests of Celtic culture prohibiting its members from taking part in a meeting of the Irish race.[24]

That a man like Blake, who had made such radical changes in the GAA in a few short years, made no enemies in the process is unlikely. Probably because of successful covering of tracks by his opponents, evidence is hard to come by; yet the sudden end in 1898 to his term of office could not have occurred without a build-up of opposition. Hostility to him from the IRB there certainly was; as early as August 1895 his resignation from chairmanship of the Meath board was forced through by an IRB majority on the pretext that Blake had supported an anti-Parnellite candidate in the recent general election. Moreover, in the absence of any other explanation, the resignation from the GAA presidency that year of the IRB man, Peter Kelly, after six years must be attributed to the fact that, like Davin in

1887, Kelly found himself out of sympathy with Blake's ideas, now adopted by the majority of the central council.

Much of the impetus for the movement which ultimately caused Blake's dismissal came from Munster and in particular from the influential Cork board, whose relations with the central council reached a record low level during Blake's period of office. For several years Cork had been one of the best organised counties in the GAA. The dissensions of the 1887–1889 period were not repeated during the Parnell crisis of 1890–1891, when Cork not only retained much of its vigour but also succeeded in keeping the Association alive in other parts of Munster, notably Limerick and Waterford. More than many other county boards in the early 1890s, Cork benefited from a fairly even balance of members belonging to the constitutional and physical force wings of the nationalist movement. Neither group was able to dominate, or to use the GAA for its own purposes. When in 1894 David Walsh of Cork city was elected Secretary of the GAA in succession to Patrick Tobin of Dublin, friction developed between the two. Walsh was supported by his county chairman Michael Deering, and matters deteriorated when Blake, in succeeding Walsh as Secretary in 1895, polled heavily against another Cork delegate.

Eventually, with the central council backing Blake and Tobin matters came to a head in May 1895. After a prolonged wrangle over the 1894 All-Ireland finals, which Blake had refereed, the council ordered a replay of one. Cork refused to comply; Deering resigned from the council; the Cork board withdrew from the Association. The central council stood its ground and Cork's secession lasted a year. During this period Cork acted in a manner suggestive of a board determined to set up a rival association. It levied affiliation fees from Limerick, organised its own competitions, awarded its own 'All-Ireland final' medals, permitted non-GAA handicappers at its athletics meetings, accepted 'affiliations' from Waterford clubs and successfully canvassed support for its defiance of the council from the Kerry and Limerick boards. Then suddenly in May 1896, after having disrupted the annual convention of that month (from which its delegates had to be forcibly ejected), the Cork board paid its affiliation fees and Deering returned to the central council.

Although the day's proceedings almost certainly set the scene for Blake's break with the GAA six months later, no detailed account has survived either of the 1897 convention, held in Thurles on 4 July, or of the central council meeting that preceded it. The convention, attended by fifty-seven delegates from fourteen counties and London, was delayed until 7.30 p.m. by the council meeting that had lasted from midday. It then became apparent that some council members had strongly attacked Blake for alleged mismanagement of the Association because he, presumably expecting a renewal of this criticism, made a detailed defence of his regime to the convention. He was, however, unable to answer adequately an allegation that he had seriously mismanaged the finances of the GAA. A special committee of three prominent delegates from Cork, Tipperary and Limerick was given the task of preparing an audit of the Association's accounts.

For the remainder of 1897 the three auditors wrestled in vain with the accounts. By December, with no report yet prepared by them, awkward questions were being asked both in the press and at county board meetings; the central council was accused of protecting Blake. Then in mid-January 1898 a special meeting of the council was called by the principal officers for Thurles for 22 January to consider the financial position. Although it was held in private, a report was supplied to the press; it admitted that the GAA was again on the verge of bankruptcy, with creditors pressing for settlement of substantial accounts. Dineen charged Blake with incompetency; after a detailed reply, Blake was dismissed by six votes to five on the casting vote of Dineen. Dineen took over as temporary Secretary until the convention of the following May, when he was elected Secretary and was succeeded as president by Deering. Blake, however, had the last word on this affair; in 1900 he published a pamphlet in which he vigorously defended his administration.

Blake's career as Secretary of the GAA ended in circumstances similar to those of Cusack's dismissal twelve years before. Like Cusack, he was forced out of office ostensibly because he had failed to look after the administration of the GAA, a state of affairs which (if true) revealed astonishing neglect by a man who had got himself made Secretary largely because of promises to reform the administrative structure of the Association. Like Cusack, however, Blake opted for a system of one-man rule; in addition, his arrogant manner, his generally inflexible attitude in management and his tactless handling of major games he refereed between them all ensured that when any shortcomings as an official became an issue he was found to have many enemies. On the other hand, his pamphlet convincingly answers many of the charges made against him, and nearly forty years later a prominent GAA figure admitted publicly to embarrassment at the recollection of the manner of Blake's dismissal.[25]

To Blake's credit it must be recorded that the period of his term of office as Secretary coincided with a welcome and large-scale revival of activity on the playing-field. It is at least arguable that, but for his work as a referee and the tightening-up of playing rules for which he was mainly responsible, this revival might not have occurred. Admittedly Connacht and Ulster remained almost entirely outside the GAA; in athletics the grip of the IAAA on the West continued; in addition, All-Ireland finals continued to be hopelessly in arrears. But almost everywhere in Munster and Leinster hurling, and more particularly football, made a remarkable recovery in the four years from 1895 to 1898. Cork, even when not affiliated, became the most active county of all; from 1894 onwards Kerry and Tipperary, now under new county bounds, regained their former positions of prominence; Limerick was second only to Cork in Munster in the number of clubs. Other counties where newly-elected county boards formed the mainspring of a revival of Gaelic games were Kildare, Offaly and Meath. Dublin too, after several lean years, returned to its old position of strength from 1896, when it awarded its first championship medals since 1890.

For the first time since the Parnell Split the number of affiliated clubs exceeded 300 in 1896. The previous year the total had been as low as 217; in 1897, the first year in which the receipts of the GAA exceeded £1,000, it rose to 360, an increase of sixty per cent in a two-year period. Among other notable events in the GAA world in 1896 were the institution of the Croke Cup inter-county competitions in both hurling and football, marking the silver jubilee of the principal patron's epis-copal appointment; a successful Gaelic tournament in London where a separate county board had recently been formed; and the reconstitution in several counties of clubs that had once been the leading ones in their areas — the Harps in Armagh, the Kickhams and the Metropolitans in Dublin, and the Arravale Rovers in Tipper-ary, to mention only a few of the best-known.

In 1897 an event with an international flavour occurred when in May the Celtic Hurling Club of Dublin travelled to Glasgow to play Glasgow Cowal Shinty Club. Two months later the Scots came to Dublin for a return game, which Michael Cusack refereed. That year too Blake edited and published the only issue of *The Gaelic News*, an eight-page tabloid with a pictorial supplement. The editorial, after explaining that the reason for the new paper was the inadequate coverage of Gaelic games in the contemporary Irish press, expressed the hope that readers would give their views on the need for a weekly paper catering for members of the GAA. But, so far as can be ascertained, no other issue of *The Gaelic News* appeared, and the weekly publication never materialised.

That such progress was made by the GAA while he was Secretary strengthens the suspicion that Blake was dismissed not so much because of any faults as an administrator but rather because he was opposed to that section of the nationalist movement from which the Association drew most of its members. Blake himself is on record on several occasions as having complained at central council meetings of attempts to use the GAA for political purposes; there is also evidence that some of the criticism directed against him sprang from his support of the constitutional movement. Up to a point Dineen, although an IRB man, loyally backed Blake's reforms. Deering supported his unanimous re-election as Secretary in July 1897 and was the only central council member out of twelve present to abstain from voting on the resolution to dismiss Blake in January 1898. To the many extreme nationalists in the GAA, however, such radical decisions as the dropping of the police rule, the lifting of the foreign games ban and the boycott of the Irish Race Convention, all associated with his regime, suggested that Blake was soft on nationalism.

Chapter 4

1898–1909

The timing of Blake's dismissal as Secretary of the GAA early in 1898, when looked at in retrospect, was symbolic, because a decision of the central council in October 1897 (which he supported) not to take part in the celebrations for the centenary of the 1798 Rising showed how out of touch with nationalist philosophy the GAA had got under Blake. The impact of this nation-wide movement of 1898 on the fortunes of the nationalist cause has been widely overlooked. It marked the beginning of the revival of nationalist agitation after 1891, and led both to the re-unification of the parliamentary party and to the Sinn Féin movement. Clearly IRB-inspired and largely IRB-controlled, the '98 centenary movement began as early as January 1897 when a small Dublin republican group, the Young Ireland League, decided to try to rally nationalist enthusiasm by sponsoring celebrations of the '98 Rising.[1] The idea spread like wildfire. Inside a few months every section of nationalist opinion had given its support. Local communities were formed on which Home Rulers of both factions, as well as Fenian and religious and cultural figures, all outdid one another in devising ways of honouring the United Irishmen of a century before.

Eventually in September 1897 the principal '98 Centenary Committee, popularly known as the City Hall Committee because of where it held its meetings in Dublin, offered two seats on its executive council to the GAA. The central council was asked to select its nominees at its October meeting. Of the nine council members present only five spoke; they revealed a fundamental division on the invitation from the City Hall Committee. Predictably, Frank Dineen and Jim Nowlan of Kilkenny, both with strong republican sympathies, were in favour of joining the committee. Equally predictably Tom Kiely, the world-famous athlete, Spencer Lyons of Limerick and Blake were against participation. A heated discussion ended with no formal decision being taken, after Dineen had ruled out a proposal by Lyons which might well have split the GAA once more. Effectively, however, the central council's indecision amounted to a severe rebuff to the City Hall Committee, although in the long run the moderate and conciliatory handling by Dineen of a delicate problem probably contributed to quite a different result. Nevertheless, this episode marked the lowest point in the nationalist commitment of the GAA.

The central council's neutral stance in October 1897 did not, however, mean that the Association or its members remained aloof from the year-long celebrations in 1898. On the contrary, the extent of the GAA's participation in the centenary movement was such as to suggest that the leading officers of the Association were now out of touch with the feeling of the rank-and-file members. This had been the case at the time of the convention of 1887; it was to be the case again in the years immediately before the Rising of 1916. Everywhere in 1898 members of the GAA were active in the various forms of local celebration, exploiting the influence they had gained in the Association and using their experience of committee work in it to further the centenary movement. Nor was this participation confined to IRB men in the GAA; in Dublin, for example, one of the most energetic supporters was Michael Cusack, who was still outside the ranks of the Fenian organisation.[2] In Dublin too Patrick Tobin was prominent in '98 work, as was Michael Deering in Cork; both were Parnellite Home Rulers.[3] In some counties the GAA county board, in spite of the absence of a lead from the central council, actively joined the '98 movement, and in several cases even led it, filling a gap caused by Home Rule apathy or by lack of local IRB organisation. Since money had to be found to finance the many '98 memorials erected throughout the country, the GAA in many counties organised special '98 tournaments in addition to its ordinary competitions. In a few counties support for the '98 movement actually generated an immediate revival of GAA activities; elsewhere, such a revival, although slower to develop, can be traced to a renewal of interest in native games in 1898.

Dublin, as the centre of nationalist activity, was naturally the focal point of the '98 celebrations. Here the GAA, without any pressure from its IRB members, had been enthusiastically participating from early in 1897. The annual convention of the Dublin board in mid-February had, without waiting for any lead from the central council, unanimously pledged its support to the movement, and asked for club delegates to attend the preliminary City Hall meeting on 4 March. One of the GAA's patrons, the Fenian leader John O'Leary, headed the City Hall Committee until its job was completed at the end of 1898. Among the more prominent figures on the Committee were P.N. Fitzgerald and Fred Allan, both leading members of the GAA almost from its foundation.[4] After the ceremonial laying of the foundation stone of the Wolfe Tone monument in Dublin in mid-August 1898, probably the biggest gathering of the whole year was for a multi-platform meeting in the Phoenix Park on 13 March. Here Cusack, who spoke in Irish, was one of the principal orators.[5] The Dublin county board also provided a meeting-place for all connected with the celebrations during the year when in June it opened the Gaels '98 Centenary Club.

When the year 1898 had ended, the small band of men who nearly two years before had started the '98 movement must have felt that their idea had succeeded beyond all expectations. All over the country '98 clubs had sprung up; countless monuments and plaques had been erected; graves and birthplaces of '98 men had been honoured; towns had vied with one another in arranging lectures and discussions, as well as visits to local historic sites. Nationalist Ireland received through the year-long celebrations an injection of national enthusiasm and an emotional tonic of patriotism that were badly needed to help it to recover from the shock of Parnell's sudden overthrow and from the disillusionment of the years following his death. Equally important, perhaps, the '98 movement, by providing a neutral platform for all sections of the still deeply divided nationalist movement, forcibly reminded nationalists of the need for unity to achieve any worthwhile success. Furthermore, a number of subsequently more prominent nationalists — particularly those who were to advocate total political separation from Britain — later acknowledged that their earliest patriotic urge had come in 1898, demonstrating that the '98 movement deserves recognition as a milestone in the cultural revival which in turn produced the political revival of the early twentieth century. In this notable and influential centenary movement the GAA, despite the initial unrepresentative decision of its central council to remain neutral, played a leading role through its ordinary members.

Notwithstanding its prominent part in the '98 celebrations, the GAA did not at once regain its old vigour. It is true that the next two years or so witnessed a renewal of activity on the playing-fields, especially in Munster, the southern half of Leinster, in Galway and Dublin. However, compared to the three-year regime of Blake, the period of about four years after his dismissal was notable for the lack of solid achievement or growth by the Association. Shortage of money, for which Blake had been blamed, continued to be a headache for the central council. Moreover, the removal of Blake himself caused a severe, if only temporary, loss of confidence in the administration of the GAA by many county boards. Factors outside the Association's control also hindered its progress during this period around the turn of the century. Among them were the conditions of near-famine in many parts of Munster and Connacht in 1898 (caused by a serious failure of the potato crop), and internal dissensions between various wings of the physical force movement, which prevented the IRB from exploiting the goodwill it had built up in 1898 and exerting its old influence in the councils of the GAA.

Within a few days of Blake's dismissal in January 1898 the Limerick county board passed an unanimous vote of no confidence in the central council, and called for an immediate special convention of the Association. In the following few weeks the Meath and Cork boards, at meetings which discussed the financial position, also called for a special convention. The central council now understandably took fright. At its March meeting it ratified a series of decisions taken by Dineen and authorised some further measures, all designed to keep a stricter supervision over the funds. In particular, two members of the council were directed to undertake an audit of the accounts left by Blake. The annual congress (held in Thurles in May) concluded a long debate on finance, in which the council came under strong attack, with a decision to call a special meeting in July of three delegates from each county board. This decision was never implemented, probably because, after difficulties encountered in concluding the audit ordered in March, the central council did not obtain details of the audited accounts until its August meeting. When these were circulated to county boards criticism of the council on this score subsided.

The attendance and county representation at annual congresses serve as a convenient barometer of the fortunes of the GAA in the first decade of the twentieth century. The figures in the Table below, particularly those in cols. (3) and (4), tell their own story. The three years following 1898 saw the Association at its weakest during the twelve-year period covered. Considering the accessibility for Munster delegates, who then accounted for a high proportion of the attendance, of Thurles (still invariably the venue for the congress), the figures for 1900 and 1901 are so low as to suggest a body once again moribund as at the time of the Parnell Split. There is reliable evidence that the older men then in control of the central council, discouraged by the growing debts and the falling-off in activities, even considered winding up the GAA. The 1903 congress appears to mark the end of this new slump in the GAA. From then on the number of delegates first, and the number of counties represented next, began to rise; by 1910 all but seven or eight of the thirty-two counties were usually represented, and the gross attendance (col. (6) of the Table) settled at around one hundred.

ATTENDANCE AT CONGRESSES 1899–1910					
(1) YEAR	(2) DATE	(3) NO. OF COUNTIES[1]	(4) NO. OF DELEGATES[2]	(5) NO. OF OFFICERS[2]	(6) TOTAL ATTENDANCE
1899	16.7.1899	8	37	10	47[3]
1900	9.9.1900	8	30	not listed	30[4]
1901	22.9.1901	10	29	10	39[5]
1902	30.11.1902	14	38	9	47[6]
1903	8.11.1903	17	60	15	75[7]
1905[8]	8.1.1905	19	70	6	76[9]
1906	27.1.1906	15	64	5	69[10]
1907	22.2.1907	19	85	2	87[11]
1908	24.2.1908	18	106	1	107[12]
1909	28.2.1909	24	78	1	79[13]
1910	27.3.1910	24	70	1	71[14]

1. The London board when represented is not included in this column.
2. Generally, but particularly for 1905–1910, where central council minutes and press reporters differ, the report is accepted because it appears to be more reliable. For 1908–1910 the Secretary is the only officer not also on a county delegation.
3. *Sport*, 22.7.1899.
4. *CE*, 11.9.1900.
5. Mins. & *CE*, 24.9.1901.
6. Mins. & *CE*, 1.12.1902.
7. Mins. & *FJ*, 9.11.1903.
8. No congress held in 1904.
9. *Sport*, 14.1.1905.
10. *Sport*, 3.2.1906.
11. *Sport*, 2.3.1907.
12. *Sport*, 29.2.1908.
13. *Sport*, 6.3.1909.
14. Mins.

These trends, and especially the unmistakable falling-off in membership around the turn of the century, are confirmed by other random figures, particularly some for counties where the Association had hitherto flourished in spite of adverse local circumstances. By late 1899 Dublin had only twenty clubs affiliated to the county board. Although this position improved in the next two years, the board organised no football or hurling championships in 1902.[6] Other counties where club championships lapsed around this period were Kildare (1898, 1899, 1901), Laois (1900), Louth (1899), Kerry (1898, 1899) and Meath (1901). Cork's total of thirty-six affiliated clubs in 1899 showed a drop of over fifty per cent since 1897 and fell to an almost incredible fifteen by March 1900, a depressing slump considering the extent of activity generated in that county by the 1898 celebrations and the prominent role it had played in GAA affairs from the start. Wexford by early 1899 was reduced to ten clubs; a year later only one Wicklow club was affiliated to the Association. Eight delegates attended the Tipperary convention for 1900; in January 1900 Galway had only eleven clubs; in April 1901, Kildare had only seven.

While such external factors accounted partly for the decline of the Association at this period, it is impossible to avoid the conclusion that the inefficiency and quarrelsomeness of some of its principal officers also contributed to the slump. The minutes of the central council around this period reveal a deplorable tendency to bickering, resulting in frequent clashes of rival personalities at a time when a potential for growth existed. An inordinate amount of time at these meetings was spent sorting out seemingly trivial disputes between county boards, with frequently no firm decision being reached, occasionally because leading members (including a president once) simply walked out when they disagreed with the majority view. In the summer of 1899 the Clare and Limerick boards were suspended in the course of an obscure disagreement with the council; inside a year the GAA was practically dead in Clare. Around the same time, no sooner had a three-year split been ended which had led to two rival boards in Waterford, than the Wexford board was suspended on technical grounds although the Association was already weak there. For most of 1899 central council meetings were hampered by friction between the Cork officials Michael Deering, Thomas Dooley and William Wrenn, and a group led by Alderman Jim Nowlan of Kilkenny and the young hot-headed Limerick man J. J. Keane of the Dublin board. Keane unsuccessfully opposed Deering for the presidency in July 1899 at an annual congress which, like that of 1900, had to be postponed several times, mainly because of delay in closing the council's accounts.

The GAA was unfortunate in losing in the period between 1899 and 1901 the services of some of its more competent early leaders. Tim O'Riordan, an early Secretary of the Association, died in January 1899; two years later Michael Deering of Cork and P. P. Sutton of Dublin, a Wexfordman who had been active with Cusack from the start, both died. Others like John Wyse Power and John Cullinane (now an MP) had ceased to take an active interest in the GAA. The renewal of parliamentary activity following the reunification of the Irish Parliamentary Party in 1900 resulted in most of the MPs who supported the Association, among them T. C. Condon of Tipperary, Eugene Crean of Cork and William Field and J. P. Nannetti of Dublin, now only identifying themselves with the GAA when publicity was likely to help their public careers. Of prominent early GAA leaders still playing leading roles in the Association only Dineen and Cusack now remained.

Another factor contributing to the failure of the GAA to build on its success in the 1898 movement was the continued lack of support for the Association in many areas from the Catholic clergy. Despite the lead given from 1895 onwards by Archbishop Croke, who though in poor health attended games in Tipperary up to three years before his death in 1902, there was at this stage and for some years afterwards a noticeable lack of support by other bishops. Two exceptions were Bishop O'Donnell of Raphoe in Donegal and Croke's successor, Fennelly, who had been an active member of the GAA as far back as 1887.[7] In Dublin, although one may interpret his attitude towards the GAA at the time as one of benevolent neutrality, the shrewd Archbishop Walsh evaded replying directly to an invitation from the central council in 1903 to become a patron of the Association. All through the 1890s, after the concerted withdrawal of clerical support at the time of the Parnell Split, there was a total absence of clerical involvement in the affairs of the GAA. This state of affairs was to last in some places almost to the end of the second decade of the new century, when changed political conditions once more made the GAA not merely safe but desirable from the clerical point of view. Even the neutral political stance adopted by Blake from 1896 to 1898 did not win back the clergy to the Association, a failure possibly partly attributable to Blake's widely known agnosticism.

Nevertheless one can find plenty of exceptions to this prolonged clerical boycott of the GAA. Here and there throughout the country were scattered, particularly from 1898 onwards, individual clergy either conscious of the beneficial social effect of organised games in rural areas remote from other forms of entertainment, or else sufficiently nationally minded to support the Association and occasionally run the risk of local episcopal disapproval. Because of the involvement in the GAA of Archbishops Croke and Fennelly, priests in Tipperary fully participated in GAA activities. Elsewhere one finds priests supporting the Association in such widely scattered places as Letterkenny in 1898, Banteer (Cork) in the same year, Glasthule (Dublin) in 1903 and Limerick in 1904, where a priest had presided at the annual county convention two years before.[8] Examples of clerical opposition to organised native games, while understandably less publicised, may also be found, especially in the years just after the turn of the century. To its credit *The Leader* usually a staunch supporter of the Church, published an acid and unanswered letter from the Secretary of the Down board of the GAA in 1904, alleging organised clerical opposition to the Association in that county. Two years later a complaint of more widespread clerical opposition to Gaelic games on Sundays also went unanswered.[9]

To make matters worse for the GAA in the years immediately before and after 1900, it found itself deprived not only of clerical but also of Fenian support. In view of the doubtful effect on the Association which IRB influence had had some ten years earlier, when it led to the withdrawal of active participation by many constitutional nationalists as well as by the Catholic clergy as a body, it is ironic to reflect that the GAA was now suffering from too little badly-needed Fenian infiltration. This state of affairs was caused largely by internal dissension inside the Fenian body, with the result that the physical force movement, like the GAA itself, failed to consolidate (much less to exploit) the gains it had made in 1898. Significantly, of the leading IRB men prominent in the early GAA Dineen was now the only survivor. Moreover, long before the rejuvenation of the Fenian organisation had been inspired by the return to Dublin from the United States of Tom Clarke in 1908, the GAA, with the aid of a timely influx of membership from the rapidly expanding Gaelic League, was well on the road to recovery.

A longside the older officials who by 1900 had become understandably gloomy about the prospect for survival by the GAA was a group of younger men determined to rejuvenate the Association, who decided that the time for positive action had now arrived. At the annual congress held in September 1901 two of this group were elected to office, Jim Nowlan of Kilkenny as president and Luke O'Toole of Wicklow as Secretary. With the two top posts in the Association now in the hands of a new, energetic and mostly younger generation of officials, the GAA at last began to show unmistakable signs of revival, although the process was to be slow and intermittent. Nowlan, imperturbable, unimaginative but devoted to Irish culture, was to retain the presidency for twenty years. O'Toole, an energetic, sociable but by no means invariably efficient organiser, was to remain Secretary for almost thirty years and was the first genuinely full-time chief officer of the GAA. Between them Nowlan and O'Toole, who found the Association at the lowest point of its fortunes, were to be instrumental in reviving it and guiding it to its first period of real expansion.

The infusion of new blood at top level did not end with the election in 1901 of Nowlan and O'Toole. Around this time P.J. Devlin and Michael Crowe both came to the fore in the GAA. An Armagh man, Devlin under the pen-name 'Celt' was to expound in print the ideals of the Association for the next quarter-century. Crowe, a Limerick man, was to work tirelessly and with much success for nearly twenty years as a referee to make the games more scientific as public spectacles. In Dublin J. J. Keane (also of Limerick), who had been prominent in Dublin board affairs for several years, began to make his forceful voice heard from 1900 onwards. In Munster Pat McGrath of Tipperary, who was to be secretary of the provincial council from 1904 to his death twenty-seven years later, also became an influential figure around this time. Since Crowe is the only one of these six of whom one can state with near-certainty that he was in the IRB, their rise to power marked the loosening of that body's grip on the early GAA.

The partial ending of IRB influence on the GAA was, however, blurred by the election to the central council around this time of another new personality. For of Thomas F. O'Sullivan of Listowel one can state with certainty that he was a leading IRB man and that he brought with him in his work for the GAA the assertive separatist ideals of the secret body, which seemed to find more acceptable expression through his attractive and dedicated manner. Furthermore, O'Sullivan came to the council with the formidable reputation of a man who had revived almost single-handed the GAA in Kerry, a county that had for a time been a bulwark of the early Association and was soon, largely through the solid foundation laid by O'Sullivan, to regain that position permanently.[10] A journalist by profession, T. F. O'Sullivan cut his formal links with the GAA when he took up a post in Dublin in 1907; although his connection with the Association was brief, his influence on it was to be lasting.

This expansion by the GAA from 1901 onwards was part of the general revival of the whole nationalist movement which began around that time. In the 1890s the bitter factional aftermath of the Parnell Split had caused many young nationalists to divert their energies into cultural activities, of which the steady growth of the Gaelic League became the most noticeable result. The '98 centenary movement, followed by the rival support by nationalists and loyalists for the opposing sides in the Boer War, the launching in 1899 with IRB support of Arthur Griffith's weekly paper *United Irishman* and the ending in 1900 of the split in the Irish Parliamentary Party, all created an atmosphere favourable to a move away from cultural nationalism towards political nationalism. By building on the cultural foundations laid by bodies like the League and the GAA, men like Griffith and Clarke gradually won support for a more outspoken, self-reliant and less conciliatory brand of nationalism than that of the parliamentary movement.

The revival of separatist philosophy in the early years of the new century, for which the GAA had been partly responsible, also helped the Association. Its loyalty to the sector of Irish culture which it had continued to foster in good times and bad was now rewarded. As the programme put forward by the young Sinn Féin organisation began to attract public support, the GAA found itself caught up in a kind of snowball effect that was to make political independence a live issue again soon. Particularly between 1907 and 1910, as Sinn Féin spread to widely separated parts of the country, prominent local members and supporters of that body, conscious of the value of the GAA in furthering their cause, pushed themselves to the front on several GAA county boards. Foremost in this new infiltration of the Association were J. J. Walsh in Cork, Austin Stack in Kerry, Charlie Holland in Limerick, Harry Boland in Dublin and Cahir Healy in Fermanagh.[11] It became clear too that Nowlan, O'Toole and others of the new leadership were ardent Sinn Féin supporters, so that from now on the fortunes of the GAA became tied to those of Sinn Féin.

It was from the ranks of the Gaelic League that the GAA in the first few years of the 1900s received a welcome, and in some places, a badly needed infusion of new ordinary members. They provided the same impetus to expansion which men like Nowlan, Crowe and O'Toole were providing just then at central council level. During the 1890s many GAA members had joined the League; from 1900 or so onwards there was a noticeable flow in the opposite direction also. In Dublin and many of the smaller towns it became increasingly common for a Gaelic League branch to set up its own hurling (or less frequently, Gaelic football) club; affiliation of this to the local GAA county board immediately involved the club members in the affairs and activities of the Association. By 1910 or so dual membership had become normal for the majority of athletically-minded urban-based nationalists; for many of them their first contact with the GAA came through their earlier involvement in the League.

An important result of this influx of Gaelic League members into the GAA was that it brought into the Association at rank-and-file level a different type of man from most of the earlier ordinary members. Until 1900 or so the bulk of the GAA membership consisted in rural areas of farm labourers and small farmers, and in the towns of tradesmen, shop assistants, barmen and the like. Now in the early 1900s there arrived from the Gaelic League branches a completely new stratum of largely non-manual workers such as teachers, commercial clerks, local officials and civil servants, who because of their higher educational attainments had been attracted in the late 1890s into the Irish language and allied cultural activities of the League. In their own clubs and on their own county boards this category now played almost as decisive a role as did the new blood on the central council in revitalising the GAA. To teachers in particular, who were to supply some of the outstanding figures in later years, the GAA was to be permanently indebted.

This influx of members from the Gaelic League led to an improved standard of administration in the GAA which lasted until political events in the second decade of the century began to have a disruptive effect on the Association. This improvement coincided roughly with the establishment between 1900 and 1903 of the four provincial councils, themselves an important development in the growth of the GAA. Under the aegis of the councils were run the provincial championships, which mark the start of the annual All-Ireland competition. Eventually each provincial council, with its own officers, came to generate a new source of income separate from the central council's, providing funds for development in its own provinces. In time the provincial councils became corner-stones of the GAA's administrative structure, bringing a welcome degree of decentralisation to balance a move to Dublin by the central council, soon to be recorded.

Shortly after his election the new Secretary, Luke O'Toole, made the first of many visits to various parts of the country to stimulate the revival or reorganisation of the GAA in counties where it had become moribund or disorganised. Michael Crowe travelled long distances to referee important games, in the expectation (duly fulfilled) that his consistent application of the playing rules would in time help to standardise the style of play and lead to a uniform local interpretation of the rules. The year 1902 in particular was remarkable for the number of counties that, under newly-formed boards, re-affiliated to the Association — Louth and Meath early in the year, Laois, Mayo, Kilkenny and Roscommon later in the Spring. In addition that year other leading counties — Dublin, Tipperary, Cork, Clare and Wexford — reported notable increases in club numbers. This trend continued in 1903 and 1904, with the revival of the once active Cavan and Armagh boards and a resurgence in Wicklow in 1903, followed in 1904 by a steep rise in the number of clubs in Limerick.

A far-seeing step taken by the central council at this time was the decision in January 1904 to rent permanent office accommodation at O'Connell Street in the heart of Dublin. Not only did this help further to improve the administration of the Association at top level, but it also marked the first stage in a gradual move away from Munster as the GAA became a more national body in the geographical sense. It also made easier the later more important decisions to switch the annual congress to Dublin and to locate the GAA's principal stadium in that city. Equally indicative of the ambitious ideas of the new men now leading the Association was the proposal, doggedly put forward on several occasions by O'Toole, that the GAA should publish its own official organ. When no action followed a motion to this effect at the 1903 congress, O'Toole repeated his suggestion the next year and succeeded in having a special committee set up to examine the commercial aspect of the proposal. It was not his fault that nothing came of it.

It was on the playing-fields, mostly those of Leinster and Munster, that the GAA made its most spectacular advances in the early years of the century, and especially between 1902 and 1906. This mainly took the form of a sudden all-round improvement in the standard of Gaelic football, quickly followed by a dramatic rise in the number of spectators at big matches. At a distance of over ninety years, and with all the principals involved long dead, it is difficult precisely to explain the cause of this major revival of native football; the most that can be done is to list what appear to have been the principal factors and admit that as between one area and another different factors probably had varying effects. The uniform refereeing of men like Crowe, Pat McGrath of Tipperary, Stephen Holland of Dublin and O'Toole and the influx of many new players between them produced a more scientific, less rough-and-tumble brand of football. The greater dedication to the promotion of Irish games as part of Irish culture generally, to some extent or in some areas stimulated or provoked by the spread of association football, probably also contributed to the revival of Gaelic football.

A few outstandingly keen fixtures, in particular the All-Ireland finals played in October 1902 and a Dublin-Tipperary challenge football match of February 1905, attracted much bigger crowds than usual. However, the climax of this resurgence of Gaelic football and effectively its coming-of-age as a popular game in modern times, came in the late summer and autumn of 1905, with the All-Ireland (home) football final for 1903, when it took three games to give Kerry a narrow win over Kildare. Never before had a final run to three matches; in the subsequent ninety-odd years of the GAA this has happened again only once, in 1931. Although precise figures were not recorded, it is generally accepted that close on 60,000 people saw one or more of the three games — the unfinished game in Tipperary in late July, the drawn match in Cork in early September and the last game (again in Cork) in late October. On all three occasions, but especially in the second and third games, it was agreed even by experts in the rival codes who attended that the standard of play exceeded anything previously seen in a Gaelic football match.

Of even greater long-term significance, however, than any improvement in internal efficiency or any rise in the numbers playing or watching football was the new role in the nationalist movement which the GAA assumed following what might fairly be called the Sinn Féin infiltration between 1901 and 1903. For the first time since 1886 the Association now became a fully-fledged component of the nationalist movement. But while twenty years earlier it was a case of the parliamentary party tactfully courting a new mass movement with an eye to votes at parliamentary elections, the position from 1903 onwards was different. The GAA, largely because of its prominence in the defence of native culture, was now an equal partner with the other group of bodies which together formed the separatist sector of Irish nationalism in the early years of the twentieth century. This state of affairs was to continue until the partial attainment of political independence in 1922.

Apart from organising native games, the GAA's participation in the nationalist movement took other forms. To funerals of prominent nationalist figures like the Young Ireland leader Gavan Duffy and the Fenian leaders James Stephens and John O'Leary (all of whom died early in the century) it sent large numbers of members, often carrying hurleys. It took a leading part in events such as those in 1903 marking the centenary of Emmet's rising. It never overlooked an opportunity, whether at local or central council level, of supporting the Gaelic League. It took a major part in the annual cultural (and later industrial) parade held under League auspices in Dublin every St Patrick's Day — which in 1903 became a public holiday following a campaign in which the GAA took part.

The GAA's close connections with the new nationalist movement led to a fresh look at the Association's policy on English games and eventually to a restoration of the ban on participation in them by GAA members. It was probably inevitable that the departure of Blake in 1898 and the resurgence of separatist ideas should revive the question of non-Gaelic games. The actual change in policy was, however, gradual and, given the emotional atmosphere of the time, the extent of reservations and even dissent on the topic surprisingly wide. Ultimately the current mood among nationalists of resistance to further anglicisation produced a decisive majority in the GAA in favour of ending all contacts with rival sports bodies.

Foremost in a three-year campaign which culminated in the re-imposition in January 1905 of the foreign games rule by the 1904 congress was a group of prominent officials, consisting partly of IRB men like Dineen and O'Sullivan and partly of younger Sinn Féin members like Pat Nash of the Dublin board. This campaign began with the successful piloting through the 1901 congress of a motion introducing a voluntary ban; the Association pledged resistance to the spread of English games, calling on Irish youth not to play them and authorising county boards to disqualify members assisting non-Gaelic games in any way. Inside three months the Dublin board, probably as a lead to others, had taken such suspending powers; by August 1902 it had used them.

At the next congress (held in November 1902) Nash for the Dublin board was instrumental in having a motion passed which changed the optional character of the 1901 English games rule into one providing for automatic suspension of members who played football under non-Gaelic codes. A year later again a motion by Cusack was passed which would have effectively continued the 1902 rule; also passed on a 25-24 vote was a Cork amendment giving each board discretion on whether to enforce the rule in its area. Little more than a year later, however, at the 1904 congress (held in January 1905) a twin decision retained the automatic suspension and rejected a Cork move to give boards an option on enforcement. The 1905 decision was effectively confirmed by the 1907 congress, which rejected by seventy votes to nineteen a Cork motion to rescind the 1904 ruling.

Meanwhile, 1903 found O'Sullivan and Nash also moving on another front in their drive to rid the GAA of all traces of what they regarded as the West British policy which Blake and his supporters had pursued. At the adjourned 1902 congress, held in January 1903, both were instrumental in having a motion passed preventing future participation in hurling or Gaelic football by policemen, soldiers and sailors, an opposing motion by Cork failing on a vote of thirty-four to twelve. Eleven months later at the adjourned 1903 congress this decision was, at the instigation of O'Sullivan, extended to cover athletics meetings held under GAA laws, and also to include men receiving pensions from British forces. Finally the 1906 congress declared any athlete ineligible for a GAA sports meeting if he had participated in any meeting sponsored by either the British military forces or the RIC.

In view of the widespread reservations of a later generation of GAA members about the foreign games ban, it is important to try to place it in its original historic perspective. Essentially a form of organised voluntary boycott of English field games played here, the ban as re-imposed in 1905 was a spontaneous reaction by leading members of the GAA (who ultimately carried the majority with them) against what they saw as a deliberate process of anglicisation of Irish society, which they were convinced ought to be resisted. So far from being regarded as a purely negative rule, the ban was to its early advocates and supporters a positive expression of loyalty to one form of Irish culture. It required GAA members not merely to indicate publicly their support of Irish games but also to withhold their support of English games. Effectively, it was a practical application in the realm of sport of the policy of de-anglicisation, which had been advocated by Douglas Hyde as far back as 1892 and by Arthur Griffith from 1899 onwards.

Around this time the GAA was directly concerned in two other events that strengthened the position of native pastimes. From about 1902 women members of the Gaelic League in Dublin had been playing their own modified version of hurling. In 1904 they established on a formal basis the game of camogie, the first competitive match being played in Navan that summer between two Dublin clubs, the Keatings and the Cuchulainns.[12] The name 'camogie' was invented by the Cork scholar Tadhg Ó Donnchadha (*Torna*); among others associated with the game from its earliest days were Professor Agnes O'Farrelly of UCD and Sean O'Duffy of Dublin. In January 1906 the last of a series of disputes with the IAAA and its satellite the Irish Cyclists Association culminated in the final break between the GAA and the loyalist-dominated bodies.

The publication in 1907 of the first *Gaelic Athletic Annual* under the editorship of Dineen was an indication of the remarkable progress that had been made by the GAA since the turn of the century. Even looked at almost ninety-five years later by a generation that has come to take for granted the value of publicity, this slim volume could have come only from an organisation that was proud of its past and confident of its future. Reflecting what might fairly be called a Sinn Féin outlook all through, it shows the strong contemporary links between the GAA and the Gaelic League, whose president Douglas Hyde contributed to the annual. With its carefully compiled lists of officials, clubs and competitions for every county, nothing proves more clearly than this courageous venture (as the Table on page 73 shows) the extent of the success of the Association in promoting native pastimes in the early years of the century. The 'years of serious disorganisation . . . endless disputes, illegalities and friction' referred to by P. J. Devlin in a critical article in 1908 were at last over.[13]

A significant side-effect of the growth of the GAA in the first decade of the century was the renewal of interest and support from sections of the community that had given the Association a wide berth for some years. As support by leading GAA officials for the revolutionary element in the nationalist movement increased, it must have occurred to observant members of the parliamentary party that they were in danger of losing some of that mass support which many of their leaders then seemed to take for granted. With some notable exceptions most Irish Party MPs were never strong on Irish culture. Indeed, one may suspect that advocates of de-anglicisation like Cusack, Hyde and Griffith would have readily included nearly every prominent Home Rule MP from Parnell to John Redmond among those in need of conversion to a policy of de-anglicisation.

As soon as it became clear to the Irish Party that the GAA was rapidly becoming an influential force in the nationalist movement steps were taken by indi-vidual MPs to show their sympathy for native games — steps in some cases quite as crude, and probably not as sincere, as those taken earlier by Fenians in rushing to join the Association. As early as July 1902 Tom O'Donnell MP attended the annual convention of the Kerry board; three months later a meeting of Sandymount Isles of the Sea club in Dublin was attended by J. P. Nannetti MP. In October 1903 Willie Duffy MP of Loughrea, who had once been prominent in Galway affairs, returned to the Gaelic council room; no less a figure than Willie Redmond MP donated some cups to the Clare board — that being the county he represented in parliament — in 1905. In Armagh William McKillop MP contented himself with a gift of one cup to the Armagh board in 1907. The following year Captain Donelan MP of Cork presented a set of medals to the Midleton club, as did J. P. Hayden MP to the Roscommon board in 1910.

TABLE OF GAA CLUBS — 1907–1908			
LEINSTER		**ULSTER**	
Carlow	12°	Antrim	18^{X}
Dublin	68^{X}	Armagh	8°
Kildare	27°	Cavan	15°
Kilkenny	26$^{\circ X}$	Derry	5^{X}
Laois	41°	Donegal	5^{X}
Longford	7^{X}	Down	10^{X}
Louth	38°	Fermanagh	14$^{X\circ}$
Meath	30°	Monaghan	17^{X}
Offaly	18°	Tyrone	13$^{X\circ}$
Westmeath	27^{X}	**TOTAL**	105
Wexford	31°		
Wicklow	12°		
TOTAL	337		
CONNAUGHT		**MUNSTER**	
Galway	36^{X}	Clare	39$^{\circ X}$
Leitrim	14^{X}	Cork	77[1]
Mayo	18^{X}	Kerry	14[2]
Roscommon	16^{X}	Limerick	—[3]
Sligo	40°	Tipperary	56^{X}
TOTAL	124	Waterford	36°
		TOTAL	222

[X] *Gaelic Athletic Annual*, 1907
[°] *Gaelic Athletic Annual*, 1908

1. *Sport*, 13.1.1906.
2. *Sport*, 14.4.1906.
3. No figures available

A similar increase in support for the GAA came from many priests once it became clear that the post-1901 regime had come to stay. By 1904 clergy in Dublin were working in the Association — a reflection of the support for the Association given by Archbishop Walsh. By 1906 there were priests holding office in clubs or on county boards in such widely-scattered places as Tyrone, Westmeath, Sligo, Donegal, Antrim, Carlow and Fermanagh. Nor was this the full extent of clerical participation. Between 1905 and 1908 priests had been chairmen at annual conventions in at least five other counties — Laois and Limerick (1905), Clare and Monaghan (1906) and Louth (1907 and 1908). When to these counties are added those others (such as Tipperary and Limerick) where the clergy had been active in the GAA even before the new departure of 1901, some idea can be gained of the extent of the break in the clerical boycott that had in many places lasted since 1889.

While the increased volume of support from influential groups like MPs and priests must have been gratifying, one may surmise that to dedicated men such as Dineen and O'Toole a marked improvement in the GAA's financial position, which would enable the Association to consolidate its gains, would have been of greater value and importance. Such an improvement did in fact occur between 1901 and 1910, although the available figures suggest that it was uneven and not of long duration. It was, however, at least adequate to enable the GAA to enter the second decade of the century not merely in a solvent state but with sufficient confidence in its own future to embark on a major programme of expenditure, before the outbreak of war in 1914 called a halt to all such activities.

Although the evidence is not plentiful, it is reasonably clear that lack of funds, coupled with mounting debts, between them hampered the work of the GAA in the three years or so following the dismissal of Blake in 1898. The gross receipts of the central council fell from £995 in 1899 to under £460 in 1900; in May 1901 the Deering administration found it necessary to call a special meeting of the central council to consider the worsening financial position.[14] Although there is no record of any action being taken then, the fact that by July Dineen had once again taken charge of the accounts is ample evidence of a continuing crisis. The congress held in September 1901, at which Nowlan and O'Toole took office, grappled firmly with the problem. While refusing to accept responsibility for debts incurred before 1894, it accepted a moral responsibility for all debts from the foundation of the Association, and set up a special sub-committee to advise on how to start to clean the slate.[15] At least one provincial council soon afterwards decided to run special competitions, the income from which would go towards reducing Association debts.

The proceedings of the adjourned congress held in December 1901 show that the sub-committee had worked speedily. Claims examined totalled £800; of these, a £450 loan from Michael Davitt at the time of the US trip of 1888, was waived. Authority was given to the council to discharge the remainder of the debts, except for £50 which were disallowed. Although by November 1903 only £114 had been paid off, it appears that between then and the congress of January 1905 the balance of £260 (including some new debts) was paid off. The Secretary's report to that congress showed that for the first time the income of the central council had exceeded £1,000. This record did not last; for each year between 1905 and 1911 for which figures are available income was even higher — £1,552 in 1906, £1,476 in 1907, £1,072 in 1909 and £1,212 in 1910. Moreover, it is an indication of the extent of Association activities in that period that the annual credit balances — £147 in 1902, £112 in 1905, £337 in 1906, £154 in 1907 and £57 in 1909 — had all but vanished by 1909, when the central council was obliged to exclude Ulster teams from a major competition for lack of funds to meet their travel expenses.

If these figures seem small to GAA members of the 1990s accustomed to thinking of an organisation whose annual balance sheet contains five-figure sums, three points ought to be remembered. The figures just given relate solely to the central council; it may, perhaps, be worth mentioning that as early as 1905 the GAA's total income exceeded £5,000, a considerable sum when converted to the values of the 1990s.[16] They also relate to a period when the numbers of matches in any year between teams from widely separated areas was low. Even so, the budget within which Luke O'Toole operated in his first ten years in office was sufficient to allow the GAA to make spectacular progress during that period. Finally, even such cursory knowledge as one can glean from contemporary press reports is enough to enable one to state that the annual income of the Association was many times greater than that of any other Irish sports body in the period before World War I.

In November 1909 the GAA was twenty-five years in existence. Luke O'Toole, now just over eight years in office, had good reason to be satisfied with the Association's progress since his election as Secretary in September 1901. The group of officials of which only he was full-time had rescued the GAA from almost certain death. In 1908 he had reported the up-to-date completion for the first time of both current championships. By June 1909 all 32 counties had a board affiliated to the central council. In October 1909 O'Toole had given the council an impressive account of the Association's finances, a marked contrast with the debt-ridden GAA he had taken over in 1901. The permanent transfer to Dublin in 1909 of the annual congress marked a significant step towards the establishment of a genuine 32-county GAA.

Yet somehow the silver jubilee of the GAA passed unnoticed, both by supporters and critics of the Association. Perhaps the omission on the central council's part is an indication of its forward-looking approach in 1909; in its work to expand the Association it was now more concerned with the future than with the past. To men like O'Toole, J. J. Keane and J. J. Walsh there was no case at all for celebration in 1909; it was to 1901 rather than to 1884 that they looked back. For them the GAA which they revived in 1901 differed so much in respect of dedication to nationalist objectives, administrative efficiency and standardised playing rules from the old Association that it was a completely new body, more replacing than succeeding that which Cusack had founded in 1884. While on this argument celebration of a silver jubilee may have been irrelevant, the leaders of the GAA in 1909 were fully aware of their Association's shortcomings.

Whatever may have been the view of the Association itself in 1909, however, the historian of the GAA looking back from a distance of ninety years is justified in treating the new departure of 1901 as an important turning-point in the Association's history rather than as the start of a new GAA. He cannot therefore avoid attempting to answer the question: what had the GAA done in its first quarter-century? Within its own chosen sphere of activity the answer is crystal-clear. It had saved the traditional national game of hurling from extinction; it had revived and standardised the distinctive Irish form of football that had been played in rural Ireland for centuries; it had gained control for nationalists of their athletic pursuits. Above all it had created in the realm of sport a sense of national identity — giving a lead that other bodies like the Gaelic League and Sinn Féin were to follow in later decades with striking success and lasting consequences.

That hurling would have been revived sooner or later is beside the point, even if true; few successful revolutions are found on analysis to have been inevitable. It is doubtful if hurling would have survived until the political settlement reached with Britain forty years later. Since the chances are that, but for Cusack's action in 1884, this ancient game would have been discarded for hockey or replaced by some hybrid, all the credit for rescuing hurling from extinction must go to the early GAA. Moreover, by 1909 the Association had done much more than merely keeping the game alive where it had survived to 1884. It had made it a genuinely national game in the geographical sense. It had introduced a standard set of rules and won acceptance of these through the GAA's authority. It had standardised hurling without the loss of local styles of play and had rid it of the dangerous elements that had crept into it. No longer could critics, or opponents such as Dublin Castle, trump up either of the old excuses for banning hurling — that the game was a risk for players or an occasion for a faction fight.

The early GAA's achievements for Gaelic football were in some ways even more remarkable than what it did for hurling. It is scarcely an exaggeration to say that by the early 1880s the various local forms of Irish football had become indistinguishable from the brand of English football played in different localities. As a result, and also because of the prevalence of varying local customs permitting practices such as tripping and wrestling, standardisation of playing rules for football was far more difficult than for hurling. Unlike hurling, football had in some of the more remote areas barely emerged from the ancient cross-country version which hundreds played. Yet by the early years of the present century a type of game had evolved under the aegis of the GAA which had been purged of the more dangerous features of the mid-nineteenth century native football. This was still sufficiently distinctive to win the support of young men not prepared to play either of the English codes, and was so scientific and orderly as a public spectacle that it had won the admiration of experts in those codes.

Not only had hurling and football been successfully revived on a countrywide basis, but the body which had been started for that purpose had established itself securely as a new force in the sporting life of the country. The GAA had barely been set up before it had to defeat a concerted move by a rival body to end its existence. Yet within a short time it had come to a working (and at times harmonious) arrangement with this rival body, the IAAA, under which each association co-operated with the other in such matters as recognition of new athletic records and enforcement of suspensions. Admittedly this co-operation came to an end in 1906; but by then the GAA, as the body to which the vast majority of athletes outside of Dublin and Ulster belonged, could claim the major share of credit both for the great increase in participation in athletics since the 1880s and for the consequent rise in standards.

Merely to list some of the major crises it survived in its first quarter century gives an idea of the resilience of the GAA, which at the end of that period was stronger than it had ever been. It took in its stride the dismissal of one of its two principal founders and the resignation of the other. It recovered from a countrywide split caused by the IRB take-over of 1887 and from mass defections of rank-and-file members following its support for the Parnellites in 1890–1891. It rejected an attempt by leading officials to wind it up altogether. It triumphed over a prolonged withdrawal of support by the Catholic clergy and over sustained apathy by the parliamentary party, to which most GAA members still gave political allegiance.

Nor ought the social benefits accruing from the success and spread of the GAA be forgotten. To a countryside that had enjoyed little in the way of genuine entertainment since the social catastrophe of the Famine, and to rural communities that knew no material luxuries and had even experienced starvation in the late 1870s, the GAA brought games and sports meetings to the remotest parish and village on a regular, orderly and organised basis such as had never previously been known. To begin to understand the social revolution effected in the 1880s and 1890s by the arrival of the GAA, one has to attempt to appreciate what the spontaneous unorganised rural games and athletic contests of pre-Famine Ireland must have meant to the millions then existing at or below subsistence level. It was this type of amenity which the GAA brought back, but on a systematic and controlled basis that made for much greater enjoyment by spectators.

Because the GAA was started at a time when any form of organised activity was liable to have political undertones, it is often impossible to segregate the social benefits from the political impact of the Association. Not the least important part of the revolution caused by the arrival of the GAA, for example, was the fact that Irish games and athletics were now controlled by representatives of the nationalist community. These pastimes now passed for ever out of the hands of people like landlords, military and police, who belonged to a class that was opposed both to nationalist political aspirations and to nationalist cultural ideals. Not only did the GAA play a major part in the organised resistance by nationalist bodies from the 1890s onwards to the anglicisation of Irish society; thanks to the Association, Home Rule was achieved on the playing-field and in the athletic arena long before it was won in any other sphere of activity.

The rise of the GAA stimulated a sense of local patriotism, in such a way that there was ultimately a cumulative effect at the top; the Association's success released and strengthened forces that helped to rebuild the nationalist movement, so shattered by the Parnell Split. Pride in parish led to pride in one's native county, and, in due course, to a stronger feeling of identity with one's nation and its political and cultural aspirations. It is one of the minor paradoxes of modern Irish history that the artificial entity of the English county, introduced by an alien administration many centuries before, never succeeded in winning popular acceptance until the inter-county rivalry of Gaelic games became permanent early in this century. The GAA also, through its system of government, starting with the parish clubs and extending through county and provincial bodies to a central council, demonstrated democracy in operation more than a decade before the introduction of elected county and urban councils in 1898 gave most nationalists their first share in real political power. Moreover, their weekly contacts in committee-rooms and on the playing-field went a long way towards reducing the danger of friction between the rising class of prosperous small farmers and the continually depressed class of farm labourers.

Another and probably equally important result of the founding of the GAA was the way in which different sections of the nationalist movement used it — or tried to do so. As had already been shown, the Association was courted in turn by the parliamentary party and the physical force organisation, each hoping thereby to further its own objectives. To the IRB the GAA was an ideal instrument to keep the separatist ideal before the public; to the Home Rule movement it was a means of strengthening the National League and of winning more votes at general elections. The importance of the GAA to the separatist cause in particular is difficult to exaggerate. By the early years of this century the Association had become an ideal bridge, across which the ideas of those who believed that constitutional action alone would never win political freedom were being passed to a later generation, which was to put those ideas to practical use with striking success.

Apart altogether from its connections with particular sections of the nationalist movement, the GAA by its successes assisted the progress of the movement, especially those sections of it which laid stress on the cultural aspects of nationality. It was, to quote one of the ablest commentators on that period, 'the first organised manifestation of the spirit which was to eventuate in the Sinn Féin movement'.[17] The Association, by implicitly emphasising the idea of a separate people, helped to give more substance to the idea of national identity and to the emotional side of nationalism in general. As it became more successful after 1900, but also even long before that, the GAA helped to foster the growth of ideas of national self-consciousness and self-reliance; Douglas Hyde's famous metaphor in 1892 about the bricks of nationality comes to mind in this connection.[18] The founders and later leaders of the GAA must be numbered among those dedicated men who, passionately clinging to the belief that the embers of national identity had never died, continued to blow until the new coals began to glow. It was on the foundations so firmly laid by Cusack, no less than on those of Hyde or the survivors of the IRB, that men like Clarke and Pearse built in the years before 1916.

In trying to assess the progress made by the GAA in its first twenty-five years, it is tempting to make comparisons with the Gaelic League. Although founded nine years later than the Association, the League would appear superficially to have achieved more in a shorter period. Furthermore, because the League kept out of politics the question arises as to whether the neutral stance of the League was a major factor in its apparently greater success. In order to put any comparison between the GAA and the Gaelic League into perspective, three facts have to be borne in mind. The League set itself specific aims in the educational field, the periodic achievement of which gives a distorted picture when set beside the single continuous major objective of the Association, the revival of native games. Secondly, early in its life the League changed course; instead of trying to preserve the Irish language along the west coast and moving its headquarters to the Gaeltacht, it decided to concentrate on the English-speaking part of Ireland, and established itself permanently in the heart of the Pale. Finally, in the six-year period from 1907 to 1912 the League enjoyed an annual income from American sources of £2,000 — at a time when the GAA's annual income was only a fraction of this.[19]

In its early years the Gaelic League benefited greatly from the neutral political stance rigidly maintained by Hyde. As he had the GAA's achievements in mind shortly before he helped to found the League, Hyde was probably anxious to avoid the type of dissension he saw the GAA endure.[20] Once Cusack was deposed union-ists and Protestants stayed out of the GAA because of its close identification with the nationalist movement from the start. On the other hand, hindsight enables us to see today that the GAA owed much of its success and permanence to its links with the nationalists. From its foundation the Association also derived most of its strength from the fact that it was a mass popular movement; this was a position to which, because of its more limited appeal, the League could not aspire. Which of the two bodies exerted the greater influence on political affairs in the pre-1922 period is a matter on which champions of the GAA and the League are unlikely to agree.

Comparison of these two bodies at once underlines one of the two major set-backs of the early GAA, its failure to hold unionist or Protestant support for the GAA, or indeed for Gaelic games in general. It is to Cusack's credit that he tried to do this; unlike the Gaelic League of the 1890s, he found himself firmly rebuffed on purely political grounds. Whether this rejection by his opponents of Cusack's non-political approach sprang from his own abrasive personality or from the high political temperature of the mid-1880s, as compared to the lower temperature ten years later when the Gaelic League was starting, is a matter for speculation. Probably each factor played a part in the result. On the other hand, it is clear that in the long run the GAA benefited because of its frank identification from the start with nationalist ideals; events were to suggest strongly that the League identified itself with the nationalist movement too late in the day.

The other major failure of the GAA in its first twenty-five years, and one for which the Association itself was wholly to blame, was its neglect of athletics. Once hurling and later football won mass popular support from 1886 onwards, athletics gradually came to occupy a secondary position with GAA officials in most areas. Meetings continued to be sponsored by the Association, especially in Munster and in Dublin; curiously, the idea of running athletic competitions on the same day and at the same venue as a hurling or football match never caught on. In due course, even in Munster where the tradition of athletic contests had never died out, a clear-cut distinction developed between officials who specialised in athletics and those who concentrated on hurling or football. Inevitably, as the games became more popular and came to draw bigger crowds, this division into two classes of officials only served further to downgrade athletics in the GAA. Occasional attempts by some county boards to encourage greater interest in track events failed.

By 1900 or so all the leaders of the GAA except Dineen, who retained a life-long interest in athletics since his own successes on the track when young, had clearly lost interest in a section of the Association's activities that P.J. Devlin accurately called 'the basis, the impulse' of the GAA.[21] Even Cusack himself, now again prominent in the activities of the Dublin board, seemed content with this state of affairs. By the time of the 1901 revival a position had been reached where the GAA's connection with athletics ended after it had issued licences for sports held under its laws and adjudicated on disputes arising from such meetings. Apart from the annual GAA athletic championships, which in the mid-1890s fell to almost incredibly low standards, the Association actively initiated no competitions what-ever. The setting up by the central council in 1905 of the Athletics Council brought about no worthwhile improvement in the status of athletics under GAA rules.[22]

As a result of this almost total neglect of athletics by the Association, the rival unionist-controlled IAAA, which Cusack in the mid-1880s had tried with consider-able success to prevent from spreading to the provinces, returned to prominence even outside Dublin. Using garrison towns where it had survived as bases for expansion, it gradually penetrated previous strongholds of the GAA all over Munster and Connacht; in Ulster it operated rigidly its own ban on nationalist athletes. Indeed, the GAA's pre-occupation with hurling and football forced it periodically to engage in discreet co-operation with the IAAA. The permanent absence from the athletic arena of prominent GAA officials led also to the return of the bookmakers, whom Cusack had successfully ejected as early as 1885. Moreover, members of the unionist community, who felt that they would not be welcome at a hurling or football match, once more came to exercise influence over local athletic affairs; occasionally, even such unmistakable trappings of ascendancy rule as the local garrison band came to be tolerated.

Almost unbelievably in spite of all these adverse circumstances the nationalist population, especially in Munster, continued to turn out athletes of world standard. The outstanding example was Tom Kiely of Carrick-on-Suir, who in 1904 at St Louis in the United States became world champion. Eventually the new blood on the central council decided to do something about the decline in athletics. A conference with the IAAA early in 1900 seems to have marked the last co-operation between the rival bodies; friction developed between them over the next few years. However, as late as 1903, although faced with the emergence of a vigorous Gaelic Cyclists' Association as a counter to the IAAA-dominated Irish Cyclists' Association, the GAA hesitated to make a final break. Many IAAA competitors took part in the GAA All-Ireland athletic championships of that year, where cycling was still controlled by the ICA. Finally in 1906, after yet another year-long dispute in 1904 between the GAA and the IAAA, the GAA decided to go it alone in both athletics and cycling. By then standards had fallen so low that it was to take over twenty years to regain Ireland's reputation in international athletic contests.

Chapter 5

1909–1922

Was the GAA once more failing to take advantage of a favourable position it had built for itself? This question is asked as the Association enters its second quarter-century in 1910, for the three years before 1913 seem at first glance to have been devoid both of spectacular progress and of solid achievements. It is true that there was no mysterious or unforgivable slump such as followed the GAA's prominent part in the events of 1898. Neither, however, can one detect before the spring of 1913 unmistakable evidence of new gains by an Association that appeared in the first decade of the new century to have left behind it for ever its early tendency to dissipate much of its energy in internal dissension.

Probably because of the striking successes and the undoubted expansion of the previous few years, what first catch the eye in the period from 1910 to 1912 are the set-backs and lapses of the GAA. An otherwise constructive annual congress held in April 1910 was marred by an acrimonious contribution by the forceful J. J. Walsh of Cork to a discussion on a long-standing local dispute over the control of the Waterford playing-field. Later in the same year the All-Ireland football final had to be cancelled because of an unresolved wrangle between the Kerry board and the Great Southern Railway company over the size of the allocation of cheap tickets to Dublin for the match. The 1911 football final was delayed until 1912, and the All-Ireland hurling final for 1911 was never played because of a dispute between the Limerick board and the central council over the venue. This dragged on well into 1912, and ultimately led to the county's suspension for its refusal to accept a council decision (which the 1912 congress had ratified) and to the award of the hurling title to Kilkenny.

However, other facts give a much brighter picture than that just drawn. The year 1910 saw a reduction, from over forty to about half that number, of the membership of the central council. It also saw the adoption by the annual congress of some important changes in playing rules, the start of a campaign to persuade leading boys' colleges to play Gaelic games and the beginning of junior inter-county matches. To mark the holding that year in Belgium of a pan-Celtic congress the hurlers of Cork and Tipperary made the only tour of Gaelic teams to the European mainland in the history of the GAA. It does not seem to have been the Association's fault that the event, while otherwise successful, was a financial flop. As the Association gave powerful support to the ultimately successful campaign to have Irish made an essential entry subject for the new National University set up in 1909, co-operation with the Gaelic League intensified.

The summer of 1911 was notable for a successful first tour of this country by a Gaelic team from the United States. A party of seventeen Irish-American hurlers, drawn from New York, Chicago and Detroit, played six matches between late July and the end of August in Dublin, Wexford, Kilkenny, Tipperary, Cork and Limerick. The visitors drew large crowds, their games bringing in an average gate of £120, a figure that would have been much higher but for surprisingly small attendances at Dublin and Cork. Expenses of the tournament, totalling over £300, were understandably high. Nevertheless there was a profit of over £400, of which three-quarters were by prior arrangement paid to the visitors in order to promote Gaelic games in the United States.

The Irish-Americans were not the only teams to bring crowds to Gaelic matches around this time. The years 1911 and 1912 saw attractive games in both codes drawing attendances similar to those for the three football finals of 1905. Over eighteen thousand watched the All-Ireland football final between Antrim and Louth played in Dublin in November 1912, when the gate of £510 was the highest so far taken by the GAA. This record did not last long; two weeks later 20,000 paid £600 to see Cork and Kilkenny in the hurling final. Since it could now claim significant wins over Tipperary (in 1910 and 1912) and over Cork (twice in 1912), Kilkenny's one-point win on this occasion marked that county's arrival as a leading hurling centre able to take on any Munster county, a position of prominence it has held ever since.

When soberly recorded in print, none of these events on the playing-fields nor the changes made in the council chamber or at the annual congress may sound exciting. Yet the 1910–1912 period as a whole, when viewed in retrospect, was one of substantial overall progress in the spread of Gaelic games. Bigger crowds than ever attended the major fixtures; they were entertained by standards of play that in both codes were higher than ever. Both football and hurling became permanently established on an inter-county basis, with the provincial and All-Ireland championships being recognised as the principal annual competitions. The decision of 1910 to try to penetrate boys' colleges was followed in 1911 by the first Colleges All-Ireland competition on a provincial basis. The same year saw the start of the inter-varsity football competition for the Sigerson Cup, which now (almost ninety years later) includes several more higher education institutions. A year later in 1912 came the first Fitzgibbon Cup games between the hurlers of the universities, a competition that (in extended form too) also still flourishes.[1]

Not the least important result of the bigger crowds was a rise in the GAA's income. This enabled the provincial and central councils to extend their activities, since sound finances ensured the prompt payment of the innumerable overhead expenses as well as facilitating awards to injured players for earnings lost or medical expenses. Furthermore, the spread and rise in popularity of Gaelic games were greatly helped by the emergence of new county teams — Kilkenny, Antrim and Wexford among them — that were able to challenge earlier champions. Little wonder that the abandonment of the 1911 hurling final, which deprived the Association of £400 in gate-money, was quickly forgotten.

Curiously, since one would have expected the severance of relations with the IAAA in 1906 to have helped the growth of GAA athletics, it was in athletics that the only major discord in the GAA occurred in the four or five years before the start of World War I. If the number of meetings held under GAA rules be taken as a fair indication of the extent of activity, athletics would seem to have been in a healthy state for several years after the 1906 decision. Following a slow but steady rise from 124 meetings in 1904 to 167 in 1907, each of the two years 1908 and 1909 saw the totals rise by about thirty to 223 in 1909. Perhaps, however, the static position suggested by the figure of 226 for 1910 was significant in the light of events in the next three years. That the GAA should have been making progress in athletics can also be argued from the unmistakable evidence around this same period of a slump by the IAAA, whose meetings outside Dublin had by 1910 or so ceased to attract entries from most nationalist competitors. Attempts in 1912 by both loyalist bodies, the IAAA and the Irish Cyclists' Association, to show that there was a general slump in Irish athletics were not convincing, nor were they supported by the extent of athletic activity in rural Ireland, including Ulster where the IAAA had always been strong.

The first signal of an impending crisis in athletics was an unsuccessful Belfast motion at the 1911 GAA congress effectively seeking the abolition of the Athletics Council, the offshoot of the central council to which control of athletics had been given early in the century. The next year there appeared in Dublin a body consisting largely of cyclists and calling itself the Gaelic Athletes' and Cyclists' Union, which proceeded to organise its own meetings in parts of Leinster. By mid-1912 it had gained considerable support in counties Dublin, Kildare, Meath, Louth and Monaghan, and was winning sympathy in a dispute with the Athletics Council over prizes. The GACU professed to want merely some form of better deal for GAA athletes; subsequent events suggest that it contained some non-nationalists, who were hostile to leading members of the Council. Although the GACU adopted some elements of GAA policy (including initially a rule barring British military and police) and protested loyalty to the GAA, it was not averse to falsely advertising its meetings as being held under GAA rules. It also advocated co-operation with the ICA and allowed, possibly even encouraged, members to play non-Gaelic games.

While the GAA could (and apparently did) dismiss the GACU as a mere splinter group, it soon found its control of nationalist athletics in danger of erosion from a more formidable body. In March 1912 a representative meeting of Munster athletes, all from the ranks of the GAA, expressed dissatisfaction at the whole system of managing GAA athletics and agreed on the need to secure genuine representation of athletes on the Athletics Council and to decentralise the system to county level.[2] A decision was taken to form a Munster Athletes Protection Association, with a governing body based in Munster controlling county committees, all to remain under GAA auspices. Basically the MAPA would be a pressure group inside the GAA; unlike the GACU, it would not promote rival meetings. Among the members of the MAPA were such influential GAA figures as J. J. Walsh and Patrick Mehigan of Cork and Maurice Fraher of Waterford.

By the spring of 1912 Irish athletics were in a sorry state, with the IAAA and ICA both in obvious decline and the athletes of the GAA deeply divided. In Leinster, for example, the Dublin board backed the Athletics Council, while the Carlow board supported the GACU. In Munster the revolt posed a more serious threat to the GAA's control of athletics. There the Cork board finally took the initiative in pressing the central council to concede some of the MAPA claims. However, far from showing alarm the initial reaction of the GAA leaders was anything but conciliatory. They were to allow matters to drift before eventually realising that some compromise was essential.

While the aggrieved Munster athletes were persuaded to delay setting up the MAPA, the Cork GAA board tried to meet the situation by putting down a motion for the 1912 congress (due in April) for a radical overhaul of the governing system for athletics. This was, however, brusquely refused even a hearing on purely technical grounds. Next the Athletics Council engaged in a dispute with, and then imposed harsh suspensions on, prominent cyclists of the GACU. Although the cause of the trouble on this occasion was ostensibly a demand by cyclists for more prizes at the popular annual Dublin Grocers Sports, it became obvious that each side was using a minor disagreement for the wider purpose of putting its case before the public.

Meanwhile, possibly dismayed by the attitude of the Athletics Council and probably heartened by support from a meeting of Limerick athletics, the Cork and Waterford athletes formally founded the MAPA in October 1912 at Dungarvan. To the two earlier objects was now added that of sending an Irish team to the Olympic Games to be held in Berlin in 1916, a matter that soon came to engage the belated attention of the IAAA also. There followed a month later in Dublin a well-attended joint meeting of the GACU and the MAPA held for the purpose of airing the various grievances of athletes and cyclists. Significantly, only a week or so later came news at the annual convention of the Dublin GAA board of plans being drawn up by the Athletics Council to reorganise the governing machinery of athletics held under GAA rules. The move forestalled a similar MAPA decision to lay its own proposals before the next GAA congress in 1913.

When the GAA's new scheme for the government of athletics was put to the congress of 1913 it was recognised as going most of the way to meet the reasonable demands of athletes for better representation at decision-making levels, and was approved without amendment. Under the new system the Athletics Council would in future have fifteen members — the three main officers of the GAA, eight elected by congress and four (one from each province) elected by athletes registered with the Association. In addition, registered athletes got the right to send to congress eight delegates, two from each province. Finally, a whole new series of inter-county, inter-provincial and All-Ireland championship athletic contests was to be staged corresponding to those in hurling and football. This reconstitution of the Athletics Council killed the MAPA; the GACU lingered on in a few places as late as January 1914 as a satellite of the IAAA.

The athletics dispute had for the greater part of two years diverted from athletics the attention of GAA athletes. What was astonishing about the whole controversy was that it raged while the GAA was having unprecedented successes in all other spheres of activity. Most of the responsibility for the dispute must rest with J. J. Keane, president of the Athletics Council, who had been permitted by the Association to run athletics almost single-handed, justifying the demands for a more democratic system of management. Whatever justification he had in refusing to treat with the GACU, a disgruntled group without clear aims, Keane's domineering and obstinate attitude to the MAPA, consisting largely of old associates in the GAA, only served to put off the day when the GAA found itself forced to concede the claims of the Munster athletes to a bigger voice in their own affairs. As so often happens in such cases, the chief casualty was what both sides to the dispute professed to have most at heart, athletics. In 1913 the number of GAA meetings fell to 154, and in 1914 to 131 — almost the same as the total for 1905 before the break with the IAAA had occurred.

As one follows the athletics controversy in the press of 1912 and 1913 one begins to suspect that it was a symptom of a deeper malaise within the GAA. The tactless and insensitive handling of its critics, especially those in the MAPA, by the Athletics Council suggests a gulf between some at least of the leaders of the GAA and many of the rank-and-file. Since the GACU was centred on counties close to Dublin, one cannot dismiss the episode as merely a difference of opinion between Dublin-based officials and those in Munster — although it may be that the latter felt that developments in Dublin, soon to be recorded, indicated too much concentration in that area. Perhaps, on the other hand, the clue is to be found in J. J. Walsh's espousal of the athletes' cause. The ebullient Corkman represented a younger generation of GAA officials which was possibly coming to feel that the central council in following, instead of leading, rank-and-file opinion, had shown itself out of touch with ordinary members.

L ooked at from any one of a number of viewpoints, the year 1913 was a memorable one for the GAA. Although it followed a period of almost unprecedented growth, that year the Association again succeeded in making significant new gains both in the council chamber and on the playing-field. The annual congress made substantial and important changes in the rules, including the reduction to fifteen in the number of players on a football or hurling team; as already recorded, it also ended the dangerous revolt by athletics. A short series of tournament games concluded by the early summer brought Gaelic football to a new peak in standard of play, and set new records for attendances at sporting events in this island. Most important of all, the financial success of this tournament enabled the GAA to purchase in Dublin a site for what was to be both its administrative headquarters and its main stadium. Finally, at a time when the Association, because of its remarkable growth and successes, was being openly courted by the Irish Parliamentary Party, it ensured its own survival when that party would be long dead by boldly taking its place alongside the new forces destined to lead the national movement.

To the ordinary member or supporter of the GAA in 1913 by far the most important events of that year were the two Croke Memorial football finals between Kerry and Louth in May and June, which remained lifelong memories for those who attended and made a permanent impact on the fortunes of the GAA. Although justifiably claiming to be the experts in Gaelic football, Kerry's footballers had not maintained the county's reputation in the years after the historic 1903 games against Kildare. Louth, a county where in relation to its size and population the game had probably been more extensively played than anywhere else since the mid-1890s, had recently proved its worth in important competitions. Following Kerry's withdrawal Louth had reluctantly accepted the All-Ireland title for 1910. The next year both counties were eliminated from the championship; the 1911 winner, Cork, which defeated Antrim, was soon afterwards beaten by Kerry for the 1912 Munster title. Kerry in turn lost to Antrim in the 1912 semi-finals; Antrim was beaten in that year's final by Louth. Against this background the meeting of Kerry and Louth in the 1913 Croke final was an event all Gaelic followers had been awaiting for long.

At Jones's Road sportsground (now Croke Park) in Dublin early in May 25,000 people paid over £750 to see the teams finish level at the low score of four points each. Between then and 29 June, the date fixed for the replay, national and provincial press coverage at a level never before experienced kept Gaelic followers tense with anticipation. All their hopes were realised when a magnificent game ended in a five-point win for Kerry. The attendance at the replay was close on 35,000, justifiably claimed as the biggest ever to watch a sporting event in any code in Ireland. The three major railway companies ran over forty trains to Dublin, carrying more than 20,000 passengers; gate receipts were almost £1,200. Special stands were erected at the GAA's expense and 200 voluntary stewards controlled the crowds, obviating the need for any policemen inside the ground at a time when uniformed RIC men were not welcome at any major Gaelic game.

In addition to the obvious beneficial short-term impact on the GAA which these great games had, they had an even more lasting indirect effect through the use to which the gate-money was put by the Association. Since the death in 1902 of Archbishop Croke the GAA had made intermittent moves to perpetuate the memory of its first patron, without whose active support, especially in the lean years of the mid-1890s, the Association might not have survived into the new century. As early as the congress of January 1905 a decision to erect a memorial to Croke had been taken; the details were left to the incoming central council, which did nothing to implement the decision.[3] Nearly two years later the congress of February 1907 passed another and similar resolution; in October 1907 the council earmarked £100 for the memorial. Once again in February 1908 (the £100 having been seemingly spent in the meantime) congress resolved to press ahead with the project. It was July 1909 before another £100 was put aside; later that year £38 was added. For three more years nothing was heard of the Croke Fund, until suddenly in the summer of 1912 it grew to £300. Of this over £100 came from the profit on the American hurlers' visit; the Munster and Leinster councils added £25 each.

By now the question of what form a memorial to Croke should take must have occurred to some leaders of the GAA. In Tipperary it appears to have been assumed all along that the money collected over the years would be spent on some local memorial, probably a statue of the archbishop; at the first sign in 1913 of a proposed departure from this course GAA officials in that county became understandably annoyed. In retrospect one cannot but sympathise with the view apparently being gradually formed by the central council that the GAA as a whole, rather than merely one area (much less one county unit), should benefit from such a substantial fund. What eventually happened was a happy compromise; but before the unveiling of the Croke memorial there were to be many bitter words between the Tipperary board and the central council. One way or another no fewer than fifteen years were to pass after the 1905 decision before Thurles got its Croke statue. Yet the central council had its stadium in Dublin within six months of the end of the 1913 tournament.

More or less contemporaneously with the growth of the Croke Fund, the GAA had also been slowly feeling its way towards a decision to acquire a stadium in

Michael Cusack, founder of the GAA.

Tipperary (Thurles), winners of the first All-Ireland hurling final in 1887. This photograph was taken twenty-three years later, in June 1910.

The 'Invasion' team of 1888. These hurlers toured the United States in that year. The figure to the left with the hammer is Maurice Davin.

James M. Ryan of Ballyslatteen, Co. Tipperary, setting up a world record for the high jump in Tipperary Town on 19 August 1895. His record of 6ft 4½ins was beaten nine days later in New York by M.F. Sweeney. The man wearing a bowler hat, to the left of jump, is the author's grandfather, John J. Bourke, GAA handicapper and judge.

The Kerry football team that won the 1903 and 1904 All-Ireland finals. In 1903 the match went to two replays before Kerry beat Kildare by 0-8 to 0-2; and in 1904 Kerry beat Dublin by 0-5 to 0-2.

A barefoot hurler from the early twentieth century. This photograph was taken in South Tipperary.

A hurling team of the early twentieth century. Notice the sharp end of the camán, before the modern curved end was introduced.

A young hurler, taken at the Glens Feis, c. 1906. The photograph was taken by F.J. Biggar, a well-known historian of the time and also a talented amateur photographer.

An early Kilkenny team with the Bob O'Keeffe Cup, awarded annually to Leinster senior hurling champions.

The opening ceremony of the international Tailteann Games in the 1920s. The photo is taken facing where the old Cusack Stand was built in 1937.

The parade of athletes before the international Tailteann Games at Croke Park in the 1920s.

Lory Meagher, hero and captain of Kilkenny's losing team in the historic three-final saga of 1931, won by Cork by 5-8 to 3-4 and watched by a gross attendance of over 91,500.

Limerick (led by Mick Mackey, holding his hurley downwards) and Cork in the 1930s. Immediately behind Mackey is the famous Limerick forward, Paddy Clohissey.

A goalkeeper saves a shot from a Kilkenny forward at Croke Park. In the background is the old Long Stand, demolished in the late 1950s.

Limerick, All-Ireland senior hurling champions 1940. This was the last hurrah for a great team: Limerick were not to win the championship again for thirty-three years. Mick Mackey is second from the left in the front row.

A youthful Jack Lynch (see box) at the start of an All-Ireland hurling final against Dublin. To the referee's left is Ned Wade (Dublin); to his right (head bent) is Terry Leahy (Dublin). On the extreme right is Jim Young (Cork).

Street celebrations after Cork won the Sam Maguire Cup in 1945, defeating Cavan by 2-5 to 0-7.

John Doyle, who won eight All-Ireland senior hurling championship medals with Tipperary in a career that stretched from 1949 to 1967, is acclaimed by supporters after a victory.

Pádraig Ó Caoimh, General Secretary of the GAA from 1929 to 1964, regarded as the architect of the modern GAA.

Christy Ring leads the Cork team in the pre-match parade before an All-Ireland final against Kilkenny.

The All-Ireland football final of 1955 between Kerry and Dublin, won by the Kingdom. The 1950s rivalry between these two sides anticipated the great clashes of the 1970s.

Dublin where its principal events could be held. For years the Association had moved from one field to another in or near the city where, even before the turn of the century, most of its biggest fixtures had come to be held — depending for some of the early period on the generosity of Lord fFrench, who owned Elm Park beyond Ballsbridge, and later on the business instinct of the friendly landlord of Jones's Road racecourse in the northern suburb of Drumcondra. In between these periods considerable use had been made of the ideal natural amphitheatre at Clonturk in Drumcondra; in less affluent times the free, if more unruly, pastures of the Phoenix Park had to be endured.

For the GAA's purposes by far the most suitable of these grounds was the City and Suburban Racecourse, popularly known as the Jones's Road sportsground. Since 1870 it had been owned by Maurice Butterly, later an Alderman of Dublin Corporation, who had laid out a course for horse-racing on it. The sport did not, however, thrive there; the field was frequently let out for athletics, boxing, walking contests, pony-trotting and (even in those unliberated days) ladies' football.[4] Almost from the start the GAA had been one of Butterly's most frequent tenants; as early as March 1896 the two All-Ireland finals for 1895 had been played in Jones's Road. Then in 1905 Butterly died; three years later the entire, now almost overgrown, fourteen-acre site was bought for £3,250 by the well known GAA man, Frank B. Dineen.

That Dineen purchased the ground because he hoped it would become the property of the GAA can be taken for granted. The year Butterly died Dineen advocated, in an anonymous newspaper article, an elaborate scheme for a major Gaelic stadium in Dublin that clearly had Jones's Road in mind. The annual congress of 1906 was urged by the GAA's auditors to set aside a special sum for this purpose. The Association itself had had to abandon such an idea in 1905 because the price asked was too high. One may surmise that Dineen bought to prevent the property from falling into hands that might not prove as co-operative as Butterly had been. One way or another Dineen for his foresight seems to deserve more recognition than he has got from a body that has not named a stadium or even a stand after him. A successful but not wealthy journalist, he had had to borrow from his bank to complete the purchase. It seems likely that he ran into trouble over repayments, because in 1910 he sold off four acres of the ground for £1,090 to the Jesuits of Belvedere College.

There are other indications of the burdens of ownership on Dineen. Between 1905 and 1908 the ground became neglected; in September 1906 it was described as derelict by a member of the central council. By the spring of 1909, however, Dineen had made substantial improvements; the pitch was re-laid and terracing accommodation increased. The financial strain must have been severe; only a year or so after the 1910 sale to the Jesuits the grounds were once again in disrepair.[5]

Against this background one may wonder if the central council's decision of late 1912 to run the Croke tournament, which came soon after a further deposit of nearly £200 had brought the Croke Fund to almost £500, was made partly with an eye on the deteriorating state of affairs at Jones's Road.

Nevertheless, although one may doubt if any sculptor would have charged so much for a statue, so far as the council minutes show the purpose of the 1913 Croke tournament was merely to bring the Croke fund to the £1,000 mark. So great was public interest in the football final that the competition exceeded all expectations, as the council found when O'Toole reported to it on 6 July. Receipts from the two tournaments totalled £2,735; after expenses of £863 had been paid, £1,872 remained, bringing the Fund in less than six months from under £500 to nearly £2,400. It would hardly be surprising in such circumstances if some of the council began to feel that, instead of a statue in Thurles, a stadium in Dublin might be a more suitable memorial to Archbishop Croke. Dineen too would have been only human if he let it be known that he expected his foresight in 1908 to be rewarded.

With more money than it had ever had before, the central council lost little time in deciding what to do with it. The 6 July meeting, which discussed what form the Croke memorial should take, revealed considerable support for a proposal (which was not voted on) that the entire fund be used to buy a ground to be called Croke Park — the first mention of this name. By nine votes to eight it was resolved to appoint a small sub-committee to confer with Archbishop Fennelly and the Thurles clergy first. As a result O'Toole, the only person available, soon after this met the Thurles administrator in the absence through illness of the archbishop. O'Toole's account to the council on 27 July of this meeting is revealing; it indicates both the strength of the Tipperary clerics' preferences for a statue and the Secretary's tactics to try to divert the Fund into grounds in Dublin.

O'Toole first sounded the priest on an earlier idea of the council that a new marble altar and stained-glass window be erected in the cathedral. Father Bannon had an answer to this opening move; there was no room for any more altars, and all the windows were already in stained-glass. It was, he firmly told O'Toole, the view of the clergy (including presumably their bishop) that a bronze statue of Croke should be erected. In addition, a donation of from £300 to £600 to rebuild the confraternity hall would be welcome. This hall, erected around 1900 partly with GAA money, had recently been destroyed by fire; although covered for only £1,000 insurance, it would cost £1,600 to rebuild.

On 27 July the central council, after a long discussion of O'Toole's report, made three important decisions. A bronze statue was agreed on unanimously. By seven votes to six a grant of £300 was authorised for the new Thurles hall, on condition that it be called the Croke Memorial Hall. Local views now having been taken care of, the rest of the £2,400 was, it was resolved by nine votes to three, to be spent on the purchase of grounds in Dublin to be called the Croke Memorial Park Ground, a title never used again. Finally O'Toole, J. J. Hogan and Crowe were directed to inspect several Dublin grounds to help the council decide which to buy. How strongly the council felt about putting its money into Dublin grounds is seen from the 9–8 vote of 6 July and the 9–3 vote of 27 July.

When the central council next met on 17 August it was advised by the three-man inspection committee that only two grounds were suitable for purchase by the Association — Jones's Road and Elm Park. The first, O'Toole explained, was 94 acres in area, was held under a lease with 500 years to run, had two houses on the site and was on offer for £4,000 from Dineen. Elm Park had fifteen acres, was freehold and had an asking price of £5,000. A decision was deferred until Elm Park was inspected by the rest of the council. By the time the council next met on 7 September Dineen, presumably fearing a decision in favour of Elm Park, had reduced his price to £3,625. Each council member was now asked to put his views in writing for the next meeting.

When the council resumed on 14 September a long discussion (which followed an adjournment to inspect Dineen's property) produced a proposal that Elm Park be bought; although seconded, the motion was not put to a vote. Three weeks now passed before the next and decisive meeting on 4 October, when a proposal by Crowe to buy Jones's Road for £3,500 got through by eight votes to seven. Dineen agreed to come down to this figure later that month; the actual sale took place on 22 December 1913. One of the two houses became O'Toole's residence at a nominal rent; he was appointed manager of the grounds at an annual salary of £75. The other house was rented to a caretaker, and O'Toole was directed to surrender the council's offices in O'Connell Street when he had had offices fitted behind the pavilion in Jones's Road.

With the central council's minutes understandably terse and all the participants long since dead, one can only speculate on the events that preceded the decision to buy Croke Park. Clearly Dineen played a major (and now hidden) role in the episode; yet it may seem that in allowing him a profit of only £250 the council treated him harshly. He, after all, could claim that but for his purchase in 1908 the GAA might never have got the grounds. In addition, he had presumably spent a considerable sum in maintaining and improving the site over a five-year period. On the other hand, he had got a fee of £10 for each big match played on his property; one may surmise, both from his colleagues' tactics over Elm Park and from the closeness of the final vote, that he proved a difficult vendor. An intimate contemporary later referred to him as 'hard to get on with'.[6] The fact that Dineen was not present at any of the council meetings in 1913 prompts the suspicion that the members had some good reason for keeping him at arm's length.

Less than thirty years after its foundation the GAA now had an ideal site for its principal grounds and administrative headquarters. Situated less than fifteen minutes' walk from the centre of Dublin and from two of the city's then three main railway stations, Croke Park was to become almost within the lifetime of the council members of 1913 the biggest and best equipped sports stadium in this island. Only forty years after its acquisition by the Association it was to hold close on 100,000 spectators at an All-Ireland hurling final, over treble the attendance at the great 1913 Croke final replay. Despite the cramped physical conditions imposed by railway lines at two ends of the ground, the modern development of high-rise buildings seems likely to ensure that the GAA will be able to remain indefinitely on this site, which in the meantime has acquired vital historical associations that serve as a permanent reminder of the role of the GAA in the movement leading to political independence.

The ink had hardly dried on the contract to purchase Jones's Road before the Tipperary board went into action. In January 1914 it instructed the solicitor to commence litigation to stop the central council from disposing, before the 1914 congress was held, of the Croke Fund in the manner already decided by the council. Even in Tipperary opinion on this drastic move was divided; the southern divisional board disapproved formally by twenty-two votes to nine. By March the Munster council had intervened and offered to mediate between the board and the central council. Eventually O'Toole skilfully piloted through congress a compromise. The central council, which earlier had agreed to raise its contribution to the Thurles hall to £500, now doubled this figure (partly with a £200 subscription from the Munster council) on Tipperary's agreeing to discontinue its law action. The result was that the central council found itself obliged to take over the £2,000 mortgage on Croke Park and could find only £1,650-odd for the purchase.

The Tipperary board drove a hard bargain and used unorthodox methods in doing so. A series of serious allegations about its tactics made in a hard-hitting speech by J. J. Hogan (chairman of the Leinster council) at the 1914 congress, went unanswered; they were almost unanswerable. Yet, until the central council decision of October 1913 to buy Jones's Road, the impression for many years had been that the Croke Fund could be used only for a memorial in Tipperary. The fact that the Munster council gave the Tipperary board its support in 1914 suggests that it was satisfied about the merits of Tipperary's case. Even after the 1914 settlement the Croke statue project continued to run into difficulties, including a serious local dispute about the actual site, until the outbreak of World War I caused a postponement for another six years.

If 1913 was a memorable year for the GAA, it was also an historic one for the nationalist movement as a whole. November saw the foundation of the Irish Volunteers, a force which less than three years later supplied almost all of the men who rose in arms in Dublin and changed the course of Irish history. The formation of the Volunteers was only one in a series of major events in Ireland in the previous four years which largely decided the type of political environment which exists in this island to the present day. The abolition in 1911 by the British Government of the centuries-old veto of the upper house of the British parliament on legislation gave the Irish Home Rule movement a new lease of life. It also brought home to Irish Unionists, especially those of Ulster, the realisation that their future under British rule was no longer secure. From the diverse reaction to these two factors emerged ten years later the two political entities of the Irish Free State and Northern Ireland.

In the short term, two general elections in quick succession put the Irish Parliamentary Party by 1912 back once more where it had been under Parnell in the 1880s, holding the balance of power at Westminster and in a position to make or break a British government. When in April 1912 the Liberal regime showed its readiness to pay the price of the Irish Party's support by introducing legislation providing for Home Rule for Ireland, it looked as if Parnell's dream of an Irish parliament was at last to become a reality. At this stage the Ulster Unionists, who had been gathering strength to oppose Home Rule, gave notice of their determination to resist, by force if necessary, their proposed inclusion in a self-governing Ireland. A self-styled provisional government for Ulster was set up; early in 1913 an Ulster Volunteer Force was formed. Eleven months later the nationalists followed this example by forming the Irish Volunteers; one of the speakers at its inaugural public meeting in Dublin was the Secretary to the central council of the GAA, Luke O'Toole.

That the chief officer of a national sporting body should participate openly in such a political event may seem surprising. However, because of the representative nature of the historic meeting in Dublin's Rotunda on that November night, O'Toole's absence would have been a bigger surprise. The platform contained men from nearly every shade of nationalist opinion — and the GAA had, after all, been avowedly nationalist in outlook since its inception almost thirty years before. For one reason only, perhaps, might O'Toole's appearance in the Rotunda be justifiably regarded as unexpected; John Redmond, the leader of the Irish Party, had sent nobody there to represent him, and it was to Redmond that the great majority of nationalists still gave almost unquestioning allegiance. As recently as 1911 at its annual congress the GAA had taken steps 'in order to secure that the Association be conducted on non-political lines'. Yet here was its Secretary helping in that capacity to start a new political movement which did not appear to have Redmond's blessing.

To understand fully why O'Toole took his seat in the Rotunda a distinction has to be made between the GAA as a body and its leading officers as individuals. For some years even before 1911 — indeed, with the notable exception of 1898, one might say from the adoption of the 1895 constitution — the Association had been carefully steering clear of party politics, as if conscious of the lesson it had learned in the period before and just after Parnell's death twenty years earlier. So far as the central council was concerned, in the twenty years before 1914 all nationalists were welcome in the GAA, which showed its consistency in this respect by running matches and tournaments for, or giving grants to, such varied causes as the Gaelic League, the AOH, the IRB through its front the Wolfe Tone Committee and (at least twice) strike-bound trade unionists.[7]

Developments after 1916, when the GAA came to be closely identified publicly with Sinn Féin and its policies, have tended to conceal the fact that, in the ten or twelve years before 1914, the GAA had come to embrace members and supporters of every nationalist body. When, for example, one finds (as in several Ulster counties as late as the spring of 1914) the Association regularly holding its meeting in halls belonging to the moderate non-political Irish National Foresters society, one may assume considerable overlapping of members between the GAA and the Foresters. Similarly, it seems unlikely that the Association in Roscommon in 1913 would have run a tournament to aid AOH funds unless the Order had some GAA members on its books. Again, it would be unwarranted to assume that there was a strong Fenian influence on the central council in 1915 just because a series of games was sanctioned in aid of a Wolfe Tone memorial or the Wolfe Tone Clubs. The council, on the contrary, appears to have had for the previous ten years or so a majority who in national affairs took their cue from Redmond.

As a body the GAA was careful never to overlook the fundamental fact that, at least up to the outbreak of war in August 1914, the Irish Party led by John Redmond still commanded the allegiance of the bulk of nationalists. The support and participation at local level of prominent parliamentarians, including several MPs, were welcomed and accepted at their face value by many GAA county boards. When in 1913 no less distinguished a person than Redmond himself turned up at Croke Park for the Croke Memorial final, he was accorded the respect due to the leader of the constitutional Home Rule movement. So was his lieutenant John Dillon, when six months later he in turn attended the All-Ireland football final. That the motives of these two leading nationalist politicians in being seen (and in being reported in the nationalist press as having been seen) at Croke Park were suspect is very likely; but the political climate of the time prevented the GAA from openly questioning these motives.

On the only known occasion when something approaching a confrontation occurred at the central council between Sinn Féin and the Redmondites, the more extreme nationalists found themselves completely outnumbered. In 1912 the central branch of Sinn Féin (effectively its executive) sent a letter to the GAA protesting about its invitations to Lord Mayor Sherlock of Dublin, a prominent Irish Party member who, Sinn Féin hinted, was using the Association to further his own political career. However, by eleven votes to two the council endorsed O'Toole's action and firmly rejected Sinn Féin's allegation. The Secretary, who strongly defended the propriety of accepting support from public figures in the parliamentary movement if to do so furthered the interests of the GAA, was authorised to reply to Sinn Féin. An attempt to dissociate the council from O'Toole's contacts with the Irish Party politicians was defeated; out of twelve leading members (excluding O'Toole himself) of the GAA present, only two sided with Sinn Féin. Only a year later the central council showed its independence in such matters by deciding to discontinue invitations to Sherlock because he had accepted the post of patron of a soccer association.

The neutral stance adopted by the Association between the various wings of the nationalist movement in no way inhibited individual members of the GAA who participated in different interests in politics, particularly at the local level. Prominent figures in the GAA so engaged in the pre-1914 period included Jim Nowlan of Kilkenny, Nicholas Cosgrave of Wexford and Lorcan O'Toole (secretary of the Dublin board), all three aldermen in their native areas. In addition J. J. Walsh and Luke O'Toole captured seats on Cork and Dublin Corporations respectively. Most of these were elected on independent tickets at a time when party labels were not normally used at local elections. A few like Nowlan (at times on the fringe of the physical force movement) and Cosgrave (a lifelong orthodox Redmondite) had been active in local politics since the time, just before the turn of the century, when on the setting up of new popularly-elected local authorities many nationalists won seats on such bodies.

While the GAA as a body might remain discreetly neutral in national affairs, it could not prevent an individual member from publicly advocating the policies of whatever organisation he belonged to. Inevitably in many such cases an impression was created (and was so intended) that the speaker's views were also those of the GAA. In the early years of the century T. F. O'Sullivan became adept at advocating the ideals of the extreme nationalists (of which he was a leading member) in such a way as to suggest that the Association (of which he was also a leading member) supported these views. In Cork J. J. Walsh, who never lost an opportunity to preach the gospel of Sinn Féin, saw the main role of the GAA as an instrument in pushing the claim to nationhood.[8] As late as January 1911, less than three months before the congress which passed the no-politics motion, Dan McCarthy, a leading member of Sinn Féin and later a president of the GAA, reminded the public that the GAA 'was not a sporting association alone . . . but . . . above . . . all . . . a national organisation . . .

to keep the bone and muscle of our country from donning the red coat or the black coat of England'.[9] In words that now seem prophetic he continued: 'We want our men to train and to be physically strong' so that 'when the time comes the hurlers will cast away the camán for the steel that will drive the Saxon from our land'.

In the eight or ten years before 1916 the Sinn Féin viewpoint on Irish affairs came to be more widely stated in public by prominent members of the GAA than did the policies of other sections of the nationalist movement. Without effecting any takeover of the Association such as the IRB had achieved between 1885 and 1887, spokesmen of Sinn Féin active in the GAA became proportionately more prominent in the affairs of the Association than did supporters of the parliamentary movement. An obvious, natural and — so far as Sinn Féin was concerned — intended result of this development was that the GAA as a body appeared to lean more noticeably towards Sinn Féin than towards the Irish Party. A number of factors combined in varying degrees to produce this effect — the influence in the GAA still exerted by Fenians like Dineen, the respect which men with Sinn Féin backgrounds (like O'Toole and Walsh) had by their work for the GAA come to command, and the fact that few prominent Irish Party men any longer actively interested themselves in the Association.

Not all prominent members of Redmond's party had discontinued their association with the GAA. As late as the summer of 1915 Thomas Lundon MP was attending Gaelic games in Limerick; in October of that same year, Augustine Roche MP was present at a GAA function in Cork city. When in 1912 it became clear that the Association's support throughout the country had reached proportions the GAA had not experienced for twenty-five years, a trend, apparently inspired by the Irish Party leaders, began with the ostensible aim of getting more Party support for the GAA — to make the Association fashionable or popular, in other words, with those in the Party who had previously kept aloof from Gaelic events. Presumably this trend stemmed from a growing fear that the Party, through its own neglect or the activities of the vocal Sinn Féin minority inside the GAA, had lost influence in the Association.

One final concerted effort to exploit the GAA's popularity was made in 1913 by the Irish Party. Redmond himself attended at Croke Park for the Croke football final in July, making some fulsome comments which showed that he had never before been at a Gaelic game. One of his wealthiest supporters, a Kerryman named McCarthy who lived in a luxurious mansion in Dunboyne outside Dublin, arranged for the entire Kerry party to stay with him. Some months later the All-Ireland football final was watched by none other than John Dillon MP, himself (like Redmond) a stranger until then to Gaelic arenas. Finally, when in October 1914 Clare won its first All-Ireland title, defeating Laois in the hurling final, Redmond's popular younger brother Willie, who by a stroke of luck was MP for East Clare, attended the game in Croke Park and the subsequent celebrations in a city hotel, and followed up a month later with a set of medals for the Clare board.

As the Irish Volunteers began to spread rapidly among the nationalist community in 1914, it became inevitable that the new movement would have repercussions on the GAA. Since the Volunteers drew most of their recruits from young active men, it goes without saying that members of the GAA, active in field games or athletics for most of the year, supplied a big proportion of the rank-and-file members of the new force. It can be safely assumed that the extent of such dual membership continued to increase as the numbers enrolling in the Volunteers continued to rise. For those in the GAA who, like Dan McCarthy, looked forward to the time to 'cast away the camán for the steel', membership of the Volunteers was taken for granted. Even for those GAA members who, because they followed Redmond, were committed to less drastic means of achieving Home Rule, it became accepted that one joined the Volunteers after leading parliamentarians everywhere in the country came to support enthusiastically the new force.

When it came to choosing between sport and politics it was not surprising that in the tense atmosphere of 1914 many members of the GAA gave preference to their Volunteer activities. Some who tried to combine sport and politics naturally found it increasingly more difficult to play football or hurling on a Sunday after a strenuous Saturday spent in military training. As a result, very soon the GAA found participation in its activities suffering in many areas. The extent of this reduction varied from one county to another; understandably it tended to hit the Association hardest in areas like Ulster, where the Volunteers were regarded as a vital bulwark against the threat of Orange domination.

In Derry, where Gaelic games had only recently taken over from soccer, both Gaelic codes had practically died out by March 1915 because of the Volunteer movement. The Tyrone board a month later found itself in much the same plight; only one club had survived in Down. Further south in Wicklow Volunteer activities had by August 1914 crowded out the local GAA calendar. In adjoining Kildare soon afterwards the GAA board found its members giving a first preference to their duties as Volunteers. The Dublin board, on the other hand, seems not to have found it necessary to curtail its fixture list. It seems possible that the proportion of GAA members in the Volunteers there was not as high as elsewhere, perhaps because of a fear of disapproval by the disproportionately large number of loyalists employers in that city. Nor did Volunteer activities affect Gaelic events to any appreciable extent in several other Leinster counties, such as Carlow and Laois.

On the question of recognising and actively supporting the Volunteers, the GAA at once found itself in a dilemma. Because the new movement had the backing of every section of the nationalist movement, the temptation to make an exception to its policy of non-involvement in party politics must have been strong. On the other hand, without any early lead from John Redmond, the Irish Party majority on the central council may have felt that to continue neutral would be the more prudent course. In view of the open support by O'Toole for the Volunteers, however, it comes as no surprise to find informal meetings being held as early as mid-December 1913 between members of the Volunteers' Provisional Committee and prominent figures in the GAA to try to persuade the Association to come out openly in support of the new force. All that was agreed was that individual members of the GAA would start local groups of the Volunteers in areas where the movement had not so far been established.

There is no evidence that the central council took part in these discussions. On the contrary, when it first made formal contact with the Volunteers at Christmas it showed its hand in unmistakable fashion by refusing to loan Croke Park for use for drilling purposes. On the other hand, the GAA president Nowlan (apparently on the same occasion) recommended members of the GAA to join the Volunteers 'to learn to shoot straight'. Although this may have been a personal viewpoint, one need not doubt that it was taken as authoritative guidance from the GAA to members, who might have been expected to follow any lead from their Association. It seems that, in keeping to its policy of neutrality (or perhaps modifying it to one of benevolent neutrality) the council accurately reflected the views of the bulk of its members. The new weekly paper *Gaelic Athlete* which, though not an official organ, seemed to enjoy support from leading GAA members and to have accurately reflected the mood of average members, several times advocated the type of attitudes which the central council actually maintained right up to Easter Week of 1916. However, when the 1914 congress allowed a member of the Volunteer executive to address them he was enthusiastically received.

Events in the political field during the second half of 1914 and for much of 1915 were to test severely the GAA's policy of political neutrality. In June, following an ultimatum from John Redmond, negotiation between the Irish Party and the Volunteer executive resulted in a substantial increase of membership of the executive to include nominees of Redmond, who gained control of the force. Some months later, shortly after the outbreak of World War I, Redmond offered the Volunteers to the British Government for the defence of Ireland and pledged the support of nationalists for the Allied cause in the war. These unauthorised actions led to a split in the Volunteers; the Sinn Féin (and associated) leaders of the Volunteers were naturally not prepared to countenance such a unilateral committal to the British. Most of the original pre-1914 executive now repudiated Redmond, and under the original title of the Irish Volunteers, seceded. The post-1914 executive members remained loyal to Redmond and continued with the majority of the force under the new title of the Irish National Volunteers.

With GAA members from rank-and-file level right up to the central council now in both rival Volunteer forces, the danger of dissension in the ranks of the

Association naturally increased. Almost unbelievably, however, no major split occurred. So far as can now be ascertained in only one county, Galway, did the Volunteer split cause a GAA split; there the Association had had its own troubles for several years which made a split almost unavoidable.[10] A suggestion by the Kerry board in October 1914, which was supported at the Dublin board's annual convention the same month, that the central council should sanction the inclusion of rifle-shooting among GAA activities, was handled with commendable discretion by the Association's chief officials at a general meeting held before Christmas to complete legal formalities connected with the purchase of Croke Park. O'Toole, arguing for a continuation of the policy of neutrality, was strongly supported by J. J. Keane who, while admitting that members could not remain neutral, pointed out that to adopt the Kerry suggestion would be to interfere with the activities of the Volunteers. Persuaded by Cork delegates that it was necessary to do so to avoid the danger of a split in the GAA, Kerry withdrew its proposal.

When four months later the GAA's annual congress, now invariably held in Dublin, coincided with a big Easter parade through the city of 25,000 of Redmond's National Volunteers, the lengths to which some of the Association's leaders were prepared to go in order to avoid a clash showed the extent of the deference then still widely shown to the constitutional movement. The congress began at an unusually early hour and the entire agenda of close on thirty motions was disposed of by lunch-hour so as to allow delegates to attend the Redmondite parade.[11] The crowded main platform at the saluting base included the veteran GAA leader Frank Dineen, making one marvel in retrospect at his reconciliation of a lifelong separatist outlook with his presence in such exalted pro-imperialist company.

The deference which the central council showed to John Redmond did not deter the Sinn Féin minority in the GAA from continuing to express publicly its belief in the ideals of the separatist cause and its lack of faith in Redmond's policy. These persistent attempts to identify the GAA with one section of the national movement provoked reaction from GAA members belonging to other sections of that movement, although this resentment was voiced surprisingly infrequently and ineffectively. The AOH monthly organ strongly attacked the GAA in December 1914; members of the Order had, it alleged, complained that the GAA was being used to further the aims of the physical force movement.[12] As for the Irish Party itself, the organ of its force, *The National Volunteers*, ran a Gaelic games column for ten months of the paper's eighteen month life. This did not prevent it from criticising the 'intriguers' inside the GAA, the 'active apostles of Sinn Féin' trying to link the GAA with the physical force movement.

While the majority of the central council might prudently take a Redmondite line, this did not prevent individual units of the GAA from taking a different line when an opportunity arose. In Derry from as early as March 1914 the county board permitted each club to decide whether or not it would support the Volunteer movement. After the split in the Volunteers in 1915 it became possible to identify particular county boards — Kildare, Roscommon and Kerry to mention three at random — as openly supporting the minority Irish Volunteers in opposition to the much larger Redmondite force. Among counties where, according to the RIC, the GAA by 1916 had become strongly nationalist (meaning influential in the separatist movement) were Cavan, Down, Kilkenny, Meath and Limerick. In Belfast, it was reported to Dublin Castle that same year, the Association, 'although nominally non-political, was in reality strongly Sinn Féin'.

The nearer one got to 1916 the greater the extent to which the younger generation in the GAA came to identify with Sinn Féin. The police reports compiled in connection with the Rising give the impression that much of the blame for the growth of what the Castle authorities regarded as disloyal activities — anti-recruiting agitation, the steady build-up of the Irish Volunteers as an efficient force, the vague conspiratorial moves by the IRB in Dublin, and so on — could be laid in many cases largely at the door of the GAA. The pages of the weekly *Gaelic Athlete*, particularly its editorial columns, provide unmistakable testimony of the closeness of the informal but effective alliance between the GAA and the Irish Volunteers at this period. It is no accident that long before the year 1916 began most of the promi-nent nationalist parliamentary politicians had stopped giving any kind of support to the GAA. Neither was it an accident that the first public official to be deported for his nationalist activities was the chairman of the Cork board J. J. Walsh, who in late 1914 was 'transferred' from Cork post office to Bradford in England.

Except for the falling-off in games in specific counties already mentioned through Volunteer activity, the intense political activity of the period from early 1914 to mid-1916 had no effect on the GAA's programmes. Right through 1914, and also for the whole of 1915, the central and provincial councils and county boards carried out their full range of championships and tournaments. Following the success of the Croke competition a few years before, the year 1915 was notable for an inter-county Wolfe Tone memorial tournament which drew big crowds, espe-cially in Munster and Leinster. The outbreak of World War I led to the occupation for several months by British military units of the GAA's principal grounds in Cork and Limerick cities; while a fall in the income of the Munster council resulted, in both cases the grounds were vacated after a few months. It is possible that the Association suffered greater financial loss from the cancellation of special train services to games in the late summer of 1914. These, however, had been resumed in time for the All-Ireland football final in November; no similar interference or disruption occurred in 1915.

❖

The Rising of 1916, which broke out on Easter Monday morning in Dublin, took everybody by surprise — the country as a whole, the people of Dublin in particular, the authorities in Dublin Castle probably most of all, even most of the nationalist bodies such as the GAA. It is true that for some months past tension had been building up in Dublin between the Castle authorities and the Volunteer leadership; on Easter Sunday itself a wave of rumours had swept the city. But nobody took them seriously; by midday on Easter Monday thousands of citizens rich and poor were enjoying the sun at Fairyhouse race-course. Back in the city centre at that hour only a handful of people was at hand to listen in amazement as Pádraig Pearse read the Proclamation of the Irish Republic from outside the front door of the General Post Office.

On the previous day, less than a mile away to the south across the river Liffey, the annual congress of the GAA was held in the council chamber of the City Hall. Some sixty-five delegates, including one each from England and Scotland, were present; twenty-three Irish counties were represented. Among the attendance were Harry Boland, energetic chairman of the Dublin board, and Eoin O'Duffy, progressive secretary of the Ulster council, both destined to play major roles in the political and military events of the years just ahead, as well as the veteran Galway chairman Pat Larkin of Kiltormer, whose associations with Gaelic games pre-dated the GAA itself and who had played in the first All-Ireland final nearly thirty years before. After a solid if uneventful day's work the delegates dispersed to their home towns; within hours of his return to Kilkenny the president, Alderman Jim Nowlan, was arrested and imprisoned for his associations with the Sinn Féin movement, now in open revolt against British Rule.

As is now well known, the Rising was universally condemned — not only by the British authorities who suppressed it but also by almost every prominent public figure and influential body on the nationalist side. The sweeping and hasty general criticisms of John Redmond were followed, when life began to return to something approaching normality, by the equally savage condemnation of the Dublin and Cork newspapers. One Dublin paper expressly urged the Castle to continue to execute the leaders; the *Cork Examiner,* almost unbelievably, dismissed the whole affair as more 'a communistic disturbance rather than a revolutionary movement'. One quarter of the Catholic hierarchy condemned the Rising; only two members, Bishops Fogarty of Killaloe and O'Dwyer of Limerick, dissented from this viewpoint.

In these circumstances it would be surprising if the GAA were found to have emerged more creditably from the immediate aftermath of the Rising than the other nationalist bodies. That the Association failed to appreciate the long-term significance of the Rising is not to its discredit. Nobody else did either, not even the more prominent survivors of those who had participated in the fighting in Dublin. For the GAA, as for most of the other nationalist organisations (apart from such obvious exceptions as the Volunteers and the IRB) it became after a few weeks a case of business as usual, even though in terms of members affected by it the Rising must have made it more difficult for the Association than for most of the other bodies to continue with its normal range of activities.

In the serious dislocation caused by the hostilities in Dublin there was little that the GAA could do except to wait and see how developments would affect the Association. With membership of the central council spread over all four provinces, control of affairs was, as usual between meetings, in the hands of O'Toole. He, because of his association with Sinn Féin, understandably kept a low profile in the month after Easter. It is in any event unlikely that a representative meeting of council members could have been called straight away. Some were almost certainly unable to reach or communicate with Dublin; in addition, not only Nowlan but several other leading GAA figures like J. J. Walsh and Harry Boland (who might have given O'Toole the support he needed) were in jail. Dineen had died suddenly shortly before. With men of this calibre and political outlook unavailable, it fell to the moderates of the central council, most of them Irish Party supporters, to cope with the exceptional circumstances created by the Rising. Their reaction to the events of Easter Week was, in retrospect at any rate, fairly predictable.

By 28 May, when O'Toole managed to assemble a meeting of the central council, a Royal Commission investigating the Rising had been meeting in public in Dublin for some days; the GAA had already been implicated in the preparations for the Rising by allegations made by the Under-Secretary at Dublin Castle, Sir Matthew Nathan. Understandably attempting to place responsibility for the Rising on the Volunteers, Nathan in a long opening statement claimed that the entire membership of the original provisional committee of 1913 was anti-British (meaning, of course, separatist in outlook) and belonged to one or more of four anti-British bodies, among them the GAA. This Association, he also said, had 'always been anti-British' and did not allow uniformed soldiers to attend its games. This line of attack was repeated by the Inspector General of the RIC, who alleged that from about 1908 onwards 'the extreme section' of the GAA had endorsed the doctrines of Sinn Féin, and by the Director of Military Intelligence, who claimed that the Volunteers had 'got practically full control' of both the Gaelic League and the GAA.

To these allegations the central council replied in a statement issued to the press. Quoting from the GAA's constitution the provision that it was to be a 'strictly non-political and non-sectarian Association' which barred the raising of 'political questions of any kind' at its meetings, and prohibited councils, committees or clubs to 'take part as such in any political movement', it went on to deny that the GAA had participated in opposition to the visit to Dublin in 1914 of the British Prime Minister. Stating that members were free to join any political organisation, the central council frankly conceded that it had many members in such nationalist bodies as the United Irish League (the controlling body of the Irish Party) and the two Volunteer forces. But it denied that the GAA had ever been used 'in furtherance of the objects of the Irish Volunteers', or that policemen or soldiers were denied admission to Gaelic events. The statement ended by protesting strongly 'against the misrepresentation of the aims and objects of the Gaelic Athletic Association as tendered to the Commission' by Nathan and others, and called for proof of the allegations.

Comment on this curious mixture of clarification and denial is almost superfluous, although admittedly easy to me ke with the hindsight of nearly eighty-five years. The main impact on the reader, and undeniably the one intended by the central council of 1916, is of the Association's obvious desire to dissociate itself from the events in Dublin in Easter Week. Nowhere in the statement is there any evidence of admiration for or sympathy with or understanding of the motives or actions of those who took up arms — nothing, for instance, of the courageous and defiant attitude displayed before a hostile audience in the British parliament a fortnight earlier by the veteran John Dillon. More important, perhaps, was the omission of any denial by the GAA that it was an anti-British body; such a rebuttal of Nathan's main premise would have discredited the other detailed evidence involving the Association. The most charitable approach to the central council's statement is to treat it as merely a reflection of the climate of nationalist opinion generally in the period just after the Rising, the long-term effects of which nobody could then be expected to foresee.

A closer look reveals evidence of haste in the drafting of the statement. The relatively unimportant topic of the Premier's visit to Dublin two years earlier was oddly given unjustifiable prominence. Yet a glance at Nathan's statement shows that he never made the allegation (that the GAA had taken part in opposition to Asquith's 1914 Dublin trip) which the central council went to such trouble to deny. On the other hand, it is probably significant that the GAA neatly side-stepped the allegations that uniformed soldiers were denied admission to GAA events. This appears to have become a widespread practice since shortly after the start of World War I. In some areas even uniformed RIC men were also kept out.

Probably the most revealing aspect of the central council's reaction to the Rising is that the event was not regarded as the main item on the agenda at the special meeting called by O'Toole for 28 May. Instead, the council resumed discussion of the Association's possible exemption from (or alternatively its resistance to) a new tax recently imposed by the British Government by way of entertainment duty on games and other sports. This new tax was to be included by the promoter of a game in the admission price he charged the public; but some exemptions were granted from the tax, as for example if the takings went to charity or the game was intended only for children. The GAA would be exempt on another ground if it could establish that its games were in furtherance of the object of reviving national pastimes (as they clearly were) and were conducted by a body which was educational and not run for profit (which the Government was disputing).

With a view to ensuring that it was not liable for the new tax the GAA had earlier in 1916 sent a deputation consisting of Nowlan, O'Toole and Dineen to London. There a group of leading Irish MPs — the leader Redmond, the chief whip Patrick O'Brien and John O'Connor and Willie Duffy (both with long connections with the GAA) had introduced the deputation to the Chancellor of the Exchequer. These negotiations proving unsuccessful, the matter had come up for discussion at the annual congress at Easter, when the council was directed to call a special congress if this were needed. At its 28 May meeting the central council decided to ask O'Connor to make another approach to the British Government. In the meantime in July county boards were instructed by the council to resist any local efforts by the revenue authorities to levy the tax, and to make the case that the new law (which had been passed just before Easter) afforded the GAA exemption from the tax. In September, having obtained legal advice, the central council altered its approach to merely requesting deferment of payment of the tax pending the outcome of negotiations in London between the GAA and the Government.

When in November John O'Connor MP reported back on his discussion in London, the affair was seen to have taken a new and more serious turn. The official British attitude had now hardened, no doubt in the light of events in Ireland. The GAA was now informed that if it wished to be exempt it would first have to make radical alterations to rules 8, 9a and 9b of its Official Guide. Since these were the rules involving suspension of a member who played or attended rugby, soccer or hockey, and debarring from membership 'police, magistrates, civil servants who have taken the oath of allegiance, jail warders, soldiers, sailors of the Royal Navy, militiamen or pensioners of the constabulary, army or navy', the central council reacted unfavourably at once. It would not agree to any such fundamental or involuntary amendment of its constitution at the behest of the British Government, no matter what the consequences. At its 3 December meeting the demand to change the rules was unanimously rejected. That this demand represented a top-level decision by the Government is suggested by the fact that, at an interview which O'Toole and J. J. Hogan had with the military authorities around the same time, it was repeated in identical terms to those given to O'Connor in London. The episode showed that, despite the moderate tone of the Association's statement on the Rising, the British recognised the GAA as one of the bodies whose policies had helped to bring about that event.

The controversy over the entertainment duty, although the first and most serious confrontation between any nationalist body and the British Government since the Rising, soon became only part of a policy of intermittent harassment of the GAA during 1916 which, if not expressly directed by Dublin Castle, was permitted by it to continue. Soon after the end of the fighting in Dublin the military authorities, now effectively governing the country, first imposed a ban on all GAA games. By mid-June this had been modified to a ban on inter-county matches; a few weeks later even these were permitted. At the same time, and for a period of from three to six months (varying from county to county) the police actively obstructed the playing of Gaelic games. In some places they insisted on clubs or boards getting permits in advance; elsewhere, they turned a blind eye when local GAA units defied them and operated without a permit. In Kerry, on the other hand, the police forced entry to games, although whether to stop the games for which no permit had been obtained or to help in the collection of the new tax is not clear.

However, in a surprisingly short time the activities of the GAA returned to normality all over the country. In Dublin (almost unbelievably, in view of the disruption to everyday life caused by the Rising) club games were in full swing again by late June, less than two months after the fighting had ended. By 1 July Croke Park was open again; a fortnight later the Munster council began its championship games. By late July those of Leinster were under way; in the middle of August the Wolfe Tone final drew an attendance of 7,000 to Croke Park; on 20 August over 5,000 people attended the annual GAA national athletic championships at Mallow. In Ulster, where the provincial council successfully thwarted efforts to obtain payment of the new tax, games were resumed in most counties by mid-August. October saw the provincial hurling championships concluded in Munster and Leinster, while counties where local activities had resumed between August and October included Meath, Kerry and Tyrone.

The controversy over the new tax was not the only major dispute between the GAA and the British authorities in 1916. For many years there had been intermittent friction between the central council (or one or more of the provincial councils) and the major railway companies, over the terms to be given by each side for special trains for major GAA games. In Cork some years earlier J. J. Walsh had his board invest in shares in one of the companies operating out of Cork. He then attended the next annual meeting as a shareholder and gave a characteristically forceful presentation of the case for fairer treatment of the followers of Gaelic games, who were providing the firm with so much profitable business.[13] In Ulster there had also been complaints of restrictive conditions for special trains to GAA matches. Later relations between the central council and the major rail firms improved so much that the GAA accepted a valuable trophy, the first of many such gifts of which the Railway Cup, still played for annually, is probably the best known survivor.

Following the Rising, however, emergency powers were used by the Castle to curtail excursion traffic. This became the basis of an apparently concerted refusal by

the major rail firms to run any more special trains to GAA games. Since a continuation of this situation, by drastically cutting attendances at Croke Park, would
seriously affect the financial position of the Association and thus hamper further
progress, the council took the matter to the highest level. A deputation interviewed
the Commander-in-Chief of the British forces, General Maxwell, in mid-November
1916, but without success. The assistance of the Irish Party was now enlisted;
Nowlan, Crowe and O'Toole crossed to London and met Redmond, Dillon and
other Irish leaders at Westminster at the end of November. Pressure from them
produced a meeting with the new Chief Secretary, H. E. Duke, who bluntly refused
to sanction special trains for any type of sport in Ireland. In spite of further extensive lobbying by Dillon this decision stood, and O'Toole re-fixed for mid-January
1917 the All Ireland hurling final which he had called off a month earlier.

Of far greater importance for the future of the GAA than its two confrontations
in 1916 with the British Government was a decision made by the central council
towards the end of that year. According to the minutes, the meeting of 5 November
unanimously resolved to appoint O'Toole and Crowe as delegates to attend an
all-Ireland convention being sponsored by Dublin Corporation 'to form a political
prisoners amnesty association'. The same meeting reached similar agreement to
accede to a request from the 'Irish National Aid Volunteer Dependants' Fund' that
the council run a tournament in aid of the fund, and for this purpose a three-man
committee was appointed to act in conjunction with the fund's committee.

Between them these two decisions represent the decisive turning of its back on
the Irish Party by the GAA and its implicit recognition of the arrival as a major political force of Sinn Féin, two years before the Irish electorate accorded Sinn Féin the
same recognition in the general election of 1918. For over twenty years, since the
adoption of its non-political constitution in 1895 after its disastrous alliance with the
Parnellites, the Association had accepted the Irish Party as the leading partner in the
nationalist movement. To this policy, despite increasing pressure from separatists
in the GAA, it had clung while Sinn Féin and later the Volunteers established
themselves as important new political bodies in the decade before 1916. The failure
of the Rising, inspired by Sinn Féin and led by the Volunteers, would seem to have
justified the stand taken up to then. Now, however, within six months of the crush-
ing of the Rising, Sinn Féin members in the GAA were asserting themselves again in
timely response to the momentous change in public opinion now taking place.

In its handling of the Rising Dublin Castle had seriously under-estimated the
force of public opinion. Through the savage repression culminating in the protracted
series of executions of the 1916 leaders and the unnecessarily wide wave of arrests
and imprisonments, the British military forces won the Volunteers friends all over
Ireland who up to Easter 1916 still stood loyally behind Redmond. By rushing head-
long into fresh and fruitless negotiations in London with the British Government

and the Ulster Unionists over the extent and implementation of Home Rule, the Irish Party only discredited itself in the eyes of its hitherto mass support among the electorate at home. Above all, in their condemnation of the Rising, Redmond and his colleagues had seriously misjudged the mood of Ireland, where the conduct of the 1916 leaders during the fighting and at their trials soon gained their cause much sympathy. To translate that emotion into solid support now became the immediate aim of Sinn Féin. In its implementation of the central council's decisions of 5 November 1916, the GAA gave a generous and helping hand when this was badly needed.

Shortly after the Rising the widow of Tom Clarke, one of the executed leaders, set up with the assistance of relatives of other dead leaders the Irish Volunteer Dependants Fund. This was followed quickly by the establishment under the auspices of Dublin Corporation of the Irish National Aid Association. The aim of both bodies was to collect money and distribute grants to help dependants of participants in the Rising. Both funds were immediate successes; in August the two bodies merged and became the Irish National Aid and Volunteer Dependants Fund. Its first secretary was a young Dubliner named Joseph McGrath, who was later to achieve ministerial rank in the Irish Free State. He was succeeded early in 1917 by a young Corkman named Michael Collins, who was destined to play a major role in the military events of the next six years.

National aid, as it came to be popularly known, became a major factor in the growth of public understanding and support of the ideals of those who had organised the Rising. Gradually support for the charitable objects of national aid led to increased commitment to the views of the dead revolutionaries. Before public subscriptions reached substantial proportions, gold sent from the United States for the Rising had been used to help dependants; then after the initial wave of public financial support had spent itself, the GAA became a principal source of national aid funds. Hurling and football games were organised all over the country and the proceeds channelled back to the national aid organisers in Dublin. The success of the national aid campaign, in which the GAA played a leading part, helped to restore morale after the failure of the Rising and to involve in the political aims of the exe-cuted leaders many who had hitherto held aloof from the separatist movement.

Looked at solely from the Association's own viewpoint, the year 1916 as a whole was understandably an unsatisfactory one for the GAA. A series of mostly unforseeable events combined to halt the steady progress of the previous four or five years — members' preference for Volunteer activities in the spring, the major disruption caused by the Rising itself in April and May, the intermittent harassment by the Government, military and police forces for the rest of the year, and above all the withdrawal of special trains. Little wonder that, when the next congress met to review the previous year's activities in mid-April 1917, it heard a gloomy financial report from O'Toole. Although the Wolfe Tone tournament of 1916 had raised £213, the ban on trains had been the main cause of a loss of £700 incurred by the central council on the Association's activities in 1916. But the council still had a credit balance of nearly £2,000.

Having failed to persuade the Association to change its policy of participation in the nationalist movement, Dublin Castle not only maintained its ban on excursion trains for Gaelic games during 1917, but revealed the partisan motive behind its attitude by permitting extra trains for race-meetings that year. Deprived of its normal income by falling attendances, the GAA now found itself unable to avoid effecting economies. The Croke Cup competition was curtailed by the voluntary withdrawal of both Connacht and Ulster; teams from the other two provinces were required to meet their own expenses from county board sources; the groundsman at Croke Park was paid off. In the autumn J. J. Walsh, recently released from jail, tried to persuade the central council to exploit the upsurge of national feeling to try to slow down the growth of soccer. An appeal was issued to GAA members to take advantage of the mood of the country to reorganise and to start new clubs in areas where the GAA was weak; the call seems to have been met with only limited success.

On the playing field 1917 brought some improvement in the fortunes of the GAA. In the early months of the year many county boards held conventions which led to a revival of activities; by Easter competitions were in progress in many places. The central council, where Harry Boland was now an influential figure, made the GAA the principal source of finance for national aid. A special sub-committee chaired by Boland sponsored inter-county hurling and football tournaments for national aid funds; the more active counties (among them Dublin, Cork, Cavan, Monaghan, Kilkenny and Roscommon) also organised inter-club ties for the same purpose. By early June, Gaelic games were nearly back to the level of 1915; in mid-August the annual GAA athletic championships were held in Limerick. By the end of the year two All-Ireland hurling finals (for 1916 and 1917) had been played; the football championship was completed with the final early in December. Despite the ban on trains 7,000 attended the Wolfe Tone memorial final in August; by late November £400 had been collected for national aid. Another indication of public interest was the re-printing in November of T. F. O'Sullivan's history *Story of the G.A.A.*; the first edition had passed the Castle censor a year before.

The deadlock over the new tax continued. Early in 1917 James Ryan, secretary of the Limerick board, was sentenced to six months in jail for refusing free admission to a match to a police officer, who seemingly wished to find out if the tax was being charged. When Ryan's solicitor produced in court secret Government documents, tending to show official bias against the GAA, he too was prosecuted and jailed for three months. The annual GAA congress, held in private for the first time, decided unanimously (after a long discussion which revealed a wide divergence of views) not to pay the tax and to convene a special delegate convention if the Government tried to enforce the law. In June, a test case brought against the Association failed; the next month another one succeeded against the officials of the Dublin board. O'Toole now called the special delegate convention; when it met in Dublin on 5 August delegates from twenty-three counties unanimously confirmed the defiant decision of the congress held three months before. So far as can now be ascertained, the British Government made no further effort to collect the tax from the GAA.

The growth of public support for Sinn Féin during 1917 was reflected in the capture of Irish Party seats in Roscommon, Longford, Clare and Kilkenny by Count Plunkett, Joseph McGuinness, Eamon de Valera and William T. Cosgrave respectively, all pledged not to attend the British parliament. In defiance of a Government ban on the wearing of the Volunteers uniform and the public carrying of arms, uniformed Volunteers in Clare, Tipperary and elsewhere appeared with hurleys instead of rifles.[14] Occupying a prominent position in the huge public funeral of Thomas Ashe, who died from forced feeding while in Government custody in September, was a large body of GAA men all carrying hurleys. Ashe, in addition to his other activities, had been a leading GAA figure in county Dublin before 1916. The closing months of 1917 were dominated by the reorganisation of Sinn Féin, when Arthur Griffith gave way as President to de Valera; the executive was strengthened by the election of figures like Collins, Boland and J. J. Walsh, the last two owing their rise largely to their earlier work in the GAA. When in mid-November 1917 the Volunteers came to hold their third annual convention they chose Croke Park as the venue; for many who attended the surroundings were familiar.[15]

The early months of 1918 saw the political temperature remaining high largely through the coercive policy of the British Government. Harassment of leading republicans, mostly taking the form of sporadic waves of arrests in the spring, was followed by the decision in April to extend military conscription to Ireland. The reaction was spontaneous. The Irish Party, Sinn Féin and the Labour movement united to oppose the measure; powerful support came too from the Catholic hierarchy, with the GAA central council adding its voice to the opposition. A one-day general strike took place in April on the issue; three weeks later most of the Sinn Féin leaders were put in jail for alleged complicity in the so-called German plot. Then in the three week period from mid-June a series of unprecedented emergency legal measures were announced by Dublin Castle which amounted to an admission of inability to govern the country on a normal peace-time basis. Thirteen counties were declared proclaimed districts; other areas became special military areas where public meetings were banned; the principal nationalist bodies were made illegal. By this suppression of all normal forms of political activity the British drove resistance to their rule underground overnight.

That any sports body, and especially one like the GAA whose policy, outlook and rank-and-file membership were so closely linked with the nationalist movement, could manage to carry out its full quota of fixtures at a time of such political tension was out of the question. Early in 1918 signs of a reduction in the Association's activities began to appear. The Kerry board, because of the involvement in Sinn Féin activities of so many of its members, found itself unable to field a team for the belated 1917 championship. Like Clare it was unrepresented at the annual convention of the Munster council, and soon afterwards was temporarily unaffiliated to the GAA. In many other counties sports meetings were called off, although whether because of the political situation or the continued failure of the GAA adequately to promote athletics in rural areas is not at all clear. Incipient grumblings in the press about the Association's record in athletics, coupled with unfavourable comparisons with past performances of great Irish athletics, failed to gather pace only because of more serious developments in which the GAA became involved in the late summer of 1918.

Nevertheless the activities of the GAA did not come to a standstill for the first eight months or so of 1918. On the contrary, right up to the end of August it continued to carry on to a surprising extent. In the early part of the year national aid inter-county fixtures were held in both hurling and football in Munster and Leinster. Most of the better-organised counties also held their annual conventions as usual — Dublin, Cork, Meath and Tipperary as early as February and March — and the central council found time to come to the aid of the Kerry board. Congress responded to an appeal from Austin Stack with an immediate grant of £100; later an inter-county football tournament was successfully organised by the council to raise more money for the county, the final attracting 12,000 people to Croke Park in June.

For the second successive year the annual congress was held in private, with the result that the nationalist public was unaware of a confrontation which took place in the Mansion House at the start of the proceedings on Easter Sunday 1918. Before agreeing to minutes of the previous congress, Harry Boland demanded details of the various deputations from the Association to the Castle authorities and the Irish MPs in London during 1916. A long and acrimonious discussion ended with the passing, by twenty-seven votes to twenty-five, of a vote of censure on the central council for such contacts; however, a substantial proportion of delegates, possibly as many as thirty, abstained. This was not the end of the matter, for although J. J. Walsh chivalrously withdrew his own nomination for the presidency in deference to Nowlan, he accused the officers of failing in their duty to members, an accusation that seems to have been partly repudiated by the majority of delegates expressing satisfaction with the council 'on the whole'. The episode, the only event of note at an otherwise uneventful congress, is revealing for the way it shows the now dominant influence in the GAA of the Sinn Féin members, who later that same year were to swing the council round in favour of a showdown with Dublin Castle, in striking contrast to the attitude of which Boland and Walsh had been critical.

Early in July, the day after Sinn Féin, the Volunteers, the Gaelic League and Cumann na mBan were proscribed, came an even more drastic order from the Castle prohibiting the holding of any public meetings in Ireland except under an official permit. Although the Government could not have foreseen it, this edict was to lead inside a month to one of the most widespread and most successful acts of defiance of British rule in the country in the six years between 1916 and 1922. The police were directed to prevent the public playing of games and other sports such as athletics. Within a week games and sports meetings were being broken up in many areas by the RIC, who in some cases even went to the length of uprooting and confiscating goal-posts. Needless to add, events sponsored by the GAA were singled out for special attention; needless too to add, the Association refrained from seeking any official permits to carry on its activities.

A special meeting of the central council on 20 July decided to organise what would be at the same time a solemn and practical assertion of the people's right to play native games, without leave or licence of any foreign power, and a mass act of defiance of the British Government. Indicative of the importance of the meeting that made this decision was the fact that the attendance included not only the members of the council but also the secretaries of the Munster council, the Athletics Council, the Dublin board and — perhaps most significantly of all in view of his prominent role in the Sinn Féin organisation — the Dublin chairman, Harry Boland. After a report by O'Toole on an interview he had had with Dublin Castle on the question of permits, two motions were unanimously passed. Under pain of automatic and indefinite suspension, no permits would be sought by any member or unit of the Association, and no member would participate in any game or athletic or cycle meeting for which a permit had been granted. Secondly, each county board was to call inside ten days a special delegate meeting of clubs to arrange for a series of (unpermitted) matches, to commence simultaneously at 3 p.m. on Sunday, 4 August all over the country.

On the reasonable assumption that news of the GAA's decision reached the RIC some time in the last week of July, this advance notice of the Association's intention to commit on a countrywide scale a technical breach of the law produced no reaction from Dublin Castle — at least until it was too late to save its face. Neither did a notice published in the national papers of Saturday, 3 August under O'Toole's name and headed 'Gaelic Sunday'. This directed all county boards to follow the orders of the central council and to ensure that on the next day '54,000 Gaels will actively participate in national pastimes all over Ireland'. Whether the British felt powerless to intervene, or whether they suspected that the GAA's move was a bluff, is a matter for speculation. In the event Gaelic Sunday succeeded beyond all the expectations of its organisers. It not only found a place in the history of Gaelic games and of the GAA itself, but became notable as the greatest single act of defiance outside the purely political sphere between 1916 and 1922.

Not only was O'Toole's forecast of 54,000 Gaels proved right; older officials of the Association who survived to recent years claim that the real figure was much closer to 100,000. In Dublin alone twenty-four matches commenced at different venues at the appointed hour. Only in Dublin was any attempt made to prevent Gaelic games; there the entry to Croke Park was barred by armed police with troops in attendance — who found themselves treated to the unusual spectacle of a camogie match on the road outside. In vain did the Government later try to argue that no prohibition on Gaelic games had been imposed. Too late in the day it was explained that the ban had been intended to apply only if a Gaelic event were used as the occasion of a political speech, something that had not in fact happened since before 1916 in any event.

Flushed with the victory of Gaelic Sunday the GAA at once resumed its activities, to find that the real gain to the Association was a sudden end to the harassment and obstruction by police that had hampered officials in their work in many areas for months. Within a week championship games were in progress again. Even in troubled Munster inter-county fixtures were carried out; early in September the GAA successfully staged the national athletic contests in Limerick. Then the great influenza epidemic struck; gradually with widespread cancellations of sports fixtures the volume of activity on Gaelic fields decreased sharply. Eventually not only had the All-Ireland semi-finals and finals in both hurling and football to be called off, but the GAA suffered many serious losses and the fatal 'flu claimed the lives of players, athletes and officials.

In November 1918 a major political development effectively and abruptly ended all activities on GAA fields for the rest of that year. Two weeks after the ending on 11 November 1918 of World War I the British parliament was dissolved. Sinn Féin decided to contest all 106 Irish seats at the coming general election in December. It at once became clear not only that this would be the Irish Party's last-ditch battle for survival against the republican organisation, but also that in choosing between the two movements the nationalist electorate would decide the future political status of their country. Both sides now mustered maximum support; in these circumstances sporting fixtures became the first casualty of the election campaign, as GAA members on both sides gave all their spare time to pre-electoral work. Within a week of the dissolution all the work of the GAA had come to a standstill; it remained so until the end of the year.

When shortly after Christmas the election results were announced, Sinn Féin was seen to have won a landslide victory and to have secured overwhelming public support for its aim of an independent republic. Of 105 candidates elected, no fewer than seventy-three were republicans (all Sinn Féin); only twenty-six (nearly all returned for seats in Ulster) were Unionists. The Irish Party was almost wiped out, winning only six Irish seats and one in Liverpool. Amongst those who lost their seats were men like William Field (Dublin), Thomas Condon and John Cullinane (Tipperary) and Willie Duffy (Galway), who had been active in or associated with the GAA almost from its foundation. Prominent, on the other hand, in the list of seventy-three Sinn Féin MPs were the names of men of the younger generation who from early in the century had also risen to prominence largely through their work in the Association — Harry Boland (Dublin), J. J. Walsh (Cork), Austin Stack (Kerry) and Joe McBride (Mayo).

Few of these were present when late in January 1919 at the Mansion House in Dublin Dáil Eireann held its first meeting, probably the most significant political event in a year that was to mark the beginning of a vital three-year period in Irish history. It was a period that was to be marked first by political action from the Sinn Féin side. This in turn was to be succeeded by open warfare in many parts of the island, leading tortuously first to a military truce, next to negotiations between the Dáil Government and the British, and finally to the Treaty of 1921. That a sports organisation, itself partly politically orientated, could manage to continue to operate fully in such a period of social and political upheaval was out of the question. What is surprising is the extent to which, and for how long, games continued to be played, often nearly simultaneously with nearby urban guerrilla warfare.

Within a fortnight of the first meeting of the Dáil came the sensational escape from Lincoln jail of Eamon de Valera, now undisputed leader of nationalist Ireland. He attended later sessions of the Dáil in April, before sailing early in the summer for the United States, where the influence of the Irish community was fast becoming a significant factor. De Valera's mission was, however, only one major development in the increasing pressure on Britain. Among others were the gradual take-over of governmental activities by the Dáil Ministry, the scathing condemnation by the Catholic bishops of British rule in June and the secret build-up under Michael Collins of an efficient counter-espionage machine. By late summer guerrilla warfare, mostly taking the form of attacks on police barracks and British forces, had broken out in places, particularly Munster. Faced with the danger of a collapse of its administrative system in Ireland, Britain reacted forcefully and in many cases brutally.

Astonishing though it may appear at first glance, 1919 turned out to be the best year the GAA had had since 1916 and probably since 1913. With the election now over and the 'flu epidemic at last on the wane, Gaelic games resumed early in January and were doubtless helped by the general release later that month of jailed republicans, who included many GAA members. By the end of February the two All-Ireland Finals deferred from 1918 had been played; in Dublin, where even the election campaign had not prevented the holding of the county board's annual convention early in December 1918, club competitions were well under way by mid-January. Most of the other well-organised counties got through their annual stock-taking during the early spring — Tipperary in February; Cork, Cavan, Limerick and Sligo in March; and Meath in April. The final of a special tournament in aid of the Republican Prisoners' Dependants Fund attracted an attendance of 20,000, including Collins and de Valera, to Croke Park early in April. Two months later the inter-county championships were in progress in Munster, Leinster and Connacht.

Off the playing-field much of the time and energy of the Association for the first four months of 1919 was occupied by a controversy with a distinctly political flavour. The question at issue was whether or not a person, such as a national teacher or a civil servant, who had taken the now obligatory oath of allegiance to the British Government, merited disqualification from membership of the GAA. At a special meeting of the central council on 7 December 1918 the four members present unanimously answered in the affirmative; all members of the GAA who had taken the oath were declared suspended pending a definitive decision at the next congress, due for Easter 1919. The council's ruling provoked widespread reaction from rank-and-file members; those affected numbered thousands who had been the backbone of the Association. While supporters of the ruling argued its validity on the strength of the GAA's stand for the national cause and on the necessity to present a united front against British rule in the coming political confrontation, the suspension met with strong opposition on the ground that to vary a qualification for membership was something that only delegates to congress could validly do.

Feeling in many counties ran high on this subject, which for a while seemed liable to split the Association. As one convention after another debated the matter, it became noticeable that no county came out unreservedly in favour of the central council, which also found its ruling openly flouted in Dublin. Among counties which, on the other hand, came out expressly against the council were such leading units as Tipperary, Cavan, Limerick and Sligo. Kerry gave its delegates to congress a free hand; not until the Meath convention of late March was there a decisive vote (sixty delegates to eleven) in favour of the council. Clearly, however, there were GAA members prepared to resign from public posts in order to remain loyal to their Association, for the central council at its meeting on 25 January 1919 found it necessary to organise a special tournament to give financial aid to such people. When the matter finally came up at the congress on 20 April a decisive majority — fifty to thirty-one — of the delegates upheld the central council's decision. The debate was conducted in a tense atmosphere and on strongly emotional grounds, with Harry Boland's speech probably swaying many previously uncommitted. In a memorable phrase, he claimed that 'the Gaelic Athletic Association owed its position to the fact that it had always drawn the line between the garrison and the Gael'.

If the 1919 congress averted a possible split in the GAA when it backed the central council on its stand over the oath of allegiance, it also healed what was easily the longest split in the Association when it welcomed back into the GAA the leading Dublin club, Kickham's. As far back as mid-1913 this club, nearly as old as the GAA itself, was pressing for reforms in the GAA which would provide grants for weaker counties and, by setting up three boards in Dublin, build on the Association's success in that city. In 1914, by refusing to affiliate with the Dublin board except on condition that its proposals were agreed to in advance, the Kickham club seceded. A year later, with only minimal and temporary support from Wexford, Galway and Sligo, Kickham's set up the rival National Association of Gaelic and Athletic Clubs — 'the five-lettered folly' to its opponents. For four more years the club stayed out in the cold, until early in 1919 its ideas for reorganisation in Dublin were accepted and that county set up separate boards for Senior and Junior activities. With congress formally agreeing to an amnesty, what had become known as the Kickham revolt came to an end.

Increased political activity in the late summer and autumn of 1919, caused by such events as the proscribing of the Dáil, Sinn Féin and the Volunteers, and the growth of violence between Irish and British forces, did not prevent the GAA from continuing with its normal quota of fixtures. For the second successive year Limerick hosted the national athletic championships. In late September what was probably a record crowd of 32,000 saw Kildare defeat Galway to win its second All-Ireland football title. Immediately after this a whole series of improvements to Croke Park, to accommodate even bigger crowds, were decided on by the central council. An architect advised on the works required; an inter-county competition in each code was organised to provide the funds necessary for the work. A special Grounds Committee was appointed, which was directed to meet weekly to supervise progress in the renovation. Among the decisions it made was one to re-sod the entire playing pitch; this necessitated the closure of the grounds for much of the early part of 1920.

Eventually, however, as the military struggle between the British forces and the Volunteers (now the army of the Irish Republic) intensified and spread during 1920, a stage was reached in the late spring when all activities of the GAA ground to a halt. This was the year when first the Black-and-Tans and later the Auxiliaries were let loose on the civilian population; the year of the burning of Cork, the sacking of Thurles and the pogroms in Belfast; the year of the assassination by Crown forces of Lord Mayor McCurtain of Cork and of the death while on hunger strike in a British jail of his successor Terence MacSwiney. It was a year of continuous raids, arrests and deportations by the British and of guerrilla warfare (including the destruction of 300 police barracks in two nights); the year of the imposition of Partition through the Government of Ireland Act; the year that witnessed the almost total collapse of the British legal system in Ireland and its replacement by the Dáil courts operated by the underground republican regime. For the GAA it was the year of Bloody Sunday.

The first quarter of 1920 saw the GAA bravely trying to carry on its work as if everyday life continued normally. Plans were made in January to hold inter-county athletic contests; at least one inter-club athletics meeting was held in Dublin in February. By mid-February the Croke inter-county competition had resumed. On St Patrick's Day the ceremonial laying of the foundation stone of the Croke statue before a huge crowd in Thurles was followed by a Tipperary-Cork hurling match and a banquet in Hayes's Hotel, where Cusack's first meeting had been held thirty-five years before. In Ulster, the only area where organised opposition to GAA events had so far manifested itself, the provincial council held its annual convention in late March. So in the same month did the Leinster council, which heard from its secretary the news that at 428 the number of clubs in that province in 1919 represented an increase of sixty over 1918. Not surprisingly congress was a quiet, if businesslike, affair. The seventy delegates heard an encouraging report from O'Toole, together with details of his ambitious plans for Croke Park. Alderman Nowlan was re-elected (for the twentieth successive year) by thirty-three votes to thirty-two for Dan McCarthy of Dublin. Of the congress decisions, two stand to this day — the fixing of a three-year maximum term for the presidency and a ruling that all future All-Ireland finals be played in Croke Park.

By early March 1920 there were signs of a falling-off in the number of Gaelic games; this trend continued into the early summer when normally the volume of activity would have been increasing. Athletics continued in Dublin to the end of the summer; but Munster had a different story to tell. There from late July GAA hurling semi-finals had to be moved from the Cork Athletic Grounds out to a much smaller venue at Riverstown. The prohibition of public meetings in that county later that month prevented any further games there; soon afterwards, as a gesture of support to the now dying Terence MacSwiney, the Cork board called off all fixtures under its control indefinitely. Soon all GAA games in Munster were cancelled; from 10 December in any event every county in that province except Waterford was under military rule. By October games nearly everywhere else in the country had also been suspended; as one contemporary commentator put it, Gaelic games had not been so disrupted by external events since the days of the Parnell Split thirty years before.

In October came a sudden and brief revival of inter-county fixtures, which the next month was to have a tragic result. Early in October 5,000 spectators, who had so far that year had little exciting fare, were entertained by a rousing challenge football match in Croke Park between Dublin and Kildare. Soon afterwards the Tipperary board issued a challenge to Dublin; a match was arranged for 2.45 p.m. on Sunday, 21 November, again in Croke Park. The events of that day, Bloody Sunday, as it came to be called inside twenty-four hours, at GAA headquarters are now a part of modern Irish history. Without advance warning from either side the Association found itself suddenly caught up in the grim military activities of both sides; more accurately, perhaps, the GAA became a convenient target for reprisal purposes by the British forces which that morning had suffered irreparable loss. Nothing more strikingly illustrates the close connections between the GAA and the republican movement between 1916 and 1922 than Bloody Sunday.

Around 3 p.m., when the crowd of under 10,000 was settling down to an entertaining game, a British military plane flew over and emitted a red signal-flare. Immediately Black-and-Tans began to climb over the walls at each end of the ground, some using ladders. At once a withering fire was directed straight into the crowd, first from small arms and then from machine-guns hastily set up on the ground just inside the main entrance. After about ten minutes an RIC officer advanced across the pitch, announcing a proposed search of spectators. An initial stampede resulted; most of the crowd was detained, and it was some hours before the search was concluded. After the shooting and subsequent stampede thirteen people lay dead around the ground, close on one hundred were injured. The dead included the Tipperary captain Michael Hogan, a young Wexford man who had been rendering spiritual assistance to Hogan, a 26-year-old Dublin woman due to get married a few days later, and three Dublin boys, aged 10, 11 and 14 years.

The Croke Park shootings were, it soon transpired, only part of a series of events in Dublin that same day. Early in the morning, with the authority of the Dáil Cabinet and on express directions from Collins, the republican counter-espionage service had executed fourteen British intelligence officers in their lodgings in the city centre, whose mission in Dublin had been the assassination of Sinn Féin leaders. Satisfied from his own efficient intelligence machine that it was a case of survival for whichever side was quicker on the draw, Collins in one carefully planned operation destroyed the centre of the whole British spy network in Ireland. Bloody Sunday proved to be the turning point in the combined political and military struggle.[16] It served notice on Britain that neither the IRA nor the underground Dáil Government would easily be broken. Once this vital message got through, there was no alternative to a compromise with Sinn Féin. Within weeks feelers went out for a truce.

At home and abroad the shootings in Croke Park were at once recognised as a savage reprisal for Collins's shattering blow to the British espionage machine. As the details of the afternoon's events were pieced together, all the evidence was seen to be against the official explanation. There were no IRA sentries around the ground, inside or outside; the firing was begun by the Black-and-Tans and not returned. Some of them, and also a few of the Auxiliaries, were drunk; at least one indiscreetly admitted that they had come for revenge. From the pre-raid survey by the plane to the departure of the last military lorry (trailing along the roadway behind it the Tricolour always flown at Croke Park), the shootings could only be interpreted as a planned act of punishment by enraged and indisciplined troops for the loss of their leading officers that morning. No official enquiry was ever held.

As for the GAA itself, like the rest of the community it was stunned by the outrage. Even before the game began Nowlan, O'Toole and McCarthy, only then hearing of the morning shootings, anxiously considered cancelling the match as if fearful of some counter-action by the British. McCarthy in particular, who worked closely with the Sinn Féin leaders, would have been fully aware of the significance of the shootings. None of the three can have been surprised at the discovery of some thirty revolvers scattered around the ground that evening; far from suggesting that some of Collins's men had come to escape detection, these weapons served only to confirm that the men of the GAA were in the forefront of the military struggle. After the shootings officials and players alike dispersed quietly. This time, unlike 1916, there was no central council deliberation, no protest to the British, no contact whatever with Dublin Castle. The GAA was justly proud of the recognition by the British, implicit in the selection of the target for the reprisal, of the Association's identity with what one of the shrewdest of contemporary observers called the 'underground nation'.[17]

The falling-off in competitions during the summer of 1920 naturally adversely affected the finances of the GAA; shortly before Bloody Sunday it found that its financial situation had suddenly deteriorated. Not only had it committed itself to expenditure of over £6,500 on Croke Park; its bank overdraft now stood at £1,700. Faced even before Bloody Sunday with an almost total suspension of fixtures, and with little prospect of a resumption of activities in the near future, the central council turned to the Dáil for assistance. In recognition of its role in the national movement the Association had been invited in 1919 to send representatives to public sessions of the new assembly; now the GAA was to test that friendship. A meeting of the Cabinet held the day before Bloody Sunday considered a formal application from the GAA for a loan of £6,000. After two further meetings on 11 and 18 December the cabinet finally approved the actual terms on 9 January 1921. The Association was to get £6,000 at five per cent interest. Its existing debt of £1,700 was to be paid by the Government. Since most of the work at Croke Park had by now been completed (but unpaid for), it is little exaggeration to say that this generous gesture by the Dáil Cabinet saved Croke Park and averted a probable bankruptcy of the GAA.

It was as well for the GAA that the Dáil regime came to its rescue when it did, for the Association was facing what was to prove organisationally its most frustrating and financially its most disastrous year since its previous near-bankruptcy twenty years before. The first six months of 1921 saw the warfare between the Irish and British forces reach a new level of intensity and ferocity. Martial law was extended in both Leinster and Munster; as outrages against both civilians and property by the British continued, the scale of activities by republican forces, which also now engaged in reprisals on property, increased. In parts of Munster, and above all in Cork, the IRA was now operating on a full-time professional basis, and although peace moves began to make progress from April onwards, Dublin remained in a state of war until after the successful destruction of the Custom House in May, which paralysed the machinery of British local government here. Finally on 11 July came the Truce, which for the first time in three years held out some hope of a political settlement between the two countries and a return to normality.

One would expect that for the GAA 1921 would be neatly divisible into two clear-cut periods — six months of inactivity followed by another six of games. No such obvious pattern emerged. Over most of the country Gaelic games did remain in suspension before the Truce; naturally this was particularly so in Munster. But Leinster and a few counties elsewhere told a different story. Dublin above all managed to carry out a programme of club games as near to normal as made no difference; it even held its annual convention on 2 January, at which sixty-six clubs were reported as affiliated. The Leinster council followed with its convention in March; towards the end of that month congress was held. Again it was a quiet affair, convened in O'Toole's rooms in Croke Park. Here a handful (twenty-seven in all, including the officers) of delegates, almost all from Leinster, and from only eight counties witnessed the retirement from the presidency after twenty-one years of Nowlan and the election unopposed of Dan McCarthy of Dublin, the only Dubliner to lead the GAA.

On playing fields here and there Gaelic games continued sporadically right through the war conditions now being widely experienced. Not only in Dublin but also in Kildare and Cavan club fixtures were successfully carried through in the early months of 1921. Football was being played at club level too in Down in March; the Meath board held its annual convention in April; by the end of June even a few inter-county championship games had been played in Leinster. While spectators may not have been deterred elsewhere, it was clear that so long as hostilities continued in the Dublin area very few were prepared to come to Croke Park again for fear of a repetition of Bloody Sunday. By mid-June 1921 the grim statistics periodically published in the Dublin newspapers showed that since the start of the year there had been 1,800 casualties, 876 of them fatal.

The announcement of the Truce on 11 July was followed by an astonishingly rapid return to normal life by the community generally, a process from which the GAA at once benefited. In Dublin especially the Croke Park terraces became filled again Sunday after Sunday. Elsewhere Gaelic events resumed immediately also; by the end of July competitions were in progress in Cavan, Mayo, Antrim and Westmeath, with Kildare, Wexford and Kilkenny restarting by mid-August, when 5,000 turned up for an inter-county hurling match in New Ross. Prominent GAA personalities such as J. J. Walsh (released after only six months of a five-year sentence) and Harry Boland (who had been on a prolonged tour of the United States) were once again free to devote themselves to Association activities. In mid-September the spectators at the Leinster hurling final at Croke Park were honoured by the first appearance in public at a social function for a long time of the now immensely popular Michael Collins.

In Munster, however, things were not going well for the GAA. The Cork board, apparently arguing that the national forces needed reorganisation lest the Truce might not last, decided that the time for the resumption of games had not arrived, and refused to carry out inter-county fixtures. At first the other Munster counties dissented; by early September the Munster council had come round to supporting the Cork action and cancelled all fixtures under its control. At a special meeting on 15 October the central council showed an apparent determination to press ahead, even without southern participation if necessary, with clearing off arrears that now stretched well back into 1920. Eventually, however, in the face of Munster's opposition it was wisely decided not to adhere to the idea of awarding All-Ireland titles to nominated counties. Meanwhile, the protracted negotiations with the British gave for some time support to the view of the Cork board that hostilities might be resumed. Then at last on 6 December 1921, came the signing of the Anglo-Irish Treaty, followed in the first week of 1922 by its ratification by the Dáil.

Chapter 6

1922–1934

With the ratification by the Dáil of the Treaty of 1921 and the setting up of the Provisional Government of the Irish Free State, a totally new situation faced the GAA. Since its foundation almost forty years earlier as a part of the nationalist movement seeking self-government for Ireland, the Association had worked and grown up in an Ireland that was politically part of Britain. As the pioneer of the cultural revival the GAA could claim to have contributed significantly to the nationalist political successes since the start of the new century. Leading members of the Association had attained high office and played prominent roles in Sinn Féin and the Irish Republican Army, the two organisations that between them had now succeeded in obtaining political independence for the greater part of this island. To mention only three; Austin Stack became Minister for Home Affairs in the Second Dáil Cabinet; Eoin O'Duffy Assistant Chief of Staff of the IRA and Harry Boland Irish Envoy to the United States.

From the early part of 1922 onwards the GAA had therefore to adapt to the fact that self-government had been won for over three-quarters of Ireland. Admittedly, controversy began at once on both the extent and the form of that self-government. Yet nobody could doubt that from now on, in an area that extends far beyond the field of activity in which the GAA had been engaged since 1884, Irishmen would be fully in control of their own affairs. Suddenly the GAA in twenty-six of the thirty-two counties found itself operating in an Ireland free of British rule, an Ireland that (to take one example particularly relevant to organisers of native sports and athletics) would now have its own police force under the control of men of nationalist outlook. Furthermore, so deeply had the Association become involved in the nationalist struggle of the previous decade that it was a certainty that some of the leaders of the new Irish State, and many of its officials (such as policemen), would be drawn from the ranks of the GAA.

In such altered, even momentous, circumstances the GAA was immediately faced with some of the biggest decisions it had ever had to make since its inception thirty-eight years before. From Cusack's time spokesmen of the Association had continually asserted that the GAA was something more than a sporting organisation; might it now safely become merely a sports body? Might it confidently assume that a native government could be entrusted with the task of advancing the interests of native sports in the area under its control? If the alien military, police and judicial institutions of Dublin Castle were now to be replaced by native institutions, could the GAA's long-standing rules effectively boycotting the Castle's institutions be abolished? Finally, how were all these questions to be answered by the GAA in relation to the new political conditions taking shape in Northern Ireland, where a regime had already been set up by Britain that seemed to most GAA members in Ulster to differ little from that of Dublin Castle before the Treaty?

At first glance it may seem that the GAA had plenty of time in which to prepare itself for (or to adapt to) the new political and social conditions. There had, after all, been a military truce since early July 1921, and over six months of tortuous negotiations between Sinn Féin and the British Government. During that period the extent of military activity by both sides had been progressively reduced. Correspondingly, the extent of social activity, such as the playing of field games, had been progressively increased, with the notable exception of Gaelic games in Munster. In reality, however, the GAA was in no position in 1921 to undertake such planning in advance. The warfare of the previous few years had disrupted the work and even the structure of the Association to an extent that only became apparent with the return of peace. With its income drastically cut, and some of its leading members (as well as thousands of its rank-and-file members) preoccupied with military or political activities, the GAA by early 1922 had been severely shaken by external events.

In the two-year period starting in the Spring of 1922 external events also were to deprive the GAA of an opportunity to make a calm and objective assessment of the impact on it of the birth of the new Irish State. One result of this was that the Association, under the guidance of a handful of leading officers, more or less drifted into a close relationship with the country's new rulers. A split inside both Sinn Féin and the IRA on the fundamental issue of acceptance or rejection of the Treaty led by the summer of 1922 to civil war. The subsequent hostilities prevented any widespread resumption of sporting activities for a year. When eventually hostilities ended it was found that some members did not resume active participation in the work of the GAA at all. Of the pre-1922 leaders of the GAA Austin Stack and J. J. Walsh concentrated on politics; Harry Boland had been killed in action shortly before the end of the war.

What now appears, admittedly with the hindsight of some eighty years, to have been an inexplicable omission on the part of the GAA in the 1922–1923 period is its failure to call a special congress or delegate convention, to assess the Association's role in the changing political and social conditions of that time and to define its attitude to the new native administration. In the past the central council had not been slow to call such a meeting to enable decisions of major importance to be made on a representative basis. Its failure to do so again in 1923 is difficult to understand, especially since the annual congress of Easter 1922 expressly empowered it to call a special congress during the year if circumstances so warranted. As will appear, a second congress was in fact held in 1922, but only for the purpose of approving important new changes in the management of Irish athletics.

To have considered it necessary to call a special congress to discuss relations with the new Government would have pre-supposed the existence of a substantial body of opinion inside the GAA either hostile to, or having doubts about, the new political regime. From the closeness of the Dáil vote on the Treaty one might be justified in assuming that members of the GAA, who after all formed a cross-section of nationalist opinion, were also equally evenly divided on this fundamental issue. However, whatever about rank-and-file members, it became clear early in 1922 that the central council as a body either supported the Treaty (and therefore recognised the Provisional Government) or else was neutral on the matter, perhaps on the understandable ground that, with a split developing, neutrality would be in the best interests of the GAA. This is not to suggest that there were no republicans (as those who belonged to the anti-Treaty side came to be known) on the council. Frank McGrath of Tipperary, Stephen Jordan of Galway and Dan O'Rourke of Roscommon, the last two later Fianna Fáil TDs, were certainly firmly on that side. These men were not yet, however, influential on the central council; in any event, they simply put loyalty to their Association before political advantage (as countless GAA members have done in the past 115 years) and accepted majority decisions.

It would be naive to think that the political views of the most influential figures on the central council could be disregarded at this formative and transitional period in nationalist affairs. Foremost among such men were the president, Dan McCarthy of Dublin, and the leading Ulster Council delegate, Eoin O'Duffy — the one a prominent pro-Treaty TD for Dublin and the other one of the highest ranking pro-Treaty IRA officers, soon to achieve even higher rank in the new National Army and later to head the new national police force. In addition, that dominating Cork personality J. J. Walsh, although no longer holding any official post in the GAA, continued to interest himself in Association affairs, even attending council meetings. When Postmaster General of the Free State he was to have many mutually fruitful contacts with the GAA.

Largely because the dominating personalities on the central council in 1922 happened to be supporters of the Treaty, the GAA quickly developed a close relationship with the Provisional Government. The fact that a substantial minority of Sinn Féin and the IRA (and therefore, one might assume, of the GAA also) had from the start major reservations about the Treaty tended to be overlooked. The further fact that the council had among its members a few prominent men like J. J. Keane, who remained neutral during the political turmoil of the 1922–1923 period, probably helped to reduce any possibility of opposition to the seeming partisanship of men like McCarthy and O'Duffy. No doubt, in view of its part in the national movement since 1916, the GAA would have become part of the new establishment in 1922 in any event; equally certainly the political outlook of the leading council members at the time made the transition all the smoother.

On the other hand, the ease with which the GAA became part of the new establishment made the Association suspect in the eyes of many members who from the start opposed the Treaty. What appeared to such men to be a partisan alliance rapidly developing between the new Government and the GAA began to put a strain on lifelong loyalties to the Association. On such people the symbolic aspect of the appointment of the wife of a founder of the GAA, John Wyse Power, to the Senate of the Irish Free State was lost; they doubtless regarded it as merely a gesture in binding the GAA closer to the Cosgrave regime. As late as February 1924, with the Civil War well over, the organ of Sinn Féin, the anti-Treaty party led by Eamon de Valera, described the GAA as a useless relic, and hinted at Sinn Féin proposals to wreck it.

The immediate interests of the GAA, especially its weak financial position, pointed to the wisdom at least in the short term of a policy of co-operation with the new administration. Before the Dáil's ratification of the Treaty, the Dáil Cabinet under de Valera had resurrected Michael Davitt's proposal of the 1880s for a revival of the ancient Tailteann Games, and had put J. J. Walsh in charge of the project, guaranteeing him £2,000 for the initial work. Assured by Griffith of the new Dáil Ministry's support, Walsh in January 1922 publicly aired the idea at an Irish Race Congress held in Paris. By mid-February the scheme had been taken over by the Provisional Government, under which Walsh held the post of Postmaster General. With him as Director, an organising committee representing every aspect of Irish culture was set up and given its own offices and secretariat; during that year grants of over £4,000 were made to this committee by the Government.

Faced with the sudden prospect of a realisation of one of the early dreams of the Association, the central council naturally eagerly supported the proposed Games. Understandably regarding the idea as its own rather than that of the Government, the GAA in its initial enthusiasm tried to get complete control of the Games. Eventually it settled for something close to this, with Walsh consulting the council regularly and even attending at, and participating in, its discussion on the Games. As the major national sports body the GAA got generous representation on the Tailteann committee, with separate nominees for hurling, football, athletics and handball. In addition, all the Tailteann athletic and cycling events were to be under GAA control.

Bound up with the Tailteann Games project was the problem of the future management of Irish athletics, which the granting of political independence had suddenly brought to a head. For years Sinn Féin leaders had been keenly aware of the propaganda value to their cause of anything that emphasised to the outside world the separate nationhood of Ireland. Now at last, if a satisfactory system of control of athletics could be established at home, Ireland could seek recognition from the Olympic Committee and get separate national representation at the 1924 Olympic Games. Alone of the GAA leaders J. J. Keane seemed to realise fully the possibilities offered by the forthcoming establishment of the Irish Free State; within weeks of the ratification of the Treaty he had moved into action. Overcoming the understandable opposition of some central council members to the prospect of releasing control of athletics to any other body, Keane got authority to draw up a detailed scheme, to be submitted for its approval to the GAA congress at Easter, for a new Irish athletics body independent of the GAA.

Congress in turn set up a special committee, consisting of six nominated delegates and the officers of both the central council and the Athletics Council, to examine Keane's scheme and report back to a special congress. At this special congress, held in May 1922, the Athletics Council recommended the adoption of the Keane proposals; forty-nine of the fifty delegates agreed and athletics, the Cinderella of the GAA since 1884, passed out of its control. Shortly afterwards the National Athletic and Cycling Association was established and the old loyalist-dominated Irish Amateur Athletics Association, Cusack's rival of the 1880s, was wound up. By the time the Tailteann Games were held athletics in Ireland were under unified control for the first time in forty years. At the Olympics in Paris in 1924 Ireland competed as a separate nation for the first time since the revival of the Games at the end of the last century. By 1924 also, with the setting up that year with GAA support of the Irish Handball Council, a period of co-operation between the promoters of this old Gaelic game and the GAA was begun that has lasted to this day.

Closely connected with the Tailteann Games also was the question of where the major field events would be held. The very nature of the project, as an international exhibition of Irish pastimes, dictated only one answer to this — Croke Park. No stadium in Ireland compared with it in accommodation both for spectators and participants, or in facilities for field games, athletics and cycling. Croke Park was, however, the property of the GAA; to stage the Games there required a cordial relationship between the Association and the Games' sponsor, the Provisional Government. Given this obvious fact, the regular contacts all through the early months of 1922 between J. J. Walsh, the Director of the Games, and the central council of the GAA can be seen to have been motivated by something more than mere support for Gaelic games. On its success in gaining the co-operation of the GAA depended the Government's plan for a Celtic cultural festival. Without Irish field games and field and track athletics such an event would lose most of its mass public appeal.

All this put the central council in a strong position in dealing with the Government. Before the formation of the Provisional Government the Dáil had voted £10,000 for the Games, on the implicit understanding that the money would be spent in making Croke Park suitable for the event. On the strength of what he justifiably took to be a promise of a grant of such handsome proportions, O'Toole had lost no time in arranging with contractors for another set of improvements at Croke Park, involving mainly two new covered stands, to hold the crowds expected for the Tailteann Games. To stifle criticism from the outspoken Walsh about the state of the ground, the central council invested in its first horse-drawn mower. By the late autumn of 1922, when the work had been completed, the £10,000 paid over by the Government was found to fall £4,200 short of the contractor's account; the GAA had to mortgage the stadium to the National Land Bank. In the meantime the Tailteann Games had been postponed to 1923; the Civil War had begun.

Depending to some extent on which side one's sympathies lie, one dates the start of the Civil War either by the occupation of the Four Courts in Dublin by the anti-Treaty forces in mid-April 1922 or by the shelling of the courts by the Provisional Government forces in late June 1922. If the matter were to be decided by reference to the extent of activity on Gaelic fields, the later date must be regarded as the more important, although this statement requires qualification because of the wide difference in the extent to which the GAA managed to carry on in different areas between April and June 1922. Taking the country as a whole, however, one of the most striking facts is that the biggest concentration of hurling and football fixtures was carried out in the months of May and June, which coincided roughly with the period of occupation of the Four Courts. Even more remarkable is the fact that, although the Dublin area bore the brunt of the fighting at this stage, and was also the centre of most of the political infighting, the Leinster council was the only provincial council of the GAA which went anywhere near to carrying out a normal season's programme of fixtures.

Because of the tense situation created by the controversy over the Treaty the year began quietly for the Association with only a few inter-county games in Ulster and some club fixtures in Dublin in January, followed by a small number of annual county conventions the next month. For most of the spring, the central council was preoccupied with plans for the change in the control of athletics, and by the related projects of the Tailteann Games and the major extensions to Croke Park. By early April, however, both the Munster and Leinster provincial conventions had been held; at each plans were made to tackle the two years' arrears of inter-county championships. The following two months saw two All-Ireland finals (those for 1920) being played off; early in June the second Munster hurling final in two months (that for 1921) was held. That same month the Croke memorial was finally unveiled in Thurles. However, the All-Ireland football final played in mid-June was to mark the end of major fixtures for either Leinster or Munster for over four months, until in mid-October the Leinster council alone resumed its inter-county championship programmes.

The summer of 1922 found the playing fields of the GAA deserted at the height of the championship season for the first time in almost forty years. Although organised fighting ended in Dublin early in July, this did not mean the end of the Civil War. The following three months were marked by equally serious fighting in places as far apart as Sligo, Limerick, Waterford, Dundalk, Kerry and Roscommon. For much of that period most of the South and West, except for Clare and south Galway, was controlled by the anti-Treaty forces of General Liam Lynch; transport and communications were seriously disrupted. So far as the GAA was concerned, its activities in most of Munster and nearly all of Connacht came to a halt, as they did also in many counties of Ulster because of an equally explosive political atmosphere there following the establishment of Northern Ireland. Almost unbelievably, games in Leinster continued both at club and inter-county level right through the season. The provincial council not only managed to complete its list of fixtures for the first season since 1916, but also went on to finish the 1921 championships.

Although most of the military activity had ceased long before the start of 1923, the political temperature remained high for most of that year. The execution by Provisional Government or Free State firing squads of over seventy opponents of the Treaty, including such prominent republicans as Rory O'Connor and Erskine Childers, in the five-month period before the formal ending in April 1923 of the war, left a scar on the political and social fabric of the new State that was to take at least two generations to heal. By the end of the war thousands of young men were in jail simply because of their opposition to the new regime. Among them, as in the case of a substantial number of the executed republicans, were many lifelong supporters or members of the GAA.

When 1923 had ended it was found that once again, in spite of all the obstacles, the GAA had managed to carry out at least a substantial proportion of its normal programme as it had done every year since 1884. Although Association activities were still at a standstill in late February, by mid-April club games had resumed in many areas, including counties like Armagh, Tyrone and Monaghan which had been seriously disrupted for much of 1922. By early July 1923 inter-county championships were in progress in three provinces, with the Connacht fixtures only a week or two behind the rest. No fewer than four All-Ireland finals — two in each code for 1921 and 1922 — were played in 1923, spaced out fairly evenly between March and October. The Munster council, whose fixtures had gone most into arrears, brought its championships once more right up-to-date. Not only Croke Park but some of the provincial venues like Limerick drew big crowds once more; the Munster hurling final and the All-Ireland hurling final marked a welcome return to the high standard that seemed to have been missing for several years.

In the bitter political atmosphere of the time, it would be too much to expect that the GAA would succeed in remaining unaffected by the Civil War, apart from the obvious effect on its games of widespread fighting in 1922 and the wholesale internment in both 1923 and 1924. Although the major impact on the Association was not to come until 1924, signs both of the times and of coming events began to be evident early in 1923. Twice that year, in March and October, the central council, in trying to steer clear of political involvement, found it necessary to impose a ban on the sale of political literature at Croke Park. On the second occasion the embargo was extended to bands not approved by the council. Collections for political purposes were also prohibited at the ground; in October an exception was made for a group of trade unionists who had been locked out by their employers.

Nor was this all. For a brief period early in 1923 the central council became directly involved in the Civil War, when an unsuccessful effort was made to use the influence of the GAA to bring the two sides together. By a unanimous decision in December 1922 the Cork county board asked the council to convene a special congress to find a way to end the Civil War. The council, at its meeting on 17 December, while being of the view that it would not be possible to assemble a representative congress, agreed to go into the matter in detail at a special meeting of the council itself. This meeting, held on 7 January 1923, produced a unanimous decision to set up a sub-committee to canvass the views of both sides in the War on the prospects for a cessation of hostilities, and to advise the full council on the possibility of holding a special congress in February. The sub-committee consisted of O'Toole, J. J. Keane, Frank McGrath and Jeremiah O'Brien of Clare.

The failure of its mission was reported to the council of 23 January by the sub-committee, which also advised against a special congress. Although the council decided to permit the sub-committee to continue its work, there is no evidence that it did. It cannot even be confirmed that it ever succeeded in meeting any of the leaders on either side. Since only one of its four members, Frank McGrath, can be identified positively as a supporter of the republican cause, one can imagine its operations being regarded with scepticism, perhaps even suspicion, by that side. At the same time the valuable role played by the Association in bringing (and keeping) men from both sides together all through the Civil War cannot be underestimated. No less partisan a figure than Eoin (then General) O'Duffy later frankly admitted the cordiality of his relations with military opponents at GAA meetings during this bitter period. When in due course the executions and the fighting ended and the jail-gates and the internment camps were opened, it was under the neutral auspices of the Association that many an old friendship which had been sundered by the Civil War began once more to be rebuilt.

Predictably the Civil War, which made such a lasting impact on the political and social life of the country as a whole, also left some scars on the GAA. That it did not split the Association is little short of a miracle and a tribute to the loyalty of both officers and rank-and-file members. However, some counties were slower to recover than others; Kildare and Fermanagh, to mention only two, remained inactive until well into 1924. Most of the Ulster counties, which had been badly disrupted even before 1920, continued in a disorganised state until well into the mid-1920s. For some years Armagh had no county board at all; Derry, which had been converted from soccer only shortly before the 1916 Rising, was for all practical purposes out of the GAA until 1929 and did not resume participation in the Ulster championship until 1933. In Munster Kerry only began to resume its full role in GAA competitions when the internment camps were finally emptied. It then became apparent that the camaraderie that had grown up behind prison-bars provided a firm foundation for Kerry's astonishing run of successes on the football field in the late 1920s.

One county only of the whole thirty-two has provided unmistakable evidence of a formal split in the GAA directly traceable to the Civil War. Early in 1923 two popular Clare players, Con MacMahon and Patrick Hennessy, were executed by a Free State firing squad in Limerick. When soon afterwards a proposal to adjourn the annual convention as a protest against these executions fell through, the treasurer of the board resigned and control of GAA affairs in Clare passed to a pro-Treaty group led by Father (later Monsignor) Michael Hamilton. A year later, shortly before the date fixed for the 1924 annual convention, delegates from twenty-five clubs (representing nearly forty teams) set up a rival county board; all its officers were opposed to the Treaty. For some months each board ran its own competitions; the ludicrous position was reached whereby it became a successful ground for an objection to a team to show that a player had played in a game run by the other board. Eventually in the summer of 1925 the Association was reunited; happily the split did no lasting damage to Gaelic games in Clare.[1]

Of much more serious dimensions was a move made in 1924 with a view to bringing all GAA games to a halt until the 2,000 captured republicans were set free from internment by the Government, presumably as a result of pressure to be exerted by influential pro-Treaty figures in the Association like Dan McCarthy and J. J. Walsh. That this move was a concerted one seems beyond doubt; also, if it was not inspired by the leaders of the anti-Treaty movement, it almost certainly had their support. In June Kerry refused to play Dublin in the 1923 All-Ireland football final, ostensibly in protest against the imprisonment of the president of the Kerry board, Austin Stack, now a leading anti-Treaty figure. Shortly afterwards Limerick refused to play Galway in the 1923 All-Ireland hurling final. In July the Cork board refused to send a team to play Offaly in the junior hurling final until the chairman of the Cork board Sean McCarthy (another leading republican) and fellow-prisoners were released. The climax was reached when in mid-July the Munster council, in a flagrant breach of the GAA constitution, decided against participation in the forth-coming Tailteann Games until all political prisoners (meaning republicans only) were released. Shortly afterwards the Connacht council took an identical stand.

Although it cannot have been surprised by this provincial revolt, the central council's handling of such a delicate matter seems in retrospect to have been unin-spiring. As if faced merely with minor disciplinary breaches, its initial reaction was to punish the offenders. Dublin was given a walk-over against Kerry; Galway and Offaly were also awarded the unplayed ties against Limerick and Cork respectively, although Galway had indicated in advance its unwillingness to take a walk-over. Then, as if belatedly appreciating the implications of the suspension of three leading counties until the next congress at Easter 1925, the council looked for a way out. By an almost unanimous decision a special congress consisting of one delegate from each county was arranged for mid-August, ostensibly to consider the interpretation of the rules under which the suspensions had been imposed. On a unanimous vote the delegates revoked the penalties on Kerry, Limerick and Cork and recommended the council to rearrange the ties and have the finals played. Thus ended in almost record time and unseemly haste a crisis which, had it developed further, might have split the GAA on political grounds just when both the Association and the country were beginning to recover from the Civil War.

In view of the disruption to both commercial and social life caused by the con-flict, it is not surprising that the Civil War caused acute financial embarrassment to the GAA for several years. As early as March 1922 the central council, which two months before had directed the Secretary to prepare a report on its financial posi-tion, found itself unable to respond positively to a letter from Michael Collins as chairman of the Provisional Government notifying the GAA of his Government's intention to collect income tax. Congress that year decided to circulate county boards on the need to raise funds for the Association. The effort cannot have been successful, since the central council later that year had to borrow over £4,000 to pay for the extensive work at Croke Park, the main immediate beneficiaries of which would be the organisers of the Tailteann festival. Only agreement by the contractors to accept payment in instalments averted financial disaster in October 1922; by the end of the year the central council was in debt to the tune of over £4,000.

Early in 1923, J. J. Keane appealed to the GAA for funds for the recently founded NACA; the central council, while repudiating any liability to subsidise what was now an independent association, promised help. It seems unlikely that it managed to keep its promise, for while the council's income for the period from March to December that year came to almost £4,800, its expenditure totalled nearly £5,000.

Some idea of how serious the Association's financial position had become is evident from the unprecedented decision to hand over Croke Park to outside commercial interests for a fortnight in June 1923 for a fête, on the understanding that fifty per cent of the takings were paid to the GAA. The Association's share amounted to £2,250, all of which was in March paid to the contractors; £34,000 had now been spent on the grounds since their acquisition just over ten years earlier. By mid-1924 the central council was out of funds; at the end of 1924 it was £3,000 in debt.

Neither the confrontation between the central council and the Munster counties nor the GAA's financial troubles prevented 1924 from being a satisfactory one for players and spectators of Gaelic games. The return to normality after the Civil War brought a resumption of sporting activities everywhere; because of arrears in 1923, competitions activity in many counties reached abnormal proportions. In Munster the championships of 1923, played in the spring of 1924, as well as those for 1924 itself, played in the autumn, attracted large crowds. After forty years Galway won its first All-Ireland title, defeating Limerick in hurling; in football Kerry in its first appearance in a final for nine years lost to Dublin in a great game. The appearance in Dublin of Army and Garda teams provided a welcome new element in metropolitan competitions; elsewhere throughout the country Garda support provided a badly-needed stimulus in areas where native games had previously not gained wide local acceptance. The success of counties new to the list of title-holders — Offaly's win in junior hurling, and the first appearance of Carlow in an All-Ireland final and of Wicklow in senior hurling — suggested a wider spread of titles in the years ahead.

It was for the pageantry and sentimental appeal of the long-delayed Tailteann Games that 1924 was remembered for long by followers of Irish games and athletics. Although sponsored by the Government and not controlled by the GAA (which lost almost £800 on the event) this festival represented the fulfilment of a dream of leaders of the Association for nearly forty years. Because most of the events, like the field games and the main athletic competitions, were held in Croke Park, the GAA could justifiably claim most of the credit for the Games' success. In addition, the organising genius behind them, J. J. Walsh, although now a member of the Government, owed his rise to prominence in the national movement to his early work in the GAA. As a cultural exhibition with mass appeal they may be regarded as one of the early (and now largely forgotten) successes of the new State. That they were so successful was due largely to the leading role in the festival played by the GAA, in providing the main stadium and in lending some of its leading officials to the various organising committees.

The Tailteann Games represented a challenging test of organising ability such as has never since faced Irish sport. Their aim was to stress the cultural identity of the Irish race and to give a new impulse to all forms of indigenous sporting activities. Spread over a sixteen-day period in August, the Games took in not only most popular pastimes but also literature, sculpture, music, several forms of aquatic and equine sport, chess, dancing, golf, tennis, billiards and even air racing. Those who worked hard on one committee or another included such distinguished figures as W. B. Yeats, Count John McCormack and Oliver St John Gogarty. Subsidiary bodies in places as far away as New Zealand, South Africa and Newfoundland, as well as in Britain, the United States, Australia and Canada ensured the attendances of visiting teams from abroad, for some of whom Dublin was a last halt on the way to the Olympic Games in Paris. From Scotland came a team of shinty players and from America the veteran patriot John Devoy. The only discordant note in otherwise harmonious proceedings was sounded by the Sinn Féin party under Eamon de Valera. It persisted in a boycott of the Games although the Government, by releasing from jail in 1924 de Valera himself and other leading republicans, had fulfilled the pre-condition demanded by Sinn Féin for its boycott to be lifted.

The Tailteann Games of 1924 marked the climax of the relationship between the GAA and the Cosgrave administration. Although the Games were to be held twice again, the circumstances were by then changed for both the Association and the Government. With the departure from public life in 1927 of J. J. Walsh the strongest link between the GAA and the Government was broken. The entry to the Dáil that year of the Fianna Fáil party helped to normalise politics. Above all, the return to active membership of the GAA of thousands of opponents of the Treaty, many of them recently released from internment, greatly strengthened the Association. They represented a new infusion of blood which was to prove valuable in helping the GAA to oppose a growing trend in the community towards anglicisation. Meanwhile, the GAA by the middle of the 1920s had reverted to its pre-1916 position of a body free of political entanglements. By continuing to operate on a 32-county basis and by adhering to its old practice of carrying on, so far as circumstances permitted, its usual range of activities even under unfavourable conditions, it succeeded in silencing most critics both outside and (more important to it) inside the Association.

Particularly to members and supporters of the GAA concerned about the cordiality of its relations with the Cosgrave regime, no single factor did more to demonstrate the Association's determination and ability to preserve its independence than its persistent refusal in the early years of the Free State to countenance any lifting of its boycott of non-Gaelic games. In order to see this now seemingly isolated stand by the GAA in its proper perspective, some appreciation is required of the existence of a little publicised and now largely forgotten anglophile feeling that manifested itself in Irish society in the years after the Treaty. Among many people there was an understandable, if often excessive, desire to show that, despite the hostilities of the previous few years, all was now forgiven on our side. Whatever the motives, it soon became evident that this outbreak of anglomania had even penetrated into official as well as social life. In the civil service, in the National Army and at most official functions it became fashionable to adopt British social habits and even to imitate British customs. Little or no effort was made to evolve or even to support distinctively Irish ways or customs.

That an organisation like the GAA, with members in every part of the country and in all walks of life, should escape such a movement was too much to expect. Even in the transitional year of 1922, before the formal establishment in December of the Irish Free State, the subject had got an airing. As if to test the reaction of rank-and-file members, the Association's president Dan McCarthy TD (a staunch supporter of the Provisional Government) admitted early that year that he favoured lifting the ban on Crown forces. Twice later in the year the GAA columnist in the Dublin weekly *Sport*, who then usually reflected what would now be called grass-roots feeling in the Association in Dublin, called for a modification of the boycott rule on foreign games. Even such an uncompromising supporter of the rule as the GAA writer P. J. Devlin ('Celt') admitted to an uneasy feeling that some watering-down of the Association's attitude towards English games might have to be faced.[2]

It soon became evident that a majority of rank-and-file members were completely opposed to any accommodation with organisers of English field games. As Crown forces evacuated the territory of the new State and as the RIC was quickly replaced by a new unarmed national police force, McCarthy's suggestion for a modification of the GAA's attitude towards British forces became irrelevant. As they saw their country facing what some of them regarded as a tidal wave of anglicisation, most leading members of the Association instinctively decided that, irrespective of how the rest of the country might react, any dilution of the GAA's policy on non-Gaelic codes was not yet justified. To soften their attitude now would, it was felt, represent a major breach of the Association's fundamental principle of fostering native pastimes to the express exclusion of foreign games.

Most GAA members who opposed the Treaty supported what a later generation came to call collectively the Ban, while those who favoured its abolition were mostly pro-Treaty members. This does not mean that one could equate supporters of the Ban rigidly with the anti-Treaty membership of the Association, or that opposition to the Ban came only from members supporting the Free State. Despite ministerial pressure only revealed twenty years later, no more enthusiastic supporter of the Ban could be found than General Eoin O'Duffy, who for ten years was one of the most popular figures associated with the Cosgrave regime. On the other hand, one of the counties that for a time showed a strong preference for abolishing the Ban was Cork, where popular anti-Treaty sentiment was strong. All that can be said with confidence is that the pattern of voting, both at county and provincial conventions and at annual congresses of the early 1920s, indicated no spontaneous nation-wide movement inside the GAA to end the Ban. On the contrary, there is more evidence than the case of O'Duffy to suggest that much of the pressure came from outside.

Nothing more clearly demonstrates how the majority of members of the GAA felt on this potentially divisive topic than the results of the congress ballots on the Ban from 1922 to 1926. Year after year early signs from county conventions of a movement to revoke the foreign games rule were followed by a decisive vote at the annual congress in favour of its retention. Despite influential sponsorship, including that of P. D. Breen of Wexford, a future president, the congress of 1922 decided against a change by twenty-one votes to twelve. The 1923 congress, in spite of strong Cork pressure, voted the same way by fifty to twelve. Perhaps because leading counties such as Cork, Dublin and Tipperary had meanwhile voted to end the ban, the now perennial motion at the 1924 congress was only defeated by fifty-four votes to thirty-two. At the 1925 congress the vote for retention rose to seventy, with only fifteen delegates dissenting; in 1926 the corresponding figures were eighty to twenty-five. At this stage the matter was sensibly shelved by a decision limiting motions to amend or revoke the rule to every third subsequent congress.

It cannot be regarded as a coincidence that the end of the annual wrangling over the Ban marked for the GAA the beginning of a five-year period notable for the progress made by the Association. The second half of the 1920s was to be a much happier time for the GAA than the first; the further away one got from the 1922–1924 period the greater was the recovery from the divisive effects of those years. Of ups and downs the GAA was to continue to have its share; the renewed political tension of the early 1930s was momentarily to test the unity of the GAA once again. However, viewed as a whole the period from 1925 to 1930 was one in which the Association not only turned the corner after a decade of comparative stagnation, but also began to assume the shape and form in which it became familiar to members and supporters for the next fifty years. By demonstrating that alone of the pre-1922 national bodies it was as strong as ever, above party politics and inflexible in adhering to its fundamental aim of fostering native games to the exclusion of foreign games, the GAA in the 1920s gained in prestige among supporters and attracted thousands of new members. This was its reward for the fact that, as Michael Collins remarked some months before his death, the GAA was 'the one body . . . which . . . never failed to draw the line between the Gael and the Gall'.[3]

At the start of this period, however, the Association suffered a major if temporary setback, which was both damaging to its public image and disruptive of its internal administration and its most popular competition. Through a series of technical objections which brought to light breaches of rules, no All-Ireland football final was played for the year 1925. All four provincial title-holders — Cavan, Kerry, Mayo and Wexford — were involved in the affair; all four were deprived of a claim to the title. Although Kerry defeated Cavan in the first semi-final, both counties were disqualified on an objection and counter-objection. In the other semi-final Mayo (nominated to represent Connacht because the provincial competition had not been concluded in time) won both on the field and in the council chamber from Wexford. Mayo's subsequent defeat in the Connacht final by Galway led to the central council's declaring Galway All-Ireland champions without any final being played. Never before or since has the GAA's principal annual competition collapsed in such circumstances.

This episode was the worst and most publicised of a whole series of objections and counter-objections with which the central and provincial councils were faced around this time. While the 1925 episode created on outsiders an impression of ineptitude by the GAA, internally just as much harm was done, in the short term at least, by a large number of other objections which that year and in the next few years were bitterly contested at all four provincial councils. Why this rash of bad sportsmanship broke out just then is not easy to explain. The growing popularity of the major competitions, especially in football, apparently led suddenly to a win-at-any-cost attitude by many counties. Probably personal animosities arising from the Civil War period were another factor. One suspects too that, because of the disturbances to its administrative machinery between 1916 and 1924, some of the trouble may be attributed to the poor calibre of officials at many levels. The bigger crowds and gate-money from 1925 onwards concealed a widespread tendency to endure mediocrity in the running of clubs, boards and councils. Evidence to support this impression of laxity is naturally hard to find; the closing of ranks at the 1926 congress to reject a Mayo motion calling for an investigation into the GAA's administration is open to conflicting interpretation.

It was almost inevitable that the exceptional circumstances of the 1919–1924 period should have produced this result. The transfer of primary allegiance by many leading GAA figures to Sinn Féin and the IRA, the casualties to and normal deaths of older officials, followed by the wholesale internments of 1923 and 1924, all left inexperienced men in charge of the Association in many areas from 1922 onwards. Even where more experienced men retained office, their main interest often lay in other spheres, with the result that the GAA was the loser. With the multiplicity of posts he held in the GAA, the NACA and the Garda Síochána, it was obvious (to take one notable example) that General O'Duffy could not find sufficient time for his GAA activities. Similarly, as the 1920s progressed it became clear that some officers were either past their administrative prime or were clinging to office largely because of the prestige and power involved.

More or less contemporaneously with this period of administrative inefficiency, the standard of play in the major Gaelic events rose. The games themselves were watched by record crowds who paid more than ever before. It was then that Gaelic football established itself as the most popular field game in this island, a position it still holds eighty years later. Dublin's dominance in the opening years of the 1920s earned it three consecutive All-Ireland titles. It was followed briefly by that of Kildare, champions in 1926 and 1927. Both Leinster counties were then completely over-shadowed by Kerry. By 1932 it had won four consecutive titles, a feat only once since equalled, and had also been victorious in six of the eight finals played since 1924. Both the draw and replay of 1926 attracted 25,000 spectators to Croke Park for the first time; when in 1929 Kerry and Kildare met for the fourth time in three years in the final, a record crowd of almost 44,000 attended.

Merely to list, in the order in which they were made or occurred, some of the more important decisions and events in the GAA in the years just before 1930 will give some idea of the progress made by the Association in that period. The congress of 1925 introduced the non-resident rule (still in force and widely availed of), under which a player may opt to play for either the county of his birth or that of his residence. It also decided to establish the National Football and National Hurling Leagues, which began in 1926 and soon came to rank permanently in popularity next to the All-Ireland championship. If the spate of inter-county objections de-tracted greatly from the spectators' enjoyment in 1925, 1926 brought ample rewards to the paying public — three Munster hurling finals and two All-Ireland football finals. The tours to the United States in the same year by the Tipperary hurlers (who scored an average of twelve goals per match against Irish-American teams) and by the Kerry footballers in 1927 began a long and rarely-interrupted series of such tours across the Atlantic.

Two more competitions which became permanent in the GAA calendar are asso-ciated with 1927 — the decision of that year's congress to establish a minor inter-county championship (for under-18s) from 1928 and the playing on St Patrick's Day 1927 of the first finals for the new inter-provincial Railway Cup, presented in July 1926 by the Great Southern Railway, whose shareholders' meetings some twenty years before the ebullient J. J. Walsh had so effectively disturbed. It was also the year in which the popular annual Whit tour to London began and the year when the Association purchased the leading Leinster stadium which later generations of spectators know as Nowlan Park, Kilkenny. On the playing-field the year was significant for the winning by Leinster counties of both All-Ireland titles, for Leitrim's first win in the Connacht football championship and for the winning of an All-Ireland title by an Ulster team for the first time with Armagh's victory in the 1926 junior football championship.

Although events and decisions off the playing-field were to prove to have been more lasting in their effects, to the followers of Gaelic sport the two years 1928 and 1929 were memorable for the high quality entertainment provided at the GAA's main stadia. Cavan, losers by a solitary point, became in 1928 the first Ulster county to reach a senior All-Ireland final for twelve years. Clare, by defeating Tipperary and forcing Cork to a replay in the provincial final, proved themselves a new force in Munster hurling. Memories of one-sided Tailteann contests of 1924 were obliterated by the international hurling match played as part of the 1928 Games between an Irish selection and a team of Irish-Americans, which reached a surprisingly high standard. In 1929 the match that overshadowed all others in a year in which games were excellent spectator fare was the football final, when the rival counties of 1926, Kerry and Kildare, again met. The attendance this time exceeded by 3,000 the record of nearly 40,000 for the 1926 replay.

The years between the Treaty and 1930 also saw the passing of the last survivors of the early office-holders of the GAA. In 1923 Maurice Crowe of Limerick and Walter Hanrahan of Wexford died. A year later came the death of Jim Nowlan of Kilkenny, who with Luke O'Toole had started the revival of the Association away back in 1902. In 1926 Andy Harty, who had been prominent on the Dublin board for decades, died. In London in 1927 and 1928, respectively, two veterans of the GAA in Britain died — Sam Maguire and Liam McCarthy, whose names are perpetuated in the two All-Ireland trophies. The deaths in 1930 and 1931 of Dan Fraher of Waterford and Pat McGrath of Tipperary, which broke the last links with the 1880s in Munster, had been preceded in 1929 by that of Luke O'Toole, Secretary of the Association for nearly thirty years, and in 1930 by the sudden death of the brilliant Kerry footballer and administrator Dick Fitzgerald.

The gaps caused by these deaths were filled by men of a younger generation who were destined to influence the affairs of the GAA for many years, and were better equipped than their predecessors to do so. Their rise to prominence was a natural consequence of the influx already referred to of rank-and-file members after the Civil War. Most of them had taken little or no part in party politics; this helped greatly to strengthen the position and influence of the GAA as a body free from political commitments. This neutral stance of the GAA was strengthened by the fact that by the late 1920s it also numbered among its membership members of all parties. A random glance at the Dáil candidates in the June 1927 election shows that this membership was diffused among Cumann na nGaedheal (later Fine Gael), Fianna Fáil, Farmers, Sinn Féin and Independents.

The names of two of the new officials call for mention at this stage; the election of each represented a break with the past. Martin O'Neill of Wexford became in 1927 Secretary of the Leinster Council for a term that was to last some forty years. With the election as president in 1928 of Sean Ryan of Tipperary the GAA got its youngest president. A solicitor just over thirty, Ryan had become a leading figure on the Dublin board and was, through a lifetime as legal adviser to the Association, and confidant of many of its leading figures, to remain an influential figure in the GAA until his death thirty-five years later.

To some of these younger officers fell the job of handling between 1925 and 1927 a delicate financial problem, involving relations between the GAA and the Government and also between the Association and the political parties. Following the establishment of the new State in 1922 the GAA had continued its pre-1922 attitude of not paying the entertainment tax introduced by the British in 1916 and successfully resisted by the Association in the following six years. Naturally the revenue authorities of the new administration could not be expected to tolerate this state of affairs indefinitely, especially as the GAA's financial position improved. In 1925 a proposal was made by the Government that the exemption which the Association had enjoyed for nearly ten years be embodied in the legislation giving effect to that year's Budget. Unfortunately for the GAA by the time the proposal had been publicly aired it was global in terms and not confined to Gaelic games — as a result, according to a leading GAA official, of pressure from Labour and Farmer TDs.

The Association believed that it alone was entitled to exemption because of its role in the pre-1922 Act and its position as the only body promoting Irish games. It resented the wide exemption given by the 1925 Finance Act and resolved not to let the matter end there. So far as it was concerned, the pressure on the Government to include other sports bodies, mainly those catering for English games, was merely a vote-catching device by TDs with constituents following those games. The Cosgrave administration, in yielding to such pressure because of its numerical weakness in the Dáil division lobby had, in the view of the GAA, turned its back on one of the organisations which had played a leading part in the struggle for political freedom.

Since 1922 the GAA had also refused to pay income tax, despite notification from the Government of the Association's liability. For their part, the Revenue Commissioners, whether because of the sensitive nature of the problem, or the financial difficulties of the GAA, did not pursue their claim. When in the light of the improved financial position of the GAA the matter was brought to a head in the mid-1920s the central council exerted pressure, both at local level and by circulating TDs, to secure support for legal exemption from income tax also. Through the intervention at the highest level of General O'Duffy, and after the receipt by the Minister for Finance of a deputation from the central council, the Government accepted the validity of the GAA case and provision was made in the 1927 Finance Act exempting from income tax the income of 'any body . . . established for . . . promoting . . . Gaelic football, hurling and handball . . . applied for such purpose'. Alone of sports bodies in the State, the GAA was permitted to enjoy this exemption for a further half-century.

Encouraged by its success in 1927 the GAA continued to keep the question of the 1916 tax under review. After the return to power in 1932 of Eamon de Valera at the head of the first Fianna Fáil Government the Association immediately exploited its contacts in that party. The result was the legalisation in the Finance Act passed that summer after the new regime's first Budget of the *de facto* exemption from entertainment tax enjoyed by the GAA from 1916 to 1927. This time the Association won a double victory. Not only was it (along with the NACA) named in the Act, but the wider exemption that had been enjoyed by other sports bodies since 1927 was taken from them. This position remained unaltered until the abolition of all entertainment duty a generation or so later.

The Dáil debates on the 1932 legislation afforded to some prominent members of the defeated Cosgrave government their last opportunity of publicly airing their views on the GAA — but for whose contribution to the national movement none of them would have been made members of an Irish parliament, a fact that a few seemed to have forgotten very soon after 1922. From the start the attitude of the Cumann na nGaedheal party had been largely one of grudging admiration. As early as December 1922 W. T. Cosgrave himself (with tongue in cheek, one suspects) hinted that the first grant for the Tailteann Games might be regarded as a loan to the GAA. As already mentioned, some of his ministerial colleagues attempted to force the GAA through Eoin O'Duffy to revoke the foreign games rule. As for Cosgrave's Minister for Finance, Ernest Blythe, whose views in 1927 were not free from ambiguity, by 1932 when in Opposition he had become quite unsympathetic to the GAA. Notwithstanding the unwavering loyalty of J. J. Walsh and O'Duffy, only a firm stand by the GAA secured for it the substantial representation it was entitled to on the Tailteann Committee, which depended on the goodwill of the GAA for the use of its principal stadium for staging the main events.

These debates of 1932 showed how little, despite the winning of political freedom, times had changed when it came to declaring one's stance on an aspect of native culture. In restrained but unmistakable language, two Unionist TDs representing Trinity College repeated what before 1922 would have been regarded as the uncompromising Dublin Castle attitude to the GAA. Of other deputies such as Patrick McGilligan (Cumann na nGaedheal), Frank McDermott (Centre) and Alfred Byrne (Independent), it has to be conceded that they openly admitted their partiality for English games and consequent antipathy to the GAA. To the central council, however, it must have been disconcerting to find such veterans of the revolution as Blythe, General Mulcahy, Michael Hayes and Peadar Doyle all inside a decade of the Treaty expressing viewpoints ranging from near-hostility (in Blythe's case) to what reasonably might be described as doubt as to the good faith of the GAA, or at best lukewarm and qualified support for it. That some leading figures in Fianna Fáil were later to prove just as unsympathetic alters the position little. The GAA deserved better of the immediate political heirs of the founders of the new State which the Association itself had helped to establish.

Not all of the GAA's problems in the 1920s arose out of its relations with the Government. Periodically disputes between either the central council or a provincial council and individual county boards broke out, with disruptive effects of varying degrees. Most of these were symptoms of the major administrative crisis already referred to. For most of 1926 and part of 1927 the Longford board, which had been suspended by the Leinster council in a disagreement over a football match with Dublin, remained unaffiliated, returning at the 1927 congress. Shortly after this the Sligo board incurred a year's suspension; this ended at the Connacht convention of May 1928. The following year found Wicklow, Louth and Waterford in troubles of a less serious nature, Donegal and Tyrone excluded from senior football and Kerry and Galway disqualified from junior football. A major confrontation between Cavan and the Ulster council in 1930 led to the county's suspension. This was only resolved that autumn by a special delegate convention of the entire Association held on the eve of the All-Ireland football final.

The most bizarre of all these disputes was that which continued between the Connacht council and the central council for at least four years, from mid-1926 to mid-1930. The trouble began when Connacht purported to suspend a prominent Galway official because (it alleged) his conviction on a criminal charge (unconnected with the Association) brought disrepute to the GAA. The central council took the opposite view. It disagreed on the question of repute because the delegate had been acquitted of a major offence, and on the suspension because he had been given no hearing. The Galway board sided with the central council, re-electing the delegate county chairman and threatening to affiliate with another province. For four years the controversy raged, with the Connacht council now evading, now defiantly refusing, implementation of a directive for reinstatement. Walk-outs, abortive mediation meetings, unauthorised suspensions, cancellation of a major fixture and even the exclusion of the press from most of one annual congress all figured in the prolonged episode. Even the ultimate resignation of the official failed to solve the dispute, which eventually ended with arbitration by the new Secretary of the GAA.

The province of Ulster, especially the greater part of it remaining under British control after 1921, presented the central council with a recurring problem of a different kind in the 1920s. The GAA had to operate there in a climate even more unsympathetic than that which it had faced in the rest of the country before 1921. As a result, the Association did not manage effectively to overcome most of the obstacles to its development in Northern Ireland, many of them discreetly placed by either central or local government, until well into the 1930s. Its claim for exemption from entertainment tax was not entertained by Stormont. The Ulster council was periodically short of money; on several occasions in the 1920s other units of the Association came to its rescue. In June 1923 the central council made a grant of £200 for organisational activities in Ulster; in 1925 the Munster council gave Ulster almost £400 raised from a special tournament. In December 1929 the central council donated another £350 to try to prevent a recurrence of the 1928 situation, when Ulster had to withdraw from junior football. The same year congress voted a £100 grant to the Tyrone board, and the next year another £100 to Down and £50 to Monaghan.

Another area in which the GAA of the 1920s was only partly successful was that of publicity. Since the death in 1916 of Frank Dineen, who had been influential in the *Freeman's Journal*, the GAA lost much of the wide and mostly sympathetic coverage it had enjoyed for so long in *Freeman* publications. Understandably the military and political news pushed sports events out of the headlines; with the collapse of the *Freeman* in 1924 the GAA lost what had for forty years been a valuable outlet for news of GAA events. Against this loss must be set an unfriendly policy adopted by the *Freeman* in the paper's last years, an inevitable outcome of the GAA's alliance with Sinn Féin. What must have been more disheartening was the discovery in the mid-1920s that the sole remaining Dublin nationalist press group, Independent Newspapers, now proved distinctly apathetic and often unfriendly to the GAA, a state of affairs that was to persist until the founding in 1931 of the *Irish Press*.

Following an initiative begun by the Gaelic League, the GAA in 1927 took the first steps on the road to publication of what would be at least partly its own organ. In the spring of that year the League called a meeting of bodies fostering various aspects of native culture; it was attended on behalf of the Association by O'Toole and O'Duffy. This conference established a Joint Committee of Irish Bodies under the chairmanship of George Gavan Duffy, a former Dáil Minister and future judge. The Committee decided to plan for the publication the following autumn of an illustrated sixteen-page weekly to contain news of interest to members of the sponsoring bodies, with the GAA and the Gaelic League filling half of each issue. There would be a board of directors nominated by the bodies participating, a full-time editor and a full-time manager, the latter being responsible for advertisements. A circulation of 16,000 was aimed at; it was planned to establish a launching fund of £5,000 before the first issue was published. Among others involved in the project at this stage were Patrick D. Mehigan (later the Gaelic sports writer 'Carbery'), Diarmuid Fawsitt, a pioneer of the Sinn Féin movement in Cork and Mícheál Ó Loinsigh of the Gaelic League, an uncle of Seán Ó Síocháin, the future Director General of the GAA.

Progress was slow, each body having its own idea on how the venture should be organised and on what the paper should contain. As so often happens in such cases, the main obstacle was a shortage of money; in April 1929 it transpired that only £500 of the planned £5,000 had been raised. Dissatisfied from the start with the Joint Committee's work, the GAA from September 1927 ran its own press bureau. This collected and disseminated to existing publications news of Association activities, in an attempt to counteract the inadequate coverage it justifiably believed the GAA was getting from the national newspapers. Then suddenly in the spring of 1931, with a new and energetic General Secretary in charge of its affairs, the Association revived the publication project. The result was the appearance in June of that year of the first number of a new monthly, *An Camán*.

Measured by any yardstick other that that of economics, *An Camán* must be rated as a moderate success at least, especially in its first year when it came out monthly. Browsing critically through its pages over sixty years later one cannot but be impressed by the high standard maintained, considering the limited field to which the paper was confined. To cater at the same time for the average member or supporter of the GAA (usually a rural reader with little time or inclination for reading) or the Gaelic League, and for the intellectual élite of both bodies, cannot have been easy. In addition, a balance had to be struck between matter in English and matter in Irish. Finally, but by no means of least importance, the paper had to adopt an independent and critical attitude towards authority. If it was to be taken seriously both by sympathetic readers and by targets of its criticism it had to be uncompromising and courageous in publishing what the sponsoring bodies thought of the deeds and words of Government, politician, churchman and other public institutions or figures, so far as these affected the aims of the sponsoring bodies.

Even a random glance through the issues of *An Camán* shows that it managed with a surprising degree of success in reconciling often conflicting interests, and in generally adopting what might be described as a policy of *sinn féin* in matters relating to all aspects of native culture. Topics covered included Government industrial policy, failures at different levels of social activity to foster the Irish language or Irish sport, occasional but valuable historical contributions and gossipy snippets from all parts of the country relating to Gaelic games and allied activities. To the editorial board, consisting of the new General Secretary of the GAA, his opposite number in the Gaelic League, Donncha Ó Briain (later a junior Minister in Fianna Fáil governments) and the president of An Fáinne, Cathal O'Toole, must go much of the credit for this admirable venture. As is always the case on such occasions, nearly all the work fell on the managing editor, a post held until June 1932 by Seán Ó Ceallaigh, who was then succeeded by Eamonn de Barra.

No publication of this kind could survive for long even in that inflation-free era without a sound financial foundation; unfortunately *An Camán* was never out of monetary trouble. From the start circulation was poor, never attaining the figure of 5,000 planned for in the initial issue. In addition, advertising revenue, while not negligible, was never adequate. As a result the paper was losing money for the whole of its career. For this reason the decision of the Joint Committee to change to weekly issues from mid-June 1932 is inexplicable. Predictably, the paper merely continued to be run at a (bigger) loss, even though the standard hardly suffered through the doubling of issues. As early as March 1932, with losses having totalled £120 in ten months and the reserve down to £200, the central council of the GAA came to the rescue with another £500 which was to last a further year. By April 1933 the paper was again in financial trouble. The end came in May 1934 when the GAA, faced with complaints that the paper was not serving the Association's needs, withdrew its financial support.

On another sector of the propaganda front the GAA met with more success. With the opening on New Year's Day, 1926 of '2RN', the Irish State radio station, the way was opened for the exploitation by the Association of this new medium of communication. Although surviving records on either side do not reveal who took the initiative, the broadcasting on 29 August 1926 of the All-Ireland hurling semi-final between Kilkenny and Galway, the first radio commentary outside America on a field game, was also the first occasion on which a Gaelic game went out over the sound waves. To calculate the part played by radio is not easy. Two facts need stressing. From the start, given favourable conditions, broadcasts from Dublin could be picked up in comparatively distant parts of rural Ireland. With the opening in April 1927 of the Cork station the position, so far as Munster was concerned, became even better.

No account of the GAA in the 1920s would be complete without a record of the appointment at the end of the decade of a new General Secretary to succeed Luke O'Toole, who died in the summer of 1929. Eleven applications for the post were received. All had close ties with the GAA; nearly all were popular figures on the playing-field or well-known officials. They included Martin O'Neill the Leinster secretary, Paddy McDonnell and Frank Burke of Dublin's recent All-Ireland football team, Ben Fay of Cavan the Ulster secretary, Hugh Corvin of Belfast, Pádraig Ó Caoimh the Cork secretary, Seán Ó Ceallaigh and Eamonn de Barra, future editors of *An Camán*. Roughly half of the applicants were from Leinster; none was from Connacht.

In retrospect it seems obvious that O'Neill, Corvin, Ó Caoimh and Fay would have been ideal for the post. All four had long administrative experience in the GAA itself, having served for substantial periods at county board level and, particularly in O'Neill's case, at provincial council level also. Corvin, who could match O'Neill and Ó Caoimh in other respects, such as proven dedication to the national movement and fluency in Irish, had the added advantage of being a chartered accountant; his qualification was widely availed of by the Association in Ulster. In the cases of both de Barra and Ó Ceallaigh academic attainment might have compensated for lack of administrative experience in the GAA.

Conscious of the vital role the new Secretary would play in the growth of the Association, the central council decided to use outside expertise to help it to select the most suitable man. To ensure a high standard of competency it insisted on all applicants sitting a four-subject examination (in Irish, English, Mathematics and Book-keeping) to qualify for consideration. A three-man board of examiners, of which only one (the chairman) was from the GAA, was set up. It consisted of Cormac Breathnach of the Gaelic League (later a TD and Lord Mayor of Dublin), Mícheál Ó Droighneáin NT of Galway, with the GAA's president Sean Ryan as chairman.

When the central council met on August 31 1929 to fill the vacancy the results of the examinations presented it with a formidable, even delicate, task. At first glance an Ulsterman seemed likely to be chosen, because Corvin had come first and Fay had withdrawn after the tests. De Barra and Ó Ceallaigh, who followed Corvin closely for second and third places, can hardly have had much support on the council against an experienced official like Corvin. However, in fourth place came Frank Burke, an immensely popular figure, one of the few to win All-Ireland medals in both codes. Burke's position was strengthened by the surprise decision by O'Neill not to sit the examination, which excluded him from further consideration.

Two rounds of open voting, in which all twenty-one delegates attending took part, quickly filled the vacant post. In the first count Ó Caoimh got ten votes, Burke nine and Corvin two. The second count gave Ó Caoimh eleven and Burke ten, Burke getting the two going to the eliminated Corvin and one delegate switching from Burke to Ó Caoimh. One glance at the voting shows that delegates voted on a provincial basis. Ó Caoimh got all the Munster votes and three of the four Connacht votes. Burke's votes consisted of those of the Leinster delegates, all the Ulster votes and one from Connacht. The delegate who changed sides was none other than Eoin O'Duffy, of whom one might comment that on this occasion, unlike most of those in his public career, he showed unerring judgement. However, this writer has been informed on impeccable authority that O'Duffy (then a leading Free State figure) was canvassed by the Pearse family (all strong opponents of the Free State) to sup-port Burke, then in charge of Pearse's school, St Enda's. O'Duffy promised to vote for Burke provided that, if Burke did not succeed on the first count, O'Duffy was then free to support another candidate. It is ironic to reflect that it was a last-minute switch by a delegate attending merely as a proxy for an Ulster candidate for the post (Fay), who had by then withdrawn from the contest and could have attended, which decided the occupancy of the important post of General Secretary for thirty-five years.

Although born in Roscommon, Pádraig Ó Caoimh had lived since infancy in Cork city, which justifiably claims him as a native. His credentials in the national movement were impeccable. Sinn Féin, the Gaelic League, the Industrial Develop-ment Association and the Irish Volunteers had all experienced his energy, ability, enthusiasm and drive. From boyhood, however, his main loyalty had been the Gaelic games and to the body that controlled them. When in 1924 peace came to Cork it was to the GAA that Ó Caoimh again gave his first allegiance after a brief spell in commerce. A man of broad vision and charming personality, whose range of acquaintances showed that he had been unaffected by the bitterness of the Civil

War, he came from Cork to Dublin in the autumn of 1929 to succeed Luke O'Toole with over ten years' experience as secretary of the biggest county board in the GAA. He had also been a leading player and popular referee.

That the central council's decision was the best was amply proved by Ó Caoimh during the next three decades. Immediately after his selection was announced Bob O'Keeffe of Laois, in a frank statement implicitly recognising the block-voting for Burke and Ó Caoimh, pledged the support of those delegates who had supported Burke. The council had shown shrewd judgement in assessing Ó Caoimh's potential. At Croke Park he was soon to reveal organisation and administrative skills of a high order. By his ability, drive and personality he was to transform the body of which he became chief officer at the age of thirty-one. In addition, as the conditions under which the GAA operated altered radically, especially in the post-war period, he was to show himself admirably able to adapt to such changed circumstances.

Pádraig Ó Caoimh was to achieve so much during his long period in office that GAA members and supporters in later years understandably came to believe that he transformed the Association single-handed from a weak ineffective body into the powerful prosperous Association which his successor inherited in the mid-1960s. Nothing would be further from the truth; Ó Caoimh would have been the first to admit this. The Association whose affairs he came to control in the dying months of the 1920s was, it needs to be stressed in fairness to O'Toole and the central councils of that decade, a very different body from that which had emerged in 1925 disorganised and inwardly divided from the Civil War. In spite of withdrawals by major figures like J. J. Walsh, intermittent bungling of important issues at central council level, excessively rigid handling of some divisive disputes and often under-standable clashes of personalities, the GAA entered the 1930s stronger than ever, with thousands of new members, its games at new high standards of play, and its critics becoming less effective as the tide of anglicisation of the 1920s began at last to ebb.

Twice in the 1920s shortly before Ó Caoimh's appointment the GAA firmly refused to be drawn into the political arena. When in mid-1929 a request was made by the nationalist-sponsored National League of the North for participation by the Association in the selection of parliamentary candidates for the Northern Ireland parliament, the president ruled that no action was called for because the matter was a political one. In the same year the central council of the GAA unanimously decided that the Association would not participate as a body in the State funeral accorded to the veteran Fenian leader John Devoy. Devoy's support for the pro-Treaty side in 1922 and subsequent association with the Free State regime had made him partisan in the eyes of opponents of Cosgrave. On the other hand, the council used the occasion of a special statement issued to members at Christmas 1933 on the eve of the GAA's golden jubilee year to urge restraint and unity on those who found themselves caught in the turbulent and bitter atmosphere which attended the rise and fall of the Blueshirt movement, in which Eoin O'Duffy played a controversial part. Although as with the GAA's mediation in the Civil War nothing came of its 1933 appeal, the Association cannot be faulted for this non-partisan intervention at a time when the possibility of another civil war seemed not too remote.

An indication of the growing influence of the GAA in the community from 1930 onwards was the greater participation in Association affairs by the Catholic clergy. As had been the case at the time of the Parnell Split thirty years before, some priests did not desert the GAA in the 1920–1924 period. Those who like Fathers Michael Hamilton of Clare and James O'Dea of Galway, either joined around this time or stayed on in the GAA, made it easier for others to join or return later in the twenties. By 1926 several priests were on delegations to congress; in the next two years more were elected to office by several county boards. That the GAA was gratified by this trend is suggested by events in 1929, when nationwide celebrations sponsored by the Hierarchy marked the centenary of Catholic Emancipation. The GAA not only agreed to the use of Croke Park for some of the ceremonies but also held a reception for the bishops and provided a corps of volunteer stewards for some of the events in Dublin, made a presentation to Archbishop Harty to mark his interest in and patronage of the GAA and sent a message to the Pope congratulating him on the conclusion of the Lateran Treaty between the Italian and Vatican governments.

In the two years after 1929 the tendency of the clergy to participate in GAA activities showed a marked increase — whether as a result of the harmonious relations between the Church and the Association during the Emancipation celebrations or simply as a continuation of a growing trend cannot be stated. Priests were elected in 1930 to the presidency, vice-presidency or chairmanship of the county boards of Wicklow, Offaly and Monaghan, and in 1932, the year of the International Eucharistic Congress in Dublin, the GAA, through its General Secretary, accepted a seat on the Stewarding Committee, provided 3,000 stewards for the Congress, permitted the use of Croke Park and ensured that no major fixtures coincided with the main Congress events.

This close relationship between the Catholic Church and the GAA, which continued in the subsequent half-century, may surprise or even trouble GAA members and supporters belonging to a later generation. In most cases, one suspects, the cause of this concern is a fear that such an apparently exclusive association (even in the realms of sport) with the Church may hinder the achievement of a united Ireland because of its effect on the majority or Protestant community north of the Border. However, the links between the GAA and the clergy must be judged in the light of the social background against which the GAA had had to operate. As all public leaders south of the Border for sixty years have found it wise to include the Church among their friends, it would be too much to expect a body like the GAA not to follow this lead. In Northern Ireland such a policy was forced on the GAA, at least until the fall of Stormont in 1972, by the existence there of a *de facto* Protestant State largely hostile to the Association.

From its foundation with the active support of a bishop with strong nationalist views, individual priests have participated in the GAA at all levels, and because this clerical presence has helped to further the Association's aims, it has always been welcomed by the GAA as a body. Anybody who has ever sat on a GAA committee knows that a priest is accepted as just another committee-man, with no greater influence than any other committee member. Doubtless priests have been instrumental in the making of particular decisions; so have teachers and politicians, to mention two other classes prominent in the GAA from the start. Apart from Croke's role in the adoption in 1895 of a politically neutral constitution, no evidence exists to suggest that the Catholic Church has ever influenced the GAA on any major decisions or important matters of policy.

Nevertheless the GAA's attitude towards the Protestant community does not appear to have been above reproach. Cusack, by his success in attracting Protestants into the Association in its early years, seems to have been ahead of his time. The GAA's subsequent long and close identification with nationalist aspirations forced Protestants to get out of it. In the following ninety-five years only a handful of them, such as Sam Maguire of Cork and London, has played Gaelic games. Until the election in recent years of Jack Boothman of Wicklow as president, no Protestant has held high office in the GAA, and there has been during that period no serious or substantial effort by the Association to attract members from outside the Catholic community. Some may see in this another example of the ambivalent attitudes of modern Irish nationalists stressed by recent historians. While aspiring to political union with the predominantly Protestant State of Northern Ireland, they have put up an almost insuperable obstacle to such unity in the form of a Catholic-dominated society.

As far as the average member or supporter of the GAA was concerned, the question of the possible wisdom of the Association's cordial relations with the Church did not cost him a thought. Not for a moment could he be expected to believe that in playing or watching the traditional field-games of his ancestors he was in some obscure or indirect way postponing the achievement of a united Ireland. For him the astonishing growth of the GAA since the mid-1920s simply showed how right was the self-reliant aggressive policy of the Association in promoting Gaelic games in every one of the thirty-two counties and among Irish emigrant communities in Britain and the United States. Should he be required to justify the GAA's policy in keeping outside the Association through its Ban players and supporters of English games, he might draw some parallel with the policy of economic protectionism then accepted by all political parties in the State.

The years on either side of 1930 itself are still regarded by many GAA members and supporters as having produced better games than any period before or since. This is particularly the case with the hurling championship. Never since 1930 has Tipperary won three All-Ireland titles (senior, junior and minor) in one year. Never since 1931 has a meeting in a hurling final of those traditional rivals, Cork and Kilkenny, necessitated three games before the title was won. Moreover, as hurling reached a new peak of popularity it was around this time too that two more Munster counties, Clare and Waterford, successfully claimed permanent inclusion among the major hurling areas. It is significant that since then only two other counties, Wexford and Offaly, can be regarded as having joined this still small group.

Tipperary's triple success in 1930 had the merit of restoring attendances for the senior final to more respectable proportions after two small crowds in 1928 and 1929. To the nearest thousand, the figures for 1927 to 1930 were 24,000; 15,000; 14,000 and 22,000. Then came the unforgettable two draws and two replays of 1931 between Cork and Kilkenny, when almost 92,000 people paid nearly £8,000 in admission money to watch the three games. Almost unbelievably, the hurling finals of 1932 and 1933 were to draw even bigger crowds and consequently higher admission-money — 34,000 and nearly £3,000 for the Clare-Kilkenny game of 1932 and 45,000 and almost £4,000 for the Limerick-Kilkenny final of 1933, with the Leinster team the victor in both cases.

In football this period was notable for the arrival among leading contenders for All-Ireland titles of two Ulster counties. One of them, Cavan, one of the oldest counties in the GAA, won the province's first senior title in either code and ended the half-century dominance in football of Leinster and Munster counties. In 1928, Cavan, in the first appearance in a senior football final of an Ulster team since 1912, had lost to Kildare by one point. Two years later Monaghan, which had lost the 1927 and 1929 semi-finals, lost heavily to Kerry in its only appearance in a senior final before or since. Then in 1933 Cavan proved its worth with a win over Kerry in the semi-final and another over Galway in the final, when a new record attendance of over 45,000 watched. Cavan's success was symptomatic of a rise in standard in Ulster football; the year before, Tyrone and Down had won lesser provincial titles.

In the administrative sphere the years before 1934 were largely uneventful for the GAA, mainly because of the continued success and growing prosperity of the Association. A good deal of Ó Caoimh's early period in office was taken up by some of the major problems already mentioned, among them the publication of *An Camán*, the Connacht council dispute, the claim for tax exemption, and ultimately preparation for the Golden Jubilee year itself. The purchase a year or two before O'Toole's death of the spacious Shrewsbury House (renamed Croke House) adjacent to Croke Park proved to be a most useful acquisition. In the grounds were two separate houses, one of which became the new Secretary's residence, leaving the other building free for offices and conference accommodation. So harmoniously did Ó Caoimh and Sean Ryan work together that in 1932 the annual congress took the unprecedented step of re-electing Ryan to a fourth consecutive annual term of office. He was to be the last Dublin nominee to head the GAA for over a quarter of a century.

Shortly after his appointment it became apparent that the new Secretary had quite a different concept of the role of the Secretary from that held by his predecessor, whose last few years had in any event been disrupted by recurrent illness. Ó Caoimh made it clear that in the first place the chief officer of the GAA in his view ought not to be a remote figure transacting routine business in an office in Dublin. By travelling widely through the country in his first few years as Secretary, actively mediating in the Galway controversy and attending numerous annual county and even several provincial conventions, he showed a readiness to be accessible that O'Toole had only occasionally displayed many years earlier. More important, Pádraig Ó Caoimh in his prefatory remarks to his first annual report showed that he regarded the General Secretary's main function as the active one of directing the Association's affairs, not just by carrying out administrative duties but by stressing its role in the social and cultural life of the country. The forceful, precise and often scholarly arguments which became a regular feature of his later reports to congress were to be found as early as Easter 1930, just six months after he took office.

One of the first major tasks which confronted the new Secretary in the autumn of 1929 was to restore order to the Association's finances. Because of O'Toole's terminal illness no records had been kept since the previous Christmas; when Ó Caoimh sought the assistance of the GAA's auditors a disturbing picture emerged. The bank overdraft on Croke Park itself had risen in nine months from £1,550 to £5,150; although the central council had in the same period reduced its own overdraft by £1,000 to £700, the combined debit balances totalled almost £6,000. By the end of the year this had been reduced to less than £4,700. Although it remained at roughly the same figure for 1930, it was cut to £1,100 by the end of 1931, only a little over two years after Ó Caoimh's appointment.

Shortage of money had been one of the GAA's problems all through the 1920s. For most of the first half of that decade it had been operating at a loss; one wonders how Croke Park would have held the record crowds of the 1927–1933 period had there been no government grant after the Civil War. It is to O'Toole's credit that persistent low incomes — as little as £300 in 1921, for example — did not deter him from developing the Association's major stadium, its main physical asset.[4] In 1925, to mention only one year at random, but one in which the Association had suffered a loss of nearly £800 on the 1924 Tailteann Games, almost £900 was spent on re-sodding the pitch and on the purchase of new turnstiles. At the time of O'Toole's death in 1929 over £30,000 had been ploughed back into Croke Park since its acquisition from Dineen seventeen years before; all this had happened during O'Toole's period as Secretary. But by 1926 things had improved considerably. In November the GAA had a credit balance of £5,750 and the 1926 surplus of £9,250 was £150 higher than the three main components of the council's liability — a bank overdraft of nearly £6,800 and loans from the provincial councils of Munster and Leinster totalling £2,250.

From then until the arrival in Croke House of the new Secretary the situation remained static. Several factors contributed to this failure by the GAA to improve its financial position. For one thing, the period from 1926 to 1930 was one in which gate-money did not significantly increase; it even fell in places. In Munster gate-money for 1927 was more than £3,500 down on the 1926 total. In Leinster the figures from 1926 to 1929 were £3,586; £3,059; £3.477 and £3,528. These showed changes varying from a fall of over £500 at the start of the four-year period to a rise of only £51 in the last year. They compare unfavourably with 'gates' of £3,088 in 1922 and £3,408 in 1924, two years in which life in many parts of the provinces could hardly be described as conducive to the success of field games. Not surprisingly, the central council's overdraft at the end of 1929 still stood at £5,000.

In the financial sense, as in most others, the GAA never looked back after Pádraig Ó Caoimh's appointment. A simple recital of the most important figures for the five-year period from 1929 to 1933 tells the story most effectively. The Association's income in each year was £8,666; £7,900; £15,500; £9,300 and £12,200, producing surpluses over expenditure of £1,660; £1,250; £7,500; £2,000 and £1,200 respectively. By far the biggest component of the GAA's income at that stage was naturally the admission-money taken at its major games; the triple hurling final of 1931 accounted for the astonishing figures for that year. Between 1928 and 1933 the value of the combined assets of the central council and the limited company controlling Croke Park rose from £28,000 to £34,000. In that period some £4,000 was spent on the stadium, and a house was purchased and a house-keeper's allowance provided for the large family of orphans who had survived Luke O'Toole, himself a widower for some years before his death. To illustrate how meticulous Ó Caoimh was, when a 'new' horse was bought in 1930 to haul the Croke Park mower, he not only valued it at £11 in his records but depreciated it by £3 for 1931!

Between 1924 and 1932 the total number of clubs affiliated rose from just over 1,000 to almost 1,700; in one year only, 1931, was this interrupted. As an indication of the strength of each province, the figures for 1928 were — Leinster 600, Munster 400, Ulster 200 and Connacht 160. While Ulster had, as already mentioned, been weak early in the 1920s Connacht declined towards the end of the decade; its total fell by forty between 1927 and 1929. Both Leinster and Munster showed an over-all expansion all through the 1920s, although the extent of the rise varied from one county to another. Dublin with 100 clubs showed no change between 1929 and

1932; in Longford the total fell sharply between 1925 and 1929; Wicklow's figure rose from nineteen to forty-two in the same period. In Munster, where Cork understandably accounted for one-third of the clubs, the total rose from just under 400 in 1929 to over 470 in 1932; Leinster's total increased between 1924 and 1932 by 200 to 650.

The year 1934, which was to mark the golden jubilee of the GAA, found the Association in an impressive position of strength and prosperity. It had manifestly achieved its twin objectives of 1884 of reviving the traditional field games of Ireland and erecting a barrier to the tide of anglicisation periodically threatening to engulf this island. Its achievements had exceeded all the expectations of the founders, who could hardly have envisaged a situation in which, inside half a century, Gaelic games would be the most widely played and followed sports in the country. It is safe to assume that none of the men who met in Thurles in November 1884 dreamed that within forty years an independent Irish State would have been established as a consequence of the political revival which followed directly from the cultural renaissance of which the GAA had been the pioneer.

Before the end of 1934 the body which Cusack and his associates had started fifty years earlier had over 1,900 clubs affiliated to it, representing a total membership of nearly a quarter of a million if each club had an average of 120 members. Not only did the GAA now flourish in all thirty-two counties; it also had for many years branches in Britain and the United States. Its assets exceeded £35,000; it had a credit balance in the bank of almost £40,000. From being harassed and obstructed for almost forty years by the agents of the British administration before 1922 (as it still was north of the Border) it had become in the ten years after 1922 a pillar of the establishment in the Irish Free State, respected, admired and even courted by public figures, lay and clerical. Yet it had succeeded in maintaining a strict neutrality in domestic politics, having learned from bitter experience that its prestige was at its lowest when the Association became the tool of any political faction.

Astonishingly, in view of the damage done to its administrative structure by the Civil War, the GAA managed to remain practically unaffected by the tensions of the Blueshirt episode. Between early 1932 and late 1934 this country had two keenly contested general elections and its first change of government in ten years. It also experienced a bitter and violent struggle on a countrywide scale, between the new government and a mass paramilitary body (led by a leading GAA figure) directly linked to the party that had lost the two elections. Once more, as had happened in 1923, members of the GAA found themselves on opposite sides; once again it was to be on the playing-fields and in the council chambers of the GAA that many sundered friendships were rebuilt. Here and there, as in Connacht (where the sudden eclipse of the hitherto influential Sean Ruane of Mayo was widely attributed to his enthusiastic participation in the Blueshirt organisation), the ill-feeling engendered by the political controversy spilt over into GAA activities. But no permanent harm was done to the Association, whose activities were hardly affected by the political controversy, in striking contrast to the disruption caused by the Civil War.

The golden jubilee celebrations of the GAA fell into two distinct parts, widely separated in time and place. For the Association as a whole the jubilee was officially inaugurated on Easter Sunday at the annual congress, held specially in Thurles, the birthplace of the GAA, for the first time for several decades. Before the congress itself began a number of formal ceremonies were held — a reception by the central council both to its own delegates and to distinguished visitors; the presentation of congratulatory messages from the Government, members of the Catholic hierarchy, local bodies and cultural associations; a religious service presided over by the Association's patron, Archbishop Harty of Cashel; and the unveiling of a plaque at Hayes's Hotel. Among the attendance were several links with the earliest days of the GAA — three members of the victorious Tipperary team in the first hurling final of 1887, Cusack's son John, a former GAA official now a leading Dublin lawyer, the veteran Corkman Tom Dooley, and from the United States John Quane of a notable Tipperary GAA family of the 1885–1895 period.

Five months later, Dublin, the city that for thirty years had been the focal point and administrative centre of the GAA, held its own jubilee celebrations. In an impressive parade through the city to Croke Park, and at the subsequent events in that stadium, the emphasis was appropriately on youth. A crowd of over 35,000, which included the head of the Government, watched a series of games played by schools teams in September. A week later, as Clare mounted its own tribute to Michael Cusack, special jubilee athletic contests were held in Dublin. A two-month industrial dispute which put all Dublin newspapers off the streets and shops deprived these Dublin events of the publicity that had attended the Thurles events at Easter. In the meantime, the two leading Dublin morning papers had each published a special supplement marking the jubilee and the Minister for Posts and Telegraphs (a son and brother of Jim and Harry Boland, both Dublin board chairmen many years before) had issued a special commemorative postage stamp portraying a hurler in action.

The golden jubilee was not without its disappointments. A plan by the central council to commission a history of the GAA fell through when a series of interviews failed to turn up a suitable writer. After struggling along for years the magazine *An Camán* finally folded up when the Association (as already mentioned) ceased to pay the major subsidy it had been contributing from the start, a decision which the taking over by the new Secretary of P. J. Devlin's *Gaelic Athletic Annual* did little to counter-balance. Nothing came in 1934 or for many years after of an ambitious project to open an All-Ireland Gaelic club in Dublin. There were justifiable murmurs of dissatisfaction at the failure of hurling to take root outside half-a-dozen counties, and only slightly less warranted criticism of the slowness of the National Leagues to improve playing standards in weaker counties and of the state of Irish athletics. However, by its courageous decision in October 1934, within weeks of the actual jubilee date, to commit itself to £30,000 on the erection of a new double-decker stand in Croke Park (the first in the country), the central council unmistakably demonstrated its confidence in the future of the GAA.

Chapter 7

1935–1950

The fiftieth birthday of the GAA in 1934 marked an important turning-point in the life of the Association. Never again were there to be any doubts about its success, prosperity or growth, or about its role in, or influence on, the cultural and social life of the community, especially in the area that was still to remain the Irish Free State for another few years. For the GAA the years from 1934 onwards were to constitute a period of almost uninterrupted success, so much so that the steadily diminishing number of survivors from the early years of the century must at times have wondered if their memories of major dissension inside the Association, or of years when it had almost ceased to function, were at all accurate or reliable. It was as if the jubilee celebrations of 1934 brought home to the public, not least that section of it uncommitted to the GAA, the fact that the Association was now a permanent feature of the Irish cultural scene.

For at least a quarter of a century after its golden jubilee the GAA continued to flourish in such a manner as to suggest that its progress could not be impeded by any exterior factor, national or international. That the relative calm in the political arena made the period between 1935 and 1950 (and even later) particularly favourable to the expansion of the GAA has to be conceded. Nothing like the protracted nationalist split of the 1890s or the Anglo-Irish struggle of 1916–1922 occurred to disrupt the Association's activities, much less to threaten its continued existence. Because the Association was now firmly and permanently politically neutral, the intermittent confrontations in the 26-county area during this period between the de Valera regime and the IRA hardly affected the GAA at all. At the worst, when such a danger arose it was quickly averted by the traditional primary allegiance to the Association of members involved in political (including paramilitary) activities.

At the beginning of this period some of the most prominent figures in the GAA used the opportunity presented by conventions or other meetings to stress the political neutrality of the Association. In the first six months of 1935 at least half-a-dozen spokesmen spoke publicly on this topic. Among them were both the outgoing and incoming presidents, Sean McCarthy of Cork and Bob O'Keeffe of Laois, the

General Secretary and Fathers O'Dea of Galway and Hamilton of Clare. The general content of their speeches apart, there is no evidence of any agreement or top-level decision to talk on politics and the GAA. The tone of these utterances shows that they were addressed more to politicians considering using the GAA than to ordinary members tempted to do so. However, despite all this influential advice the Kerry board withdrew from all competitions for 1935 following a decision by the 1934 county convention explicitly linked to the imprisonment of republicans by de Valera.

When, just five years after the GAA's golden jubilee, another world war involving all the major States lying geographically nearest to Ireland broke out, the Association was to find itself gaining from the consequential stresses produced in this country. The unanimous determination of the community south of the Border to remain neutral in the global conflict, and the closing of ranks necessitated by the rigours of the so-called Emergency, together with the almost total suspension of foreign sports contacts which the country's isolation from 1939 to 1945 entailed, between them were to result in increased interest and participation in Irish games, from which the GAA naturally benefited. One of the unexpected, but not un-welcome, effects on Irish culture of World War II was to be the temporary halting of the ever-threatening forces of anglicisation, to the consequent advantage of bodies like the GAA.

For a body like the GAA the current political and social climate in its area of operation is never irrelevant. For this reason the dominance of the political scene in the twenty-six counties for most of the fifteen-year period ended in 1950 by Fianna Fáil not only made life easier for the Association in that area, but constituted another factor favourable to the expansion of the GAA. Contrariwise, in Northern Ireland life was made that much more difficult for the GAA because of the area's permanent dominance by an anglophile (and thus anti-nationalist) political regime, whose cultural outlook was unacceptable to every member of the Association. South of the Border, because Fianna Fáil was always the biggest political party, it was naturally the one to which most members of the GAA involved in public affairs gave their allegiance. In any event, despite the fact that a few prominent figures in Fianna Fáil were never friendly to the GAA, that party more than any other since 1922 has been unequivocal in its support for native culture. In addition, from its foundation in 1926 Fianna Fáil has drawn much of its support from rural areas; since the GAA had also done so, there had inevitably been a substantial overlap of membership between the two organisations.

In marked contrast, the Fine Gael party taken as a whole, while always having prominent members either involved in GAA activities or openly supporting the Association, has from the mid-1930s appeared to be less enthusiastic in its com-mitment to the aims and policies of the GAA. Part of the reason for this is probably that the party has for much of that period drawn a good deal of its support from those sections of our urban communities whose favourite sports are soccer or rugby. After the initial honeymoon period of the early 1920s, and especially since the retirement from public life in 1927 of J. J. Walsh, relations between the Cosgrave regime and the GAA became gradually less than cordial, if not downright cool. The attitude of Cumann na nGaedheal (the predecessor of Fine Gael) revealed in the Dáil debates already mentioned, cannot have endeared the party to those then in charge of the GAA. To surviving officials from pre-1922 days this unsympathetic approach must have brought back memories of the lack of support for native games for long displayed by most of the Irish Parliamentary Party under John Redmond.

At the same time, the lukewarm attitude of the founder and leader of Fianna Fáil to Gaelic games was for many members of the GAA a continuing source of disappointment. Although reared in a part of rural Munster always devoted to Irish culture, Eamon de Valera had, through his long association with Blackrock College in Dublin, developed an early and lasting attachment to rugby football. This partiality for what has remained essentially an English and bourgeois brand of football was at variance with the strong nationalist outlook of Fianna Fáil. Moreover, because rugby football in this country has always been almost exclusively the favourite field sport of the more affluent sections of our urban communities, de Valera's lifelong liking for rugby seemed to conflict with his professed sympathy for the less well-off sections of our rural areas.

To a greater extent than has been the case for earlier periods of the Association's history, some account of the major events on Gaelic fields must form an initial part of any attempt at a survey of the GAA in the decade after its golden jubilee in 1934. Such an account may be in danger of deteriorating into a mere chronicle of games or a list of new contenders for provincial or national titles, or of the winners of such titles. The risk has to be taken; without some references to the great games of the time, the full extent of the change that came over the GAA cannot be understood. Since 1922 it had concentrated much of its energy on regaining that position of organisational strength which it had unavoidably lost between 1916 and 1922. Now in the mid-1930s, largely as a result of its success in making the two games it controlled an integral part of the social and cultural life of the community, the GAA established itself as the most successful, most popular and most resilient of the Gaelic cultural bodies that had triggered the revolutionary changes in the Irish political scene which culminated in the Treaty of 1921. The rise to prominence of new counties in all four provinces formed a major factor in the increased public support for the GAA.

Another reason for concentration initially on events on the playing-field is that, at least in the years just after 1934, comparatively little of lasting importance happened in the committee rooms and council chambers of the GAA. It is true that crises of varying dimensions continued to occur; in particular, two in the late 1930s (soon to be related) did little to help the image of the GAA held by non-members. Playing rules were occasionally examined and sometimes revised; special problems like those associated with the slow growth of hurling were analysed, many new stadia were acquired and developed in the provinces. But examination of the central council's minutes for the period from 1935 to 1945 shows that an almost monotonous routine of minor problems — transfers, county declarations by players not residing in the county of their birth, National League fixtures for each round of that competition, appointments of referees, to mention some at random — took up by far the greatest proportion of time at central council meetings.

One of the new formal investigations into any aspect of the GAA's activities undertaken during this period was carried out by the Congress Hurling Commission of 1940, which produced an interim (and only) report a year later. This body concentrated exclusively on two related problems, the supply of ash for hurleys and the number of members who regularly played hurling. Inquiries by the six-man Commission, which included the president, the General Secretary and Fathers O'Dea and Lee of Galway and Limerick, suggested that timber supplies were adequate but needed to be made more freely available. In an effort to increase the number of players, concentration on the primary schools was urged; county boards were advised to enlist the co-operation of retired teachers and organisations like Muintir na Tíre to ensure permanent competitions for the under-eighteen age group. However, largely because of its restricted terms of reference, this Commission made no effort to assess the cause of the failure of hurling to spread to new areas in the fifty-five years following the foundation of the GAA.

The year 1935 was remarkable for the fact that attendance records at both All-Ireland finals were broken, and also because for the first time a sports fixture in this island drew over 50,000 spectators. Cavan, by defeating Kildare (which has only twice since reached a senior semi-final) before a crowd of 50,400, won its second senior football championship. Limerick, which had beaten Dublin on a replay in 1934, lost the hurling title to Kilkenny before an attendance of over 46,000. Thus the combined attendances at both 1935 finals was close to the 100,000 mark, a fact that stands favourable comparison with the 90,000 figure for the three-game hurling final of 1931. In football the year 1935 was notable also for two other events — the first success by Connacht in the Railway Cup competition, and the sudden if brief emergence after fifteen years of Tipperary as provincial champions. As a result of the Kerry board's withdrawal from all Munster competitions, Tipperary reached the All-Ireland semi-final, only to be narrowly beaten by the ultimate winners of the competition, Cavan.

The record attendance at a hurling final established in 1935 lasted only a year. When Limerick and Kilkenny again met in the 1936 final over 51,000 watched. This remarkable crowd for a hurling match was 1,000 higher than the figure for the

1936 football final, although that might have been expected to attract a record crowd. Mayo, the winner, which had monopolised recent National League titles, was in its first final, while the loser Laois was in its first final for forty-four years. In 1937 the return by Kerry to its first football final in five years, when it defeated Cavan on a replay, was the occasion of a new record attendance of 52,000. The following year Kerry, in yet another draw-and-replay series, showed that county's crowd-pulling power when nearly 70,000 came to the drawn game and another 47,000 to the replay; this time Kerry lost, Galway being the winner this time. In 1938 also Mayo won its fifth successive National Football League, and when in 1939 it scored its sixth win in this competition it established a record that has not since been equalled in over forty years in either code of the League.

In hurling 1939 saw the first appearance of Cork in a senior final since the unforgettable three-game series of 1931. In a remarkable game remembered by all who attended it as the thunder-and-lightning final because of the sudden storm which broke over Dublin during the game, Cork lost to Kilkenny, its rivals of 1931. Cork's return to prominence can now be seen as giving notice that a revival of Cork hurling was on the way. The late 1930s also gave signs of future achievements by other counties, some new to GAA titles. Meath, which was to have to wait till 1949 for its first senior All-Ireland victory, won its first Leinster championship in forty-four years in 1939, and retained the title the following year. Roscommon's three All-Ireland football wins in 1939 (minor), 1940 (junior) and 1941 (minor) were to be followed by two senior All-Ireland titles later in the 1940s. Waterford, on the other hand, after losing its first hurling final in 1938, was to have to wait another ten years for its first success in the senior championship.

The 1930s were memorable also for long runs of consecutive appearances in All-Ireland or League finals, producing major games of a standard of play and a degree of entertainment and excitement long remembered by spectators. In hurling the decade was dominated by the achievements of Limerick led by the inimitable Mick Mackey, who is accepted as the most colourful player the game has produced. In the All-Ireland hurling finals played between 1932 and 1940 Limerick appeared in six. Although winning only three All-Ireland titles, Limerick around this time won five consecutive League titles (1933 to 1937) out of six League finals in which it appeared. In football no county — not even Kerry — approached Mayo's achievements. From 1934 to 1941 it won seven League finals, six of them in consecutive years. In the 1930s Mayo also won three All-Ireland titles — junior in 1933, minor in 1935 and senior in 1936.

Another feature of the 1930s was the success of counties new or almost new to GAA honours. In this category probably none evoked more popular appeal than the Laois footballers, whose Leinster title in 1936 (the first of three in succession) was their first such success in forty-seven years. Although heavily defeating Cavan in the semi-final, they themselves were beaten in the 1936 final by Mayo. In 1937 Kerry defeated Laois by a single point in a replayed semi-final and again in 1938 by only two points at the same stage — since when Laois have been Leinster football champions only once. Other newcomers around this time were Sligo, Wicklow and Longford; they took the junior football titles of 1935, 1936 and 1937 respectively. Wicklow in 1936 captured its only All-Ireland title so far by winning the junior football championship; Louth, which was to have to wait forty-five years before its next senior football final after 1912, won two junior All-Ireland titles and two minor titles between 1932 and 1940.

The memorable games of the 1930s, which in football included several drawn games at the semi-final or final stage, together with the rise of counties that had never before won provincial or national titles, had an invigorating effect on the fortunes of the GAA. Major titles were seen to be no longer the monopoly of a small group of counties whose skills in either code had been accepted as traditional and immune to challenge. Once such an immunity was successfully challenged Gaelic games in one or both codes received an immediate impetus in counties outside the 'traditional' group. It was, to mention a few examples at random, the great games of the 1930s that proved conclusively that Limerick and Waterford could break the dominance of Munster hurling by Cork and Tipperary, that Kilkenny could no longer disregard the challenge of a Dublin team built round non-Dublin hurlers, and that an Ulster county was now just as likely as one from one of the other three provinces to win the senior football championship.

The GAA also shared in and benefited from what might be called the national euphoria of the years between de Valera's accession to power in 1932 and the outbreak of World War II in 1939. This was the period when the new Government, building on the foundations laid by its predecessors, consolidated the country's position and status in the international sphere and, by gradually breaking the various links between the Free State and Britain, put an unmistakably republican stamp on the young Irish State, a process culminating in the Constitution of 1937. The successful economic policy, climaxed by the Anglo-Irish Trade Agreement of 1938, increased the sense of national identity and emphasised the apparent triumph of the old Sinn Féin policies. It was inevitable that a body like the GAA, promoting a major and popular aspect of native culture, should have shared in this upsurge of national feeling. It was in this period that the major Gaelic fixtures established themselves as accepted features of the social calendar — a state of affairs that has not altered since.

To the leaders of the GAA all this was a recognition of the part the GAA, both as a body and through many thousands of its members, had played in the events leading to the setting up of the State in 1922. That they got greater recognition from Fianna Fáil governments than they had from Cumann na nGaedheal administrations merely signified an unfortunate lapse on the part of the later Cosgrave cabinets rather than any kind of partisan link between the GAA and the de Valera regime. Similarly, if the 1930s saw the Catholic Church, through many of its bishops and priests, taking more interest and greater participation in the Association than before, such a development was understandable both in the light of the close links between the GAA and nationally-minded clerics from Croke onwards and because of the desire of the Church to keep a watchful eye on any organisation catering for youth. The GAA of the 1930s never felt any need to explain or defend the prominent and respectable niche it had carved for itself in contemporary Irish society; it had done no more than receive its due.

This whole atmosphere of success comes clearly through from Pádraig Ó Caoimh's annual reports to congress during the second half of the 1930s. Each year he was able to single out for special reference some new achievement by the Association — the record number of major new stadia (including Cusack Park in Ennis and Fitzgerald Memorial Park in Killarney) opened in 1935, the record number of counties participating in the championship in 1936, the astonishing organisational success in 1937 when a major building operation obliged the GAA to find a venue outside Dublin for the All-Ireland hurling final. Significant too was the confident tone of the General Secretary when he occasionally strayed outside the field of Gaelic pastimes — reminding delegates of the Association's role in stemming the tide of anglicisation; on another occasion emphasising that the promotion of games was but a means towards the end of creating a new Ireland that would not be a 'little shadow England', and stressing the close connection between the promotion of native culture and the support of genuine native industry.

Another picture of the progress of the GAA during the early years of Ó Caoimh's period as Secretary, when everything seemed at last to be going right for the Association, may be obtained from the financial accounts presented by him each year to congress. In none of the six years from 1935 to 1940 did the income of the central council fall below £14,000; in two years (1937–1938 and 1938–1939) it exceeded £20,000. For 1937–1938, the fiftieth year of All-Ireland championships, gate-money from major games under the council's control came to a record £20,000. In 1938–1939 three All-Ireland finals, including a replay in football, drew a combined attendance of 153,000. The balance to the council's credit at the bank (the excess of assets over liabilities) grew from £38,000 in 1934–1935 to almost £60,000 in 1937–1938; it passed the £80,000 mark in 1940–1941.

TABLE OF GAA CLUBS 1935–1945										
	1935	1936	1937	1938	1939	1940	1941	1942	1943	1944	1945
Cork	147	143	138	134	149	160	157	173	160	170	182
Tipperary	108	97	88	90	101	111	108	109	109	100	105
Clare	54	54	54	58	60	60	60	56	60	66	70
Limerick	72	73	72	76	80	80	83	81	90	87	100
Kerry	6	44	48	56	61	59	61	58	60	60	67
Waterford	40	40	40	47	65	63	60	66	82	79	91
MUNSTER	427	451	440	461	516	533	529	543	561	562	615
Dublin	100	100	110	110	110	80	84	80	90	90	90
Meath	66	67	63	56	59	57	56	63	69	82	84
Louth	36	36	36	33	32	32	30	34	42	36	40
Longford	18	19	20	18	15	14	13	13	12	17	17
Westmeath	40	45	45	45	39	45	47	49	56	52	56
Laois	60	60	60	60	60	60	60	60	60	60	60
Offaly	94	89	52	48	48	50	50	50	50	60	60
Kildare	48	46	43	43	41	44	42	41	45	48	48
Wicklow	42	36	35	33	30	32	36	39	48	41	52
Carlow	38	38	40	40	40	40	40	26	26	28	26
Wexford	72	72	70	65	65	73	67	72	82	93	107
Kilkenny	65	60	61	57	56	63	60	61	66	80	75
LEINSTER	679	668	635	608	595	590	585	588	646	687	715
Galway	96	88	86	86	86	97	88	89	105	102	129
Mayo	65	60	60	65	66	65	65	65	65	68	65
Sligo	38	36	36	36	36	36	36	36	36	36	36
Leitrim	38	37	37	29	35	38	35	45	39	36	45
Roscommon	56	56	56	56	56	58	78	76	56	56	56
CONNACHT	293	277	275	272	279	294	302	311	301	298	331
Down	28	30	30	25	25	23	25	25	30	33	42
Antrim	57	50	50	44	53	48	53	49	68	90	77
Monaghan	26	21	20	30	26	26	16	18	18	21	29
Armagh	32	34	30	26	30	30	30	30	30	30	48
Derry	16	20	27	29	31	21	19	17	25	39	36
Tyrone	39	28	28	30	32	32	38	29	28	23	28
Fermanagh	16	17	23	22	28	23	17	19	18	19	19
Cavan	40	33	39	37	33	39	38	40	44	44	44
Donegal	33	30	24	35	26	31	33	30	24	21	36
ULSTER	287	263	271	278	284	273	269	257	285	320	349
TOTALS	1686	1659	1621	1619	1674	1690	1685	1699	1793	1867	2010

* Source: Annual Reports to congress by General Secretary

However, a study of the Table on page 161 suggests that the undoubted and substantial increase in public support for the GAA from the early 1930s onwards reflected in record attendances failed to translate itself into greater participation in the Association itself. If it be accepted that statistics of club numbers form a reliable indicator of the numerical strength of the GAA, it has to be conceded that this Table reveals no pattern of steady growth by the Association in the 1930s. The position is even worse than the Table would suggest, because the average annual number of clubs for the four-year period 1930–1933 (1,670) was slightly higher than the corresponding figure for the four-year period 1935–1938. Moreover, to cover a longer period from the jubilee year of 1934 to 1941 (the statistics for which relate to 1940, the first year of the wartime Emergency) the figures at the foot of the Table show that the total at the end of the period was marginally lower than at the start — a surprisingly poor achievement at a time when the Association was enjoying greater public support than ever before and when conditions for expansion were so favourable.

Nor is this all. Closer examination of the totals for the thirty-two counties produces an even more unfavourable result. For four years after 1934 the figures declined steadily, with the total for the three years from 1936 to 1938 being almost 350 lower than that for the three years from 1931 to 1933. It was to be a full ten years before the elusive 2,000 (almost reached in jubilee year) was to be passed for the first time. Of the four provinces, Connacht and Ulster showed almost no change over the seven years from 1935 to 1941, which was roughly the period between the jubilee and the outbreak of the war. Leinster surprisingly fared worst of all, with a drop of ninety-four clubs or fourteen per cent in the same period, largely accounted for by the falls of forty-seven per cent, sixteen per cent and twenty per cent in Offaly, Dublin and Longford respectively. Munster alone of the four provinces enjoyed an almost uninterrupted rise in the provincial total; only 1937 showed a drop on the previous year. There, however, the growth came nearly exclusively from two counties, Waterford (probably because of its hurling success) and Kerry, where the total began at an artificially low level because of the political background already referred to.

Some other curious conclusions emerge from the Table. Mayo's football successes led to no appreciable increase in club numbers. In Roscommon the county's senior football successes were preceded by a substantial, but only temporary, rise in club numbers. Other counties whose All-Ireland final appearances failed to yield results in the shape of a rise in club numbers were Limerick and Kilkenny in hurling and Kerry and Cavan in football. That the existence of a large number of clubs in a county did not necessarily lead to any championship wins is proved by the figures from several counties — Leitrim, Wexford and Westmeath, to mention a few at random. The spread of clubs shows Munster, the cradle of the GAA, still by far the strongest numerically with an average of almost ninety clubs per county in 1940 compared to fewer than sixty per county for Connacht and about fifty and thirty for Leinster and Ulster, respectively. Understandably, larger or more populous counties like Cork, Galway, Dublin and Tipperary accounted for a high proportion of the relevant provincial total.

Because this Table suggests a state of affairs inside the GAA quite different from the public image of the Association at the time, it naturally casts doubt on the assumption (implicit in the use of such a table) that club numbers form a reliable guide to the numerical strength of the GAA. Pádraig Ó Caoimh in some of his annual reports in the 1930s appears to have placed equal if not more reliance on other indicators of the Association's progress or success — an increasing number of competitions, high standards of play and bigger attendances (producing usually a higher income) to mention a few. Nevertheless, not only has the club been the basic unit of the GAA since its foundation, but it is probably a better guide to the extent of activity inside the Association than figures of attendances or higher income. Both of these reflect support deriving at least in part from outside the Association, since many spectators are not members. No inconsistency exists between the mass public support enjoyed by the GAA from 1930 or so onwards and the apparent failure by the Association to expand numerically in the 1930s. It was, after all, a period of high emigration, especially from the countryside, where the Association had always been strongest.

To many members and supporters, and especially to tens of thousands of ordinary playing-members in rural parish clubs, probably the most impressive achievement of the GAA in the 1930s was the erection of the Cusack Stand in Croke Park. By any test it was an important event in the history of the Association. The ambitious scale of the project and its successful execution probably did as much for the public image of the Association as it did for the morale of the rank-and-file members. Conceived in the golden jubilee year of 1934 as a necessary expansionary move and a permanent tribute to the GAA's founder, the Cusack Stand became on its completion at once a symbol of the new prosperity and permanence of the Association and solid proof of the leading position in Irish sport attained by the GAA.

After the initial decision to build the stand was taken by the central council in October 1934, nothing more was done for a further year. Then late in 1935 it was decided to name the new stand after Michael Cusack. According to Pádraig Ó Caoimh in his annual report to the 1936 congress, it would be 'the most extensive scheme . . . ever undertaken by the Association' and would involve 'a covered double-deck stand' (the first of its kind in Ireland) and 'the terracing of Hill '16' to produce 'an estimated accommodation for 30,000'. An exchange of land with the Jesuits, who owned the adjoining sportsfield, would be necessary. By Christmas

1935, after tenders had been invited by press advertisement, eight Irish firms had tendered in sums ranging from £34,000 to £45,000 for the contract.

On the advice of its engineer, the central council accepted a tender of £41,000 from the Limerick firm of McCaffrey and O'Carroll. The contract concluded between the GAA and this firm required the work to be concluded within eighteen months from February 1936. On this basis the council expected to be able to stage the 1937 All-Ireland finals in the reconstructed stadium. By the late summer of 1937 the greater part of the new stand apart from the roof and the seating had been built. However, a strike in the building industry held up work for the best months of that year. It was August 1938, two-and-a-half years after it had been begun, before the work was finished.

By the time the president, Pádraig MacNamee of Belfast (the first Ulsterman to head the GAA) formally opened the Cusack Stand before the start of an All-Ireland semi-final in August 1938, the cost of the entire project had exceeded £50,000. At an early stage extensions to the work costing £8,100 were agreed to by the GAA, bringing the original estimate to over £49,000. Ultimately the bill presented to Nicholas O'Dwyer, the Association engineer, in October 1938 totalled £58,700, of which he disputed nearly £7,800. A protracted arbitration was necessary before a substantial reduction was achieved by the GAA. To meet this unprecedented bill the central council had in July, 1936 created a debenture for £35,000 in favour of the wholly Irish-owned Property Loan and Investment Company. By effecting substantial economies in expenditure over the next few years Ó Caoimh managed to reduce this debt year by year. By 1941 it was down to £22,000, by 1944 to £6,000. The following year it was wiped out.

Partly because of the building strike, the prolonged work at Croke Park from early 1936 to mid-1938 caused little disruption to major games. Since the present practice of playing both All-Ireland football semi-finals in Dublin had not been established, it was necessary to find an alternative venue for only one final, that in hurling for 1937. With commendable initiative the central council decided to play the match, between Tipperary and Kilkenny, in the new Fitzgerald Stadium in Killarney. Local enthusiasts performed an organisational miracle and won the admiration of the thousands of spectators who made the long trip to Kerry. Neither the GAA nor the GSR Company was able to avoid the understandable congestion and delay caused by the handling of almost forty special trains at one small rural station. In every other respect this first final to be played outside Dublin for nearly thirty years was a success, although the game itself disappointed.

During the period when the Cusack Stand was in course of erection a new personality who played a big part in popularising both hurling and football entered the world of Gaelic games. In the twelve years since the first radio broadcast of GAA events Radio Éireann had had several commentators, ranging from the sports journalist Patrick D. Mehigan ('Carbery') to Father Michael Hamilton of Clare. Then one August day in 1938 a teenage Dublin schoolboy, the son of a popular Clare-born Dublin GAA official, was given charge of the commentary on the football semi-final in Mullingar. Mícheál O'Hehir became an almost essential part of the annual Gaelic championship season, bringing the major games not only into remote rural homes in every corner of this island but also half-way around the globe to emigrant Irish communities. While his talent as a broadcaster proved unique and ideal, O'Hehir would have been the first to admit that he owed a special debt to the encouragement and friendship in those early years of his career as a commentator to the GAA's General Secretary Pádraig Ó Caoimh.

Such success as the GAA achieved in the 1930s is rarely gained without some unforeseen consequences for the body concerned. The bigger crowds that came to watch Gaelic games must have included at least some who were either previous or potential supporters of rival games. Similarly, the spread of hurling and football to new areas must have been, to some extent at least (especially in urban areas), at the expense of those same rival games. Two consequences were to follow over a period of years. First, there were to be attracted into the GAA some players (and later some officials) who for different reasons, such as the absence of previous connections with the Association, did not feel so strongly as did older members on some of the means used to achieve the GAA's objectives — on the Ban, to mention only one obvious example. Secondly, the astonishing growth in support for the GAA, which presumably involved a corresponding lack of support (or at least a slower rate of growth) for rival sports bodies, would in time understandably cause some degree of envy among followers of non-Gaelic codes. This feeling came to manifest itself principally in attacks from outside the Association on the rules comprising the Ban; these were naturally seen as the biggest obstacles to growth by the GAA's rivals.

Two now almost forgotten, but then controversial, episodes of the late 1930s suggest that there already existed inside the GAA a small number of people at least — players, officials and active supporters — who were not fully in sympathy with the strict enforcement of the Ban. The first concerned a prominent Tipperary hurler, James (later Colonel) Cooney of Carrick-on-Suir, then an engineering student at University College, Dublin and a member of the UCD team. In mid-February 1938 Cooney attended an international rugby game in Dublin; when the matter came to the knowledge of the Tipperary board he admitted his breach of GAA rules. Since he incurred an automatic three-month suspension Cooney was dropped from all teams by his club and county. In due course he was reinstated by the Leinster council. So far as the Tipperary board was concerned that was the end of the matter; Cooney's return had come in time for the impending Munster championship.

However, when shortly after Easter the central council held a routine meeting to approve of 'declarations' (formal written statements by players not residing in their county of birth of their intention to play either for that county or the county of residence) the president, in reply to a query from a Tipperary delegate, ruled that the date of a declaration was not that on which it was signed but that on which it reached the council. For Cooney and the Tipperary board a serious situation now suddenly developed. Although he had signed the declaration form ten days before he had suspended himself by attending the rugby match, the Tipperary board had not forwarded it to the central council until shortly before Easter. As a result of the council's ruling the declaration was invalid, since Cooney was debarred from all GAA activities (even making a declaration) while suspended. He was therefore ineligible for the Tipperary team for the 1938 Munster championship.

Naturally incensed at being deprived of the services of one of its best players because of what it understandably regarded either as a mere technicality or a wrong interpretation of the rules, the Tipperary board reacted strongly. Since the central council ruling had not been a formal one based on a full hearing, it was decided to challenge it openly by playing Cooney in the forthcoming championship game against Clare. Clare in turn announced the intention of formally objecting to Cooney should the occasion arise; in due course Clare lost the match on the field but was awarded it in the council chamber by the Munster council. The presidential ruling seems to have been prompted by a suspicion (voiced beforehand to Tipperary by Pádraig Ó Caoimh) that Cooney's form had been back-dated to ensure his return in time for the Clare game. Tipperary, however, seems to have had a grievance over the rejection of its counter-objection to a Clare player said to have attended the rugby match with Cooney. The only evidence for this, a statement by Cooney, was ruled out because of his status as a suspended member.

If the Cooney case suggested anything of general application to the GAA, it was that a rule providing for automatic suspension without a hearing was an unwise one. One may speculate on whether or not, given favourable circumstances, an opportunity might have been found at the 1939 congress to amend this rule. By then circumstances were quite unfavourable. Early in 1938 the new Constitution of the State, which had been approved by the people at a referendum held in 1937, came into operation. In an unusual gesture all the political parties agreed to the unopposed election as first President of Ireland of the distinguished Gaelic scholar and founder of the Gaelic League, Douglas Hyde, who had never been involved in politics. Hyde, then in retirement, had been largely forgotten by the public; probably not one in a hundred members of the GAA realised that he was for many years a patron of their Association. When late in 1938, in his capacity as President of the State, Hyde attended an international soccer match in Dublin hardly anybody in the GAA considered the implications of his attendance.

On 17 December, however, at the last meeting of the central council for 1938, a Connacht delegate moved for the Galway county board a resolution asking the council 'to consider the position of a patron whose official duties may bring him into conflict with the fundamental rules of the Association'. When the delegate for Roscommon (Hyde's native county) loyally commenced to defend Hyde, the president halted him and effectively ended the brief discussion by formally ruling with regret that, because a patron was bound by the rules, 'such a person ceased to be a patron of the Association'. Nothing quite like this had happened in the GAA since the removal of its founder Cusack from the post of Secretary fifty-two years earlier; when he made his ruling Pádraig MacNamee probably did not realise that history was nearly repeating itself. While Hyde had not been at the early meetings of the GAA, he and Cusack had been closely associated in work for Irish culture, and in particular for the Irish language, before 1884.

Within a few weeks of the council ruling it became clear that opinion inside the GAA, even down to what a later generation would call grass-roots level, was divided and disturbed over the action of the council in 'expelling' such a distinguished figure from the Association, as the average member naturally came to describe it. In Connacht especially a surprisingly unexpected depth of feeling for the State's new President revealed itself. Discussions in mid-January 1939 by two Mayo divisional boards were followed shortly afterwards by a unanimous call at the county's annual convention for the restoration of Hyde as a patron. The north Kerry board followed suit. At the Roscommon convention Dan O'Rourke, a future president of the GAA, described the council's action as unwise. Gradually, however, feeling subsided; only two other counties, Roscommon and Kildare, followed Mayo's example. At some other conventions, including those of Wexford and the Munster council, the central council was strenuously defended, its decision on Hyde being even formally approved. Ultimately at the Association's annual congress at Easter Mayo withdrew their motion and Roscommon did not move theirs. A vote on the Kildare motion produced only eleven delegates in favour, with 120 against and five abstentions.

Sixty years after the event it is easy to be wise. But in the absence of an explicit statement in the GAA's rules, it is doubtful if a patron of such a voluntary body is also a member solely because of his patronage. In any event, the central council could easily have side-stepped the issue by ruling that there was no proof of Hyde's membership in 1938. Alternatively, the presidential staff might have been informally alerted to the probable implications of patronage of the GAA, leaving it to Hyde himself to decide whether or not to continue as a patron. Since he had earlier taken a keen interest in GAA affairs, Hyde could hardly have been ignorant of the rule; it was open to him to give up his patronage before attending Dalymount Park. Instead, by choosing to attend a function forbidden to members of a body of which he was a patron, he acted imprudently.

Exactly why MacNamee decided as he did remains a mystery. Presumably Ó Caoimh, when he got the Galway motion in advance, discussed it with the president since it raised the possibility of a confrontation between the Association and the President of the State. One would have thought too that, because of the delicacy of the matter, there would have been consultation with any other council member within easy reach. However, most of the eighteen delegates who attended the mid-December 1938 meeting are now dead; a few of the survivors have indicated that they were not consulted beforehand. Some of them are known to have later regretted the ruling; so too did MacNamee himself. Paddy Mullaney of Mayo, who admittedly attended the meeting only as a proxy, participated in his county's unanimous call to restore Hyde. As will shortly appear, both Ó Caoimh and a later president conceded that 'the Hyde incident had been most unfortunate' — which is probably as close as the Association could be expected to go towards admitting that a wrong decision had been made.

One interesting side-effect of the Hyde case was the temporary reopening for the first time in several years of discussion inside the GAA on the Ban. It became apparent that opinion even among prominent personalities in the Association was not at all as inflexible as was often believed by outsiders in favour of the permanent retention of the prohibition on members playing or attending excluded games. In Tipperary, for example, where the loss of Cooney was naturally still resented, no less prominent figures than Father (later Canon) Fogarty, the president of the county board, and Johnny Leahy, the popular county secretary, both publicly questioned the value of the Ban. In Ulster the provincial secretary, Gerry Arthurs of Armagh, contemplated the possibility of the ultimate removal of the Ban by a majority decision of the GAA. So also did the General Secretary himself, in an otherwise trenchant defence in his annual report for 1938 of the policy of fostering unqualified allegiance for native games on a voluntary basis.

Neither his handling of the Cooney case nor that of the Hyde case ought to be taken to suggest that Pádraig MacNamee was an inadequate leader of the GAA. On the contrary, few GAA presidents of modern times acquitted themselves so creditably in a post that demands a combination of qualities which include tact, personality, firmness and idealism. Coming to the highest post in the GAA from many years' work for the Irish language in Ulster, MacNamee's dream (still largely unrealised) was of a broad federation of organisations working for the various aspects of native culture, which would be more effective than any of its components alone in dealing with bureaucracy in both parts of the country. Another episode later in his term of office, soon to be recalled, suggests that MacNamee visualised the GAA taking a more positive role in the public life of the community than any of his predecessors. The GAA recognised MacNamee's qualities; he was elected to a fourth term of office, an honour never since accorded to any GAA president.

Seven years after the central council meeting of December 1938 which decided that President Hyde was no longer a patron of the GAA, the unhappy episode again obtruded itself into relations between the Association and the State in a series of frank exchanges about which neither the ordinary member of the GAA nor the general public has ever been told. In the summer of 1945 Hyde retired at the end of his seven-year term and was succeeded by Seán T. O'Kelly, the nominee of the Fianna Fáil party, who defeated Fine Gael and Independent nominees in a three-candidate election. Shortly afterwards the president of the GAA, Séamus Gardiner of Tipperary, instructed the General Secretary to arrange a courtesy call by the Association's chief officers on the new head of State, who like Hyde had also been a GAA member many years before. When Ó Caoimh endeavoured to make an appointment no reply was received from the Presidential office; instead, he got from the Taoiseach, Eamon de Valera, a request to meet him in Government Buildings. On 10 August Gardiner and Ó Caoimh presented themselves to the head of the Government in his office in the presence of a senior civil servant. By now both GAA men must have guessed the reason for their summons.

According to the official account of the meeting, the Taoiseach explained that he had been asked to call it by President O'Kelly, who (according to de Valera) felt that he 'could not ignore the slight which had been offered to Doctor Hyde by the GAA when he was removed from his position as patron of that body'. Consequently the Taoiseach felt it was essential that precautions be taken to avoid any future embarrassment in the relations between the President and the GAA. De Valera expressed it as his view that representatives of a national organisation like the GAA should be received by the President; he in turn should be invited to its major games. But because the President represented all sections of the community, the GAA must appreciate that acceptance of such an invitation carried no implication to restrict himself regarding invitations from other sporting bodies, which the Taoiseach made clear would be accepted by President O'Kelly.

Dealing specifically with the Hyde case, de Valera argued that the GAA should on Hyde's election have drawn his attention to the implications for him of the Ban and obtained his permission to continue him as a patron. In the Taoiseach's view, had this been done Hyde would have resigned his patronage. Moreover, in de Valera's opinion, the central council should resist any attempts by members to criticise a President publicly for any actions conflicting with GAA rules. Gardiner and Ó Caoimh agreed to return to the Taoiseach after conveying his views to their council, confining themselves at this stage to commenting that the Hyde case 'had been most unfortunate, but . . . that the responsibility for failing to acquaint him with the possible implications of his position as patron lay as much with his advisors as with the GAA'.

A special meeting of the central council held in private a week later on 17 August considered the discussion between its officers and the Taoiseach. After a long debate a motion was passed by a majority vote indicating the council's acceptance of 'the principle . . . that representatives of a national organisation such as the GAA should be received by the President . . . that he should be invited to its principal functions' and that 'he cannot in any circumstances put himself in such a position as to seem, by implication or otherwise, to discriminate against any section of the community'. A five-man deputation, to be led by the president and the General Secretary, was appointed to convey the council's decision to the Taoiseach. It was expressly instructed to 'explain to the Taoiseach the council's inability to agree with the Taoiseach's view as regards rights of members to express criticism'.

Formal notification of the passing and terms of the resolution was sent by the General Secretary in a letter on 21 August to the Taoiseach, who at once arranged for a second meeting with the GAA for 24 August. At this meeting not only was the right of members 'to express criticism' (presumably of the President of the State or anybody else) asserted, but Gardiner and other members of the GAA party emphasised to the Taoiseach that the central council's decision (embodied in the resolution, which the president explained to de Valera) would not necessarily bind future central councils. The meeting ended with the Taoiseach indicating that he would communicate with President O'Kelly, who would decide whether to meet the GAA, and expressing the hope that should the President attend Croke Park he would be received in a fitting manner. On this point Pádraig Ó Caoimh immediately reassured de Valera.

For giving a later central council of the GAA an opportunity to back down quietly from the almost untenable position represented by MacNamee's ruling of December 1938 the Association was in a sense indebted to President O'Kelly's initiative (if it was his) in the summer of 1945. Since it was reasonable to expect that some, perhaps many, presidents of the new State would be either members, or former members of the GAA, a situation could hardly be permitted to continue in which, so long as the Ban lasted, periodic confrontations would occur between the head of State and the country's leading sports body. In such circumstances the officers of the GAA in 1945 (some of whom, like MacNamee, were still in office from 1939) deserve credit for the tact and good grace with which they accepted the way out of the impasse so opportunely presented by President O'Kelly.

The central council minutes clearly hint that for some like Father Hamilton the decision of August 1945 was not easily accepted. Probably resistance to de Valera's proposals was caused by resentment at his insensitive approach. His proposition that 'acceptance of a position as patron of an organisation did not necessarily connote membership' was reasonable. However, to suggest that it was the GAA's duty to get Hyde's permission to continue him as patron and to tell him of the implication of the Ban was quite unreal. No patron of such a body has his position examined periodically. Above all, by arguing that invitations to Croke Park should not be withheld in disapproval of a President's relations with other bodies, and by urging the GAA not to criticise a President publicly, the Taoiseach was proposing to deny to thousands of GAA members 'the right of the citizens to express freely their . . . opinions' guaranteed by the new Constitution of the State, of which he himself was the principal author.

This private confrontation in 1945 between the GAA and de Valera was only the last in point of time of several disagreements between the Association and the Fianna Fáil governments of the pre-war and wartime periods, that had reached a climax in 1943. Among some leading members of the GAA a growing sense, partly of disillusionment and partly of resentment, over what they felt was a lack of sympathy for the objectives of the GAA by a few influential figures in the Fianna Fáil party developed in the years after de Valera's accession to power in 1932. Because of the strong republican element in the Fianna Fáil party, the GAA had understandably expected that from 1932 onwards the new political regime would give unqualified and even exclusive support to native pastimes, and would also display a more positive degree of support than had the Cosgrave administration for the Association, as the leading body promoting native sport.

In anticipation of a more cordial atmosphere than that which had existed in the closing years of the Cumann na nGaedheal administration, and in the interests of the Association of which he was chief officer, Pádraig Ó Caoimh had cultivated a close relationship with de Valera himself. However, by the late 1930s Ó Caoimh and some of his principal associates on the central council had become disheartened to find from time to time what they felt was a lukewarm attitude towards the GAA both by de Valera himself and by some of his ministerial colleagues. The suspicion of the GAA naturally centred on a small number of politicians such as Oscar Traynor and Sean MacEntee, whose partiality for non-Gaelic games was widely known. To its dismay the Association found that, as had been the case with the Cumann na nGaedheal party in the years just before 1932, the feelings of prominent members of Fianna Fáil about the GAA varied in individual cases from enthusiastic support to total apathy or even (so it seemed to the GAA) latent hostility.

Typical of the friction that occurred between the GAA and the Government in the years of the Emergency was that which arose over the position and status of Gaelic games in the Army. With the substantial increase in the strength of the Defence Forces caused by the mass recruiting drives of the early 1940s, inevitably more and more soldiers came to play either soccer or rugby. In the GAA, however, the feeling grew that these games were being actively encouraged at the expense of Gaelic football and hurling, ironically a total reverse of the position that had obtained in the days of General O'Duffy under the Cosgrave regime. Predictably, many officers of the GAA became convinced that the real villain behind the scenes was the Minister for Defence, Oscar Traynor, a former member of a Belfast professional soccer club. In time each side came, somewhat grudgingly, to respect the rights of the other, but not before allegation had been followed by counter-allegation, until finally the central council, in a strongly-worded statement unanimously approved after a special two-day meeting in May 1943, accused the Minister of falsehoods and reminded the public that the Irish army from 1916 to 1921 had been 'almost exclusively' recruited from the GAA — the 'almost' being a barbed reference to Traynor himself.

Associated with its periodic bouts of disillusionment with Fianna Fáil's attitude to the GAA was a similar feeling in the Association about the party's daily news-paper, the *Irish Press*, which from the start was closely supervised by de Valera himself. From the start the Association had nursed a justifiable grievance against influential organs of nationalist opinion for the often inadequate support some of them gave to a body sponsoring Irish culture — without which, as GAA spokesmen from Cusack onwards argued forcibly, no independent Irish nation-State could hope to prosper indefinitely. All along there had been newspapers outside Dublin — the *Examiner* of Cork, the *People* of Wexford and the *Democrat* of Dundalk among them — which never wavered in their support for the GAA from its foundation. In Dublin, however, the *Freeman's Journal* group had rarely given the Association the prominence its activities deserved in the forty years before that paper's demise after the Civil War. Similarly, in the various publications of the *Independent* group, which politically took a strong pro-Sinn Féin line in the years just before 1922, coverage of GAA events remained at a low standard right up to 1931.

The foundation in the autumn of that year of the *Irish Press* led rapidly to a complete change of attitude to the GAA by the national press, or at least by that portion of it concerned with sport. Not only did the new daily paper give extensive and sympathetic coverage from the start to Gaelic games; within a short time also the sports columns of the *Irish Press* as a whole came to be regarded by followers of sports in general as superior to those of its rivals. As a direct consequence of this, the other morning dailies, especially the *Irish Independent,* were quickly forced to raise the standard and increase the column-space of their sports reports and commentaries, particularly those relating to GAA events, in which the new national paper had excelled from the start. Needless to say, all this healthy commercial rivalry was extremely gratifying to the GAA, which now found its games getting more and better treatment in all the national papers than had ever previously been the case. In short, the Association had at last been accorded the fair play it had so long been denied by the press; for that it had to thank the Fianna Fáil organ.

As the years went by, however, and the GAA increased in popularity with the sporting public there were some in the Association who apparently felt that the column-space allotted to Gaelic games in the national press should also increase. The principal critic of the papers was Sean McCarthy of Cork, a Fianna Fáil TD, who in July 1938 with the support of the president Pádraig MacNamee succeeded in having a decision made by the central council that, after advance notification, the council would cease advertising in the Dublin dailies, in protest against their persistent neglect of native pastimes. But the advance notice, which was probably intended to produce promises to do better in the future, misfired. The news editor of the *Irish Press* and the sports editor of the *Independent* both replied, the first defending his paper and the other offering a meeting. The council then decided to try to effect a meeting with the *Irish Press*. It seems that later it had second thoughts on this, perhaps feeling that the publicity given to its protest might itself effect an improvement.

As in the case of the controversy over the position of Gaelic games in the Army, one gets an impression that the GAA was to a large extent asserting its independence. Curiously, apart from one other central council member, it does not appear that MacCarthy's dramatic proposal received much support. Pádraig Ó Caoimh, who normally offered advice in such important cases, remained uncharacteristically silent. Perhaps he was not satisfied that the GAA's case was a strong one, bearing in mind the normal commercial restraints under which daily papers catering for all sections of the community had to operate. Some of the figures quoted by the *Irish Press* were impressive. They showed from a spot-check that from the foundation of the paper its main rival, the *Independent*, had increased its coverage of Gaelic games no less than ten-fold, and that in a month chosen at random the *Press* coverage was still more extensive than that of its main competitor.

If the GAA felt that its activities were being inadequately covered by the more important sections of the national press in the 1930s and 1940s, it has to be said that the Association's own efforts to project a favourable public image as a leading cultural body met with little success. The only venture that achieved a high standard, the quarterly review *An Ráitheachán*, which first appeared in June 1936, failed to last beyond five issues. Devoted to all aspects of native culture and published from the Secretary's office at Croke House, this now forgotten publication attracted during its brief career a number of eminent contributors, including the scholar Douglas Hyde, the writer Daniel Corkery, the poetess Alice Milligan, the novelist Maurice Walsh and the painter Sean Keating, as well as Irish writers such as Shan O Cuiv and An Seabhac, the young Bryan MacMahon and the future President Erskine H. Childers. Internal evidence points to Ó Caoimh as the editor of this high-quality journal, which stands favourable comparison with anything sponsored by the GAA in the following forty years.

In December 1942, five years after the collapse of *An Ráitheachán*, appeared the first edition of what was probably both the most curious and the most commercially successful publication ever sponsored by the GAA. *National Action*, a 130-page booklet written by the anonymous Josephus Anelius, ran to three editions (totalling 16,000 copies) inside eighteen months. With its fourth edition (carrying the author's real name) in 1947, its sales must have easily passed the 20,000 mark. Described as a plan for national recovery, it contained a laudatory preface in Irish by the president of the GAA, Pádraig MacNamee, who commended its ideas to every citizen concerned about the survival and future prosperity of the Irish nation. Joseph Anelius concealed the identity of Joseph Hanly, a Galway man, a senior civil servant and a Sinn Féin veteran who, after writing two booklets on farming in the early 1920s, followed in 1931 with a longer and wider-ranging booklet entitled *The National Ideal*, a survey of the contemporary political, social and economic scene in Ireland containing some of the ideas expanded in the controversial booklet sponsored by the GAA eleven years later.

Basically what Hanly advocated was a totally new system of government, borrowing a few of what he believed to be the better features of some of the continental regimes. The National Government which he envisaged would be subject to surveillance by a novel form of Opposition, drawn from elected parish councils. Periodically after a pre-determined programme had been carried through the Government would vacate office, thus avoiding any risk of permanent totalitarianism. The whole radical transformation from the existing form of democracy based on the British system could, Hanly believed, be peacefully effected through the machinery of the referendum in the 1937 Constitution. That the *National Action* programme contained some sound ideas — on agriculture, for example, a subject on which Hanly had specialised for long — is undeniable. Equally undeniable is the fact that many of his proposals were impractical and too idealistic to win widespread support. In addition, in some spheres he was almost purely negative or critical in his approach; given the validity of much of his criticism, he frequently offered no positive or constructive alternative.

On two counts the GAA's sponsorship of such a controversial publication left the Association wide open to criticism. It appeared to be a clear breach of the GAA's fundamental rule prohibiting participation in politics. Secondly, on a particular (and not unreasonable) interpretation, *National Action* advocated the replacement of the existing system of government by a single-party regime, such as was then associated in the public mind with the fascist or communist regimes which controlled Germany, Italy and Russia. Not surprisingly, the GAA was widely attacked, even from inside the Association, on both counts. The two main Dublin morning papers wondered how the Association reconciled its sponsorship with its no-politics rule. Leading members of the GAA such as Dan O'Rourke of Roscommon, a Fianna Fáil TD, a veteran of the GAA and a future president, bitterly resented the implicit rejection, by a body for which many of them had spent a lifetime working, of the existing political parties, to one or other of which they were equally sincerely attached.

Although approved by a majority of delegates attending the 1943 congress, the extent of opposition to *National Action* seems to have caused the central council to reconsider the wisdom of its sponsorship. In a statement issued only a month after congress it admitted the existence of valid grounds for criticism of the booklet and implicitly accepted that its advocacy of a single-party system was a breach of the GAA's constitution. It is difficult to avoid the conclusion that the whole episode constituted a rare error of judgement on the part of Pádraig Ó Caoimh, whose defence of the venture and anger at criticism of the booklet strongly suggested that he had played a major part in the adoption of Hanly's programme. Although equally indefensible, MacNamee's support for *National Action* is easier to understand in the light of his open and sincere advocacy of a unified policy, led by the GAA, by the major bodies dedicated to various aspects of native culture.

Probably no previous war affected the lives of so many ordinary people in so many parts of the world as did the Second World War. Not only was this second global conflict in a quarter of a century of much greater dimensions than its predecessor from 1914 to 1918; it also affected the lives of even non-combatants, including those in non-combatant states like Ireland, to a far greater extent than World War I had done. In such circumstances one expects to find that for a sports organisation like the GAA life became gradually more difficult from September 1939 onwards. It would seem inevitable that such fringe or non-essential activities as field games would be among the earliest to be restricted as a result of the outbreak of war, even in a country like this which, although not directly involved in the war, lay geographically close to the warring States.

It soon became clear that the Government's policy of neutrality, which had been agreed on in advance by all the political parties, could not prevent the war from having some effect on Irish life. Within hours of the outbreak of hostilities special meetings of both the Dáil and the Senate were summoned at which a national emergency was declared arising out of the commencement of the war. Special legislation to ensure essential supplies and services was speedily passed; the temperature of party politics suddenly dropped. Since it was widely believed that aerial warfare would become a major feature of the conflict in Europe, plans were put in hand to protect life and property from air-raids. Recruiting for the defence forces began on a big scale; reserve officers were called up for training. Within months the impact of the war had been felt. Irish ships had been sunk; an occasional stray bomb had been dropped on Irish territory from unidentified planes, rescued passengers from ocean liners sunk off the Irish coast had been landed at Irish ports.

Nevertheless, it was almost two years before the war made any major impact on the GAA. Even then a serious cattle disease had a temporarily more disruptive effect on the events run by the GAA than the war had. The last quarter of 1939 and the whole of 1940 passed without any noticeable curtailment of the programme of the central council or the provisional councils. In the summer of 1939, as some of the statesmen of Europe desperately tried to avert what has since been regarded as an almost unavoidable resort to arms, while others headed seemingly purposefully towards the same conflict, the footballers of Galway and Kerry sailed across the Atlantic in what none of them realised would be the last 'American tour' for a GAA team for many years. Four months later, as Hitler's troops pounded their way across Poland, the All-Ireland finals drew attendances of 40,000 and 46,000 respectively. Cork, whose win over Limerick had drawn a record 40,000 to the Munster final two months earlier, lost the hurling final to Kilkenny; Kerry defeated comparative new-comers Meath by only two points.

The following year, 1940, is remembered by many who lived through it as that in which Hitler's army and air force blasted their way westwards across Europe, over-running half-a dozen countries and chasing the British forces off the continental mainland from the beaches at Dunkirk. For followers of Gaelic games, however, it holds far more pleasant memories. In Munster Cork and Limerick had to play twice in the provincial hurling final before Limerick came out on top. Two weeks later in Croke Park a record crowd (33,000) for two All-Ireland semi-finals played at the same venue on the same day watched Kerry defeat Cavan and Galway defeat Meath. By the last Sunday in September Limerick had regained the hurling title for what was to be the last time for thirty-three years and Kerry had retained the football title, before attendances of 49,000 and 60,000 respectively. So far not a single GAA competition in any grade had been interrupted by the war, mainly because transport facilities still continued at the pre-war level.

By the middle of 1941 the war had at last begun to affect life in this country. Transport, the first sector of the economy to be hit and the most seriously disrupted to the end of the war, had been curtailed, mainly because of the shortage of coal as a result of falling exports from Britain. As early as Easter the quality and quantity of petrol available had begun seriously to affect long-distance bus services; later in the year petrol became generally scarce. Imports too began to run at an exceptionally low level, forcing the Government to try to make our economy self-sufficient in respect of essential commodities. In May Dublin had its only major air-raid of the war; over thirty people were killed in the North Strand bombing adjacent to Croke Park. The GAA's General Secretary, Pádraig Ó Caoimh, whose home was nearby in Clonliffe Road, was one of scores of residents who spent the night ferrying injured people to city hospitals. By October the train services on many main lines had become erratic at best; coal was rationed to a half-ton a household a month; at Christmas supplies of petrol dried up altogether for some time.

Now at last the GAA also began to be affected by the wartime conditions. Because of the transport situation the junior championships were cancelled altogether; they were not to be resumed until the war was over. Later in the year both National Leagues were abandoned for the same reason, after special trains planned for some big games did not run. In Britain the Association's programme was severely curtailed and in places came to a halt. Attendances began to fall. Although 20,000 watched the annual Railway Cup games in Croke Park on St Patrick's Day, 1941, only 8,000 attended the Munster hurling semi-final. Most significantly of all, perhaps, when those traditional football rivals Dublin and Kerry played drawn and replayed All-Ireland semi-finals in mid-summer, only 16,000 and 15,000 spectators turned up. Contrary to expectations, however, Kerry and Galway attracted 45,000 to the football final; some weeks earlier only 26,000 had come to the hurling final, although Dublin was one of the contestants.

In one important respect the 1941 hurling final was unique. Neither contestant (Cork or Dublin) had won its provincial title that year; each had been nominated by its provincial council to ensure that the All-Ireland final could be played by the customary time in early September. This unusual and probably unprecedented situation came about as a result of the foot-and-mouth epidemic of that year, which caused widespread disruption of sporting activities in Munster. Spread over a ten-month period beginning in February 1941, this worst-ever outbreak of the dreaded cattle disease in Ireland, although confined largely to Munster and south Leinster, resulted in the enforced slaughter of over 19,000 cattle and 5,000 sheep. In an effort to reduce the extent of the epidemic, which could be spread by human contact with affected animals, the Department of Agriculture was obliged to resort to stringent compulsory measures, including the cancellation not only of animal fairs but also of many sporting fixtures.

For the GAA the most serious aspect of the foot-and-mouth disease was the fact that the half-dozen worst-hit areas included most of the major hurling counties. As the epidemic reached its climax in mid-summer (the period reserved for provincial championships), it became impossible to either the Munster or the Leinster council to complete its programme in time for the All-Ireland semi-final stage, normally fixed for August. To ensure that the hurling final for 1941 would not fall through, Dublin and Cork were nominated as finalists. To some extent, the low attendance at the final probably reflected the artificiality of the pairing more than the current transport difficulties. The final did not end the central council's difficulties for that year; when in late autumn the cattle restrictions were lifted and the belated Munster hurling final between Cork and Tipperary was re-fixed, Cork (now All-Ireland champions) was decisively defeated.

So far as the supply of goods and services hitherto regarded as essential was concerned, 1942 was the first year of real hardship for most Irish people, especially those who, because they lived in towns or cities, were unable to augment food and fuel supplies from their own or local resources and were dependent on public transport to travel to and from work. In addition to coal and tea (rationed from the previous year), bread, butter, clothing, gas and soap were now all rationed. As petrol became permanently scarce, a severely reduced urban and provincial bus schedule was added to an already unreliable provincial rail service. Before the spring was out private cars (except when used for essential purposes such as funerals and medical treatment) were put off the roads altogether.

Gaelic games, or at least attendances at them or the prosperity of the body controlling them, could not remain unaffected by such conditions. The principal figures in the annual financial report presented to congress give some idea of the impact on the GAA of the travel restrictions operating in the period from 1942 to the end of the war three years later. For 1940, although the income of the central council rose by only £300 on the 1939 figure, the council had a surplus of £6,700 compared to £4,400 for 1939, as a result of reduced expenditure itself caused by the initial wartime transport difficulties. For 1941 income fell from over £15,000 to £11,200, gate-money alone being down £3,000 on 1940. As a result the council's surplus of income over expenditure was a mere £2,150. The figures for 1942 tell their own story. Income at £7,600 was down by £3,600 on the previous year; because expenditure (£4,950) was down by £4,100, there was a surplus of £2,650. Not until 1944 did the central council's income or surplus return to anything like that of pre-war days. What is surprising is that never during World War II did it incur a loss on any year's operations, no matter now curtailed these were.

Predictably, attendances at major games began to fall from mid-1942 onwards. Although played in Cork city, the Munster hurling final that year attracted only 24,000 spectators. One of the two All-Ireland football semi-finals drew a mere 8,000, although Dublin was a participant and the game was played at Croke Park. The All-Ireland hurling final itself was watched by only 27,000. Yet it is possible to find more cheerful statistics even for 1942. The second football semi-final attracted 20,000, even though the contestants (and therefore their home supporters) had to come from as far away as Kerry and Galway; the final drew 37,000 spectators. If the Leinster council's income was lower than for thirteen years and the Munster council's down £4,600 on 1941, in Ulster (six counties of which were, after all, technically at war) Tyrone alone of the nine counties failed to report a surplus of income over expenditure — and in its case the loss was negligible.

Gradually the GAA, mainly through the loyalty of its supporters, adapted to the abnormal circumstances. Since other competitions such as the National Leagues and the junior championships had been called off indefinitely, the public was forced to take more interest than usual in the senior championships, both at club and county level. Club games in particular enjoyed a boom for several years and occasionally drew bigger crowds than major inter-county games. To try to reduce the fall in attendances neighbouring counties were often paired off, even in early rounds of provincial championships. Soon the public came to display an incredibly tenacious loyalty to the games by taking to the old-fashioned pedal bicycle in tens of thousands. Eventually officials came to take it for granted that, given a good pairing at final or semi-final stage, no shortage of conventional transport would keep away a substantial crowd. For some supporters it became almost an excursion rather than an endurance test to travel many miles to and from a championship fixture. At major stadia parking attendants now collected more in tips from cyclists than they had ever obtained from motorists. In long journeys parties of cyclists travelling to important Gaelic games commonly made overnight stops in guesthouses, friendly farmhouses and even open fields.

The extent of public support for the GAA even under wartime conditions became manifestly clear in 1943 and 1944, when new record attendances were achieved that astonished many both inside and outside the Association. The whole seven-year-period from 1943 to 1950 was marked by a series of record attendances at All-Ireland finals and semi-finals, with hurling finals and major provincial games in both Munster and Leinster also attracting bigger crowds than ever. As a result, the GAA found itself in the enviable position of facing the immediate post-war period, as life slowly returned to normal, in a position of greater popularity than ever before and enjoying the higher income associated with bigger crowds. In addition, the years between 1943 and 1950 were memorable for supporters of Gaelic games, particularly for followers of football, by many matches at the final or semi-final of the All-Ireland championship which compared favourably with some of the great games of the late 1930s. They were also made more attractive by the rise, and in a few cases, the success of several new counties.

For the first time since the turn of the century the exciting possibility of new champions became an almost permanent feature of the annual football competition. It was in the second half of the 1940s that followers of Gaelic games saw the welcome break-through by 'new' counties which has continued through the succeeding decades and has made the GAA All-Ireland football championship the most popular and most open sporting event in the country. Before the mid-1940s Cavan alone had succeeded in establishing itself as a real threat to the traditional winners of the Sam Maguire Cup. By 1950 Roscommon had also made the break-through; Meath had won its first senior title; Carlow's performance suggested that it too might soon win a senior title. In hurling Waterford had at last won a senior All-Ireland championship; Wexford was beginning to show what only later came to be recognised as initial evidence of future greatness; Dublin enjoyed a brief period of dominance in Leinster.

The year 1943 was notable in Gaelic arenas for the appearance in each final of a county that had never before got so far in the code concerned — Antrim in hurling and Roscommon in football. Antrim's first appearance in a senior hurling final was the result of a freak defeat in Belfast of an unprepared Kilkenny side; wartime conditions notwithstanding, a near-record crowd of almost 50,000 came to see the Ulster team trounced by twenty-seven points by Cork. Roscommon in its first All-Ireland final was watched by 68,000, only 1,000 short of the record attendance established in 1938. For the replay, in which it defeated Cavan, the figure was 52,000. The following year, 1944, the new Connacht and All-Ireland champions retained the national title when they beat Kerry by a bare two points before a record crowd of 79,000, the same margin by which Kerry had defeated the new Leinster champions Carlow before a record semi-final attendance of 41,000. Two years later Roscommon was back again. In the 1946 final it held Kerry to a draw before nearly 76,000 people and lost the replay before 65,000. That year it was associated with two new attendance records — that of 51,000 for the semi-final (against Laois) and that for a replayed final which exceeded the 1943 figure by 16,000.

After Roscommon's two titles in football Cork (narrowly defeated by Cavan in the 1943 semi-final) in 1945 won its first All-Ireland senior football title for thirty-five years. Between the two codes Cork dominated finals in the seven years from 1939 to 1946; since it won the hurling championship every year from 1941 to 1946 except 1945, the football win that year enabled the future Taoiseach Jack Lynch to collect six All-Ireland medals in consecutive years, a feat never equalled before or since. Even Lynch's achievement, however, was bettered by an even more famous Cork player of the same period, the inimitable Christy Ring, acknowledged as the greatest of all hurlers. Ring, by 1954 had collected eight senior All-Ireland hurling medals, a feat later equalled by the Tipperary hurler John Doyle. The period from 1947 to 1949 saw the arrival of two more counties new to senior titles in either code — Meath which, after its defeat by Kerry in the 1947 football semi-final (which set a new record of 66,000 for a semi-final), returned in 1949 to win its first title, and Waterford, which won its first hurling title in 1948 by defeating Dublin.

These greatly increased attendances at major games, achieved under wartime conditions and mostly before private motoring had recommenced, naturally reflected themselves in a return to a position of financial growth, shown by the annual financial statements to congress from 1945 onwards. For 1945 the central council's income totalled £17,000, the highest for any year since 1940; in addition, the surplus of £8,500 for 1945 was not far short of the corresponding figure of £9,000 for 1939. In 1946 the financial position of the Association suddenly improved substantially. Income reached the record figure of £23,000, and a record surplus of over £12,000 was achieved despite the paying-off of the balance due on the Cusack Stand. In the last three years of the 1940s surpluses of £15,700, £17,750 and £13,000 were achieved; by the end of the decade the assets of the central council totalled almost £167,000, with liabilities of only £4,500. A significant feature of the annual accounts around this time is the reappearance of figures of investment in new or existing grounds; between 1942 and 1947 this type of grant seems to have been suspended.

Probably the most impressive achievement of the GAA in the immediate post-war period was the successful transfer to New York in 1947 of the All-Ireland football final. In its own way this proved to be as powerful a morale-booster and as significant a milestone in the Association's history as the Cusack Stand venture of ten years earlier. Because of wartime conditions and the steep rise in emigration to Britain, the early and mid-1940s had seen a marked fall in Irish emigration to the United States, with a resultant slump in the playing of Gaelic games by the Irish and Irish-American communities in New York, Boston and other major cities of that country. From time to time attention was drawn, at congress and elsewhere, to the deteriorating plight of the games across the Atlantic. Nothing had been done about it by the time around 1946 when the influential Canon Michael Hamilton of Clare became the champion of the American wing of the GAA. Even then it seemed that he was pleading a hopeless case. GAA members with no American connections were naturally unenthusiastic. Some of those with such connections doubted if Gaelic games there merited support from home, partly because of occasional disturbing evidence of semi-professional aspects of the organisation of the games in some States.

In those circumstances the decision of the 1947 congress to ask the central council to consider the feasibility of playing the football final of that year in New York came as a surprise to many rank-and-file members. The easy passage of the motion from Clare was largely attributable to the persuasive emotive case made by Canon Hamilton. Even so there remained many in the GAA, including some at the higher officer level, who felt that somehow the project would never materialise. To many the idea of playing what had become the biggest national sports event of the year outside the country bordered on the unthinkable. Some also wondered if the sponsors of the idea had given any thought to the possible effects on the average Gaelic spectator, who would now be deprived of the customary climax to his seasonal championship fare. However, despite the formidable obstacles outlined to the central council on 23 May by a party (including the General Secretary, himself quite lukewarm on the venture) which had discussed the idea for a month in New York with local officials and potential supporters, a proposal by Vincent O'Donoghue of Waterford (a future president of the GAA) to abandon the whole idea was lost by twenty votes to seventeen. The New York Polo Grounds was fixed as the venue.

With a decision to play the match in America now irrevocably confirmed, what was possibly the most strenuous half-year of his life began for Pádraig Ó Caoimh. Clearly a move to New York was essential; before that he had to complete as much as possible of the normal high-season work at Croke Park. Fortunately he was able to leave behind him in Dublin a newly-trained full-time assistant in the person of a young Cork teacher Seán Ó Síocháin, who within little more than a year of his appointment as assistant to Ó Caoimh found himself acting as chief officer of the biggest sports body in the country for what was normally its busiest three-month period each year. In the meantime the central council succeeded in persuading the former president Pádraig MacNamee to travel to New York ahead of Ó Caoimh. The enthusiastic Belfast official sacrificed the entire of his annual leave as a teacher to take the Secretary's place in putting the administrative machine into motion in New York. In addition, a whole team of prominent Irish-Americans led by the Mayor William O'Dwyer of New York, a native of Mayo, at once put their talented experience at the disposal of MacNamee.

In spite of the excellent ground-work done by MacNamee and the various local committees before Ó Caoimh's arrival, it took the Secretary almost another two months, working a seven-day week and often a seventeen-hour day, to complete the arrangements for what would be an unprecedented and unique sporting venture. To ensure the success of the event from both the commercial and the promotional viewpoints a whole set of arrangements had to be made which were never required for a game in Ireland — a reception for the Irish party on its arrival, a banquet for 1,500 guests, a New York mayoral reception for the American sporting press, as well as boat and plane reservations for a party of sixty-five and a wide variety of forms of advance publicity. In order to guard against the creation of a black market in tickets it was decided not to release any to local ticket agencies; instead, a permanent booking office was opened in a New York hotel and had to be staffed daily. In addition, the baseball pitch at the Polo Grounds required alteration to suit Gaelic football. Radio coverage for the home country, with Mícheál O'Hehir in the commentator's box, received high priority. After encountering a whole series of technical difficulties, this major problem was solved only at a late stage. The GAA had to pay all the expenses incurred by Radio Éireann, since the station had made no provision in its estimates for such a costly broadcast.

One thing which could not be guarded against, of course, was unfavourable weather. Heavy rain the night before the match in mid-September kept many New Yorkers at home. Only 35,000 out of a possible maximum of 54,000 watched Cavan defeat Kerry by seventeen points to thirteen in an exciting game which was heard on radio by tens of thousands in this country. However, it became evident soon after the Irish party had returned home in October that the venture had succeeded in its two main objects. It attracted wide publicity in the United States and led to a revival of interest and participation in Gaelic games there. Moreover, the efficient management of Ó Caoimh, MacNamee and their voluntary local assistants (led by John 'Kerry' O'Donnell of the New York GAA) was handsomely rewarded by a profit of over £10,000. This enabled the central council to make a grant of £2,000 towards the promotion of the games in the United States.

Chapter 8

1950–1980

Whether a survey of a body like the GAA still flourishing after 115 years should include the most recent decades is arguable. Despite the widely accepted practice of historians nowadays of bringing the recent past within the scope of their study, it is often difficult in the case of an organisation such as the GAA to say of recent events which are more important than others, and nearly impossible to assess accurately the impact on such a body of events whose effects are probably not yet fully apparent. In another decade or so, when the recent past has become the not so recent past, a future historian of the GAA will almost certainly find that changes of emphasis and revised judgements are called for.

To end the story of the GAA at any point of time before the early 1970s, however, would involve the absence of even a factual record of some of the greatest successes achieved and most important decisions made in the whole history of the Association. If a history such as this is to claim to be complete, these successes and decisions, because of their extent and likely long-term impact, make some kind of survey of the last quarter-century or so in the life of the GAA essential, no matter how subjective it may prove. The Association itself in its eighty-fifth year took stock of what might be called its material position. Accordingly, it seems appropriate to try to define the new role it has assumed in the contemporary Irish cultural and social scene — or at least to supply the facts from which the reader may make his own definition.

As most people familiar with Irish sport know, the GAA in the last thirty years or so has achieved successes in the sporting world that its founders 115 years ago could not have dreamed of. Judged by the ordinary standards of the average sportsman, fortune seems to have smiled more favourably on the Association in the quarter-century ending in the mid-1970s than it had ever done before. The standards of play in the two field games which the GAA controls have remained high; as a result, attendances at Gaelic games in the early part of this period soared to levels never reached before or since. This period has also seen the rise of several new counties in Gaelic football and the return to prominence in hurling after several decades of at least two counties. Probably the two most striking examples are Down in football and Wexford in hurling.

However, to suggest that the GAA's successes since 1950 have been largely fortuitous is seriously to underrate the part played in bringing about those successes by the Association itself. The astonishing progress reflected in an annual income of over £645,000 and by an attendance of over 90,000 at one match was not achieved by accident. It was the reward of efficient administration and prudent management by the GAA's officers, both voluntary and full-time, all over the country. Many of these were men from humble walks of life who, often instead of seeking advancement in their own occupations, devoted all their spare time to work for the Association, and usually never got a single trophy or medal for doing so.

If the successes of the GAA in the past quarter-century can be attributed to any one person, that person was the Association's longest-serving General Secretary, Pádraig Ó Caoimh, who died half-way through the period as he was beginning to guide the GAA through another vital period of adjustment to new external factors. To 'Paddy O'Keeffe', as he had become affectionately known long before 1950 to thousands of officials, players and ordinary members or supporters throughout the thirty-two counties and as far away as San Francisco and Melbourne, must go much (if not most) of the credit for making the GAA the prosperous and influential organisation it is today. As chief officer of the GAA Ó Caoimh was, of course, the servant of successive central councils in carrying out the wishes of rank-and-file members expressed at annual congress. However, the permanence of his position, together with the trust reposed in him by successive officers from presidents down to club secretaries, enabled Pádraig Ó Caoimh to use to the full his exceptional administrative talents to make himself the architect of the modern GAA.

While enjoying all this good fortune the GAA was undergoing changes in both its internal structure and its external image which in the long run will probably prove to be of greater significance for the Association. The intermittent bouts of illness suffered by Ó Caoimh made it clear that an organisation of the size of the GAA could no longer be efficiently managed by one chief officer with one assistant, no matter how dedicated or energetic both might be. The adjustments necessitated by the death in the mid-1960s of the General Secretary ultimately produced a congress decision to conduct an investigation into all aspects of the Association, particularly its administrative structure. The report of the Commission which carried out this inquiry led in the early 1970s to a wide diffusion of power from the central council and to the appointment of additional staff to the head office at Croke Park — in short, to a streamlining of the GAA's administrative machine.

A development that was probably of even greater importance was the realisation by the GAA from the early 1960s that a national body whose activities impinged on the spare time of all age groups and both sexes had social obligations to the

The building of the new Hogan Stand in Croke Park in the 1950s was one of the largest construction projects undertaken by the Association to date.

The late Jim ('Tough') Barry, successful trainer of many winning Cork teams.

Mick O'Dwyer, later the famous Kerry trainer, in action at Croke Park (on right) against Dublin.

The victorious Down football team of 1960 which defeated Kerry by 2-10 to 0-8 before an attendance of almost 88,000, to bring the Sam Maguire Cup across the Border for the first time. Kevin Mussen, the Down captain, has the ball at his feet.

Mick O'Connell of Kerry goes highest against Down. In the opinion of many, O'Connell was the greatest mid-fielder in the history of football.

Midfield action in the Cork-Wexford All-Ireland hurling final of 1954, with Christy Ring (with hand outstretched) in the centre of the picture. Nick O'Donnell, reckoned by many to be the greatest full-back in hurling, is on the right. Cork won this match, their last championship victory for twelve years. Wexford, however, went on to dominate the mid 1950s, winning the next two championships with one of the most glamorous teams in the history of hurling: its central figures were the three Rackard brothers, Bobby, Billy and Nicky.

Eddie Keher was Kilkenny's outstanding forward from 1959 to the mid 1970s. He is seen here in action against Cork in an All-Ireland final.

Kerry's Seán Walsh jumps with Brian Mullins of Dublin
in the mid 1970s.

Jack O'Shea of Kerry, in the opinion of many the greatest Gaelic footballer of the modern era.

The Kerry/Dublin rivalry of the mid to late 1970s produced a series of stunning matches which confirmed the position of Gaelic football as the most popular spectator sport in Ireland

Ger Cunningham, the talented Cork goalkeeper of the 1980s, blocks an opposing forward's shot.

Hill 16 in Croke Park, full of Dublin supporters.

John Egan of Kerry retains possession in the All-Ireland football final of 1980.
The Kerry team of the late 1970s and early 1980s was arguably the
greatest in the history of the game.

Kerry 1982. This great team was going for an unprecedented five All-Ireland victories in a row, and were denied only by a goal from Offaly's Seamus Darby.

Martin Furlong, the Offaly goal-keeper, shows his delight at Seamus Darby's winning goal in the 1982 All-Ireland final.

GAA President Paddy Buggy (left) unfurls the Association's centenary year banner in 1984.

Cyril Farrell, central to the revival of Galway's hurling fortunes in the 1980s and 1990s. Galway won the Hurling championship in 1980 for the first time since 1923, and went on to win again in 1987 and 1988.

Crossmaglen, Co. Armagh: the GAA ground partly occupied by British forces for over a quarter of a century for use as a helicopter pad.

Nicholas English, the central figure in the revival of Tipperary hurling from the mid 1980s onwards. A brilliant forward, English spearheaded the Tipp revival that brought them All-Ireland success in 1989 (their first in eighteen years) and 1991.

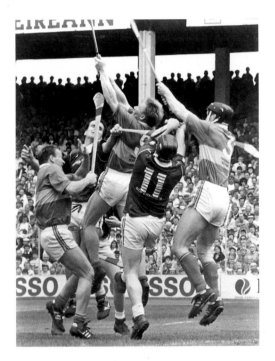

Action from the 1991 All-Ireland hurling semi-final between Galway and Tipperary.

Dublin -v- Meath 1991 in the Leinster championship was the greatest saga in the history of Gaelic football. It took four matches to separate the teams and even then Meath won by only a single point. In this photograph Tommy Carr of Dublin fields the ball while challenged by Meath's Brian Stafford.

The old Cusack Stand, built in 1937, is demolished to make way for the new Cusack stand of the 1990s.

Camogie has remained a vibrant part of the Association in modern times.

Ollie Baker 'loses' his camán in the 1997 All-Ireland hurling final against Tipperary which Clare won by 0-20 to 2-13. The revival of Clare hurling — their All-Ireland victory of 1995 was their first in eighty-one years — captured public imagination like little before it. It was central to the phenomenal revival of public interest in hurling in the 1990s.

D.J. Carey of Kilkenny, one of the great hurlers of
the modern era.

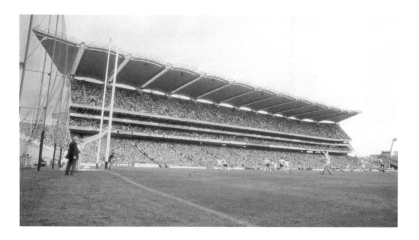

The new Cusack Stand in Croke Park during the Clare/Offaly All-Ireland
semi-final of 1998. Offaly, along with Clare and Galway, had emerged in the
1980s and 1990s to challenge the traditional hurling powers. Offaly won the
championship in 1981, 1985, 1994 and 1998.

community beyond the organisation of football and hurling for adult males. In the last few years of his life Ó Caoimh advocated the adoption of the basic concept of the parish GAA club becoming the focal point of leisure activities generally for the entire parish, young and old, male and female. Since then the Association has, especially in the 1970s, developed the idea of the social or community centre. It has also branched out into participation in a whole range of cultural activities, from the provision of normal club facilities for retired players and their families to the sponsorship of *Scór* talent contests.

Three other factors have contributed to the successes of the GAA in the period since 1950. The nationwide revival of other forms of native culture, especially traditional music and the Irish language (typified by the rise of such bodies as Gael Linn and Comhaltas Ceoltóirí Éireann), which marked the 1950s and 1960s and has since continued to flourish, spilled over into a rise in the popularity of native games. The existence of a well-organised body possessing an experienced administrative machine and adequate financial resources ensured that this greater support for Gaelic games endured. Above all, the GAA has elected to its presidency men who possessed the exceptional vision and personality required to pilot the Association safely through a period of radical change in Irish society.

From the start of this century the GAA has contributed to all forms of Irish culture, especially the language. Within the Association itself, at meetings, through its rules and in many other ways, the language is encouraged at every level. Close ties are maintained with the various bodies comprising the language movement; in some areas there is a considerable amount of dual membership. The GAA Coiste na Gaeilge has as its sole function the promotion of the language. Critics of the GAA who argue that it merely pays lip-service to the language overlook the fact that there is a limit to the contribution which a sports body can make to a cause such as the revival movement. They also ignore the very substantial material assistance that has been provided for many years by the Association to the language bodies, including in particular the proceeds from the annual Oireachtas hurling competition and the provision of Gaeltacht scholarships.

From the late 1950s onwards, as some long-accepted views came to be questioned and more conciliatory attitudes gradually took root in Irish life, doubts began to grow inside the GAA about the wisdom or necessity of continuing the prohibition on members playing or attending English field games. For the first time in twenty-five years the Ban came under attack from members of the Association, rather than from usually hostile outside critics. Partly through genuine concern for the possible divisive implications for the Association of abolishing the Ban and partly because many felt the Ban to be a fundamental principle, the anti-Ban campaign was slow to gather speed. When it did so it provoked some lively, even occasionally bitter, public debate. By the end of the 1960s, however, it was fast becoming a question, not of whether to end the Ban, but of when it would be best to do so. There was a complete absence of acrimony at its ending in 1971.

Although to many outside the GAA following the fortunes of the Association the ending of the Ban was regarded as the most significant event in the GAA for generations, most members and supporters soon forgot the whole episode. To them it was only one aspect of an evolutionary process that has been going on for many years as the Association adjusts to major changes in the society in which it operates. Above all, the quiet removal of the Ban was accepted by both sides as a triumph for the democratic system which has operated in the GAA from its earliest years. Yet among many both pro- and anti-Ban members there is a feeling of disappointment that the impact of the abolition of the Ban has not been as spectacular as opponents of the Ban had forecast. For example, no boys' school has so far displaced rugby from the dominant and usually exclusive place it occupies in many of them, a matter that is as much a reflection on the parents who patronise such schools as on those who run them.

Today the GAA enjoys a more favourable public image than ever. Some idea of the extent of its achievements in the past thirty years in the fiercely competitive world of sport may be gained simply by listing a few of the principal obstacles it has either overcome or seems at present likely to overcome. These include the intro-duction to thousands of Irish homes almost overnight of television entertainment with a substantial non-Irish element and a strong Anglo-American bias; the equally sudden elevation of soccer football to the status of a world-wide field game by tele-vision; the growing inroads being made on amateur sports by professionalism; and the problem of violence among spectators now having to be tackled by many sports bodies.

It is no accident that Jack Lynch, the politician who in his heyday scored a bigger political victory than any since the foundation of the State, owed his entry to public life to his prowess on the playing pitches of the GAA. Similarly, it is signifi-cant that the late Cardinal Ó Fiaich had to the day of his appointment as cardinal been active in the inner councils of the GAA. A number of factors have together contributed to the acquisition of a new look by the GAA, which has earned it an enviable place in the contemporary cultural and social scene. These include its new popularity with sports followers, especially many in urban areas previously slow to support Gaelic games, its demonstration that it can move with the times and adapt to new conditions without any change in fundamental principles or aims, and its part in the recent revival of native culture. Between them they enable the GAA to look forward with confidence to the early decades of what will soon be its second century of promotion of native Irish pastimes.

❖

On the playing-fields of the GAA the 1950s began, as they were to end, with the arrival of a new Ulster claimant to national football honours. Armagh's victory in the Ulster senior football final of 1950 was its first win for sixty years; although the county failed at the All-Ireland semi-final stage (but only by six points and to Mayo, then probably the best team in the country), it was to return to do much better three years later. Since then Armagh has rarely been altogether out of the reckoning in football in Ulster, the province which captured the biggest headlines in Gaelic football in the 1950s. Although it has yet to win a senior All-Ireland title, as recently as 1977 the county reached its third senior football final.

That Armagh's performance in 1950 was a creditable one is suggested by the fact that its conqueror Mayo not only went on to win the All-Ireland final that year but also retained the title in 1951. In both finals the attendances (76,000 and 78,000) were close to the record crowd of 79,000 that had watched the 1949 football final. In 1952 the same two counties that had contested that final, Cavan and Meath, had to play twice, before a combined attendance of over 125,000, before the Ulster team emerged winners of the fifth final it had contested in ten years. When in 1953 Armagh reached its second senior football final, losing narrowly to Kerry, a new record attendance of 85,000 watched. This figure was exceeded two years later when over 87,000 came to see the 1955 Dublin-Kerry final, establishing a record that was not broken until the 1960s. Kerry had contested the 1954 final too. This was won by Meath, which in the 1950s also won a National League title (1951), a junior All-Ireland football title (1952) and a minor All-Ireland football title (1957).

Several notable 'football firsts' occurred in 1956 — among them Kildare's first Leinster senior title for twenty-one years, Tyrone's first Ulster senior title and Monaghan's only All-Ireland win (junior football) in any grade of either Gaelic code. Most significant of all was the first appearance in a senior football final for fourteen years of Galway. Its defeat of Cork brought Galway its first All-Ireland win since 1938 and its first victory in four finals; it had narrowly lost those of 1940, 1941 and 1942. Although hindsight enables us now to see the 1956 win as heralding the revival of Galway football, the county had yet to lose two more finals before its most glorious era dawned in the mid-1960s.

For Cork, the loser of both the hurling and football finals of 1956, the following year was to be another poor one. The county had the misfortune in 1957 to be opposed in the football final by a formidable Louth team, whose victory was that county's first senior All-Ireland title for forty-five years. Outside of Cork Gaelic followers overlooked the possibly unique fact that this leading county in Gaelic games had now lost three consecutive All-Ireland finals. Another casualty of Louth's brilliant football in 1957 was Tyrone, which has since three times reached a senior All-Ireland final.

After Tyrone came Derry. In 1958 this Ulster county, whose only major victory had been a National Football League title won shortly after the end of World War II, captured its first Ulster title of any kind. Unfortunately it came up in the final against a talented Dublin team, which took its first senior football title in sixteen years and began a revival of Gaelic football in the capital that has lasted to this day. The following year Derry reached the final of the National League, defeating Leitrim in that county's first appearance in Croke Park. Unlike Leitrim, Derry was to return to Croke Park in the 1970s. In 1959 also, when Fermanagh won its only national Gaelic title (junior football), yet another Ulster county, Down, won its first senior provincial title. Although it then failed at the All-Ireland semi-final stage, Down was destined in the 1960s to produce the most popular and most successful football team ever to cross the Border.

The increase in popularity of Gaelic games in the 1950s is reflected in the attendance figures for some of the major games for that period. Twice in that decade, in 1953 and 1955, the attendance record for the football final was broken; on two other occasions, 1954 and 1956, the hurling final was attended by over 83,000 spectators. Provincial finals too, in particular those of Leinster and Munster, now began to draw crowds of up to and occasionally over 40,000. In addition, the annual Railway Cup games on St Patrick's Day, which have since fallen sharply in popularity, still retained their off-season attractiveness for followers of both games in the Dublin area.

In spite of all these impressive football statistics and the successes by new football counties, it was for hurling rather than for football that many followers of Gaelic games will remember the 1950s. Above all this was the period of the remark- able revival of hurling in Wexford, which before 1951 had not won the Leinster senior hurling title since the end of World War I thirty-three years before. Although losing to Tipperary in the 1951 All-Ireland final, Wexford returned in 1954. That year the final against Cork, which Wexford also lost, drew a crowd of 85,000, the largest ever to attend a hurling game.

Eventually Wexford's new hurling skills brought well-deserved rewards to what was probably one of the most powerful teams of the past thirty years. In 1955 before 73,000 spectators Wexford defeated Galway to win its first senior hurling title for forty-five years; the next year 83,000 spectators saw it retain its title by defeating Cork. Nor was this all. In 1956 Wexford added the National Hurling League title to its All-Ireland title of that year; in 1958 it won the League again. Even this was not the last that hurling followers saw of a county that has continued to add much colour and excitement to the national game. Since 1958 Wexford has added to its list of hurling successes eight more Leinster and three more All-Ireland titles. All this represents an astonishing performance by a county where, for much of the thirty-year period between 1920 and 1950, the standard of play had fallen very low.

Wexford's resurgence, which was to be sustained into the 1960s and weakened only slightly in the 1970s, has significantly affected in the past thirty years Munster's previous dominance of the hurling world — and that in spite of the rise of Waterford, which won two All-Ireland titles in that period. In the 1940s Munster won nine All-Ireland titles, Kilkenny alone in 1947 preventing a clean sweep by that province. The 1950s and 1960s, with Wexford and Kilkenny winning eight titles, saw Munster's total fall to seven and five respectively, with Leinster's rising correspondingly to three and five, a trend also discernible in National Hurling League titles. Because of Cork's dominance from the mid-1970s this trend was not maintained in the hurling championships of the 1970s.

Memories of the 1960s are still so fresh for most followers of Gaelic games that few need to be reminded that it was the period when, mainly through the achievements of Down and Galway, Gaelic football reached new high standards of play. In 1960 Down made Irish sporting history by becoming the first (and until the 1990s the only) county from north of the Border to win a senior All-Ireland title, when it defeated Kerry by double scores before nearly 88,000 people. Such was the impact of this victory that when in 1961 Down retained the title (by a single-point win over Offaly) a crowd of over 91,000 came to Croke Park, setting a record now unlikely ever to be broken because of the reconstruction at the stadium. Seven years later in the 1968 final Down repeated its 1961 win over Kerry.

The football finals of 1962 and 1963 saw two Connacht teams lose — Roscommon (in its only appearance in a senior final, before 1980, since its victories in 1943 and 1944), which lost to Kerry; and Galway, whose narrow defeat by Dublin before an attendance of 87,000 gave that county its second senior football title in six years. For Galway 1963 marked a turning-point; the county went on, with what is accepted as having been one of the most stylish teams of modern times, to win the finals of 1964, 1965 and 1966. Kerry was defeated twice and Meath once. Meath, now loser of three finals since its first win in 1949, returned in 1967 to defeat Cork, since then liable any year to challenge successfully Kerry's dominance of Munster football titles. Back also came Kerry; after being beaten by Down in 1968, it defeated Offaly in the last senior final of the '60s.

The 1960s showed the extent to which the standard of Gaelic football has been levelled upwards in the past thirty years. With a combination of good juvenile or minor material and efficient training and dedication, almost any of the thirty-two counties can now hold its own against the leading traditional football counties. Of the ten All-Ireland titles from 1961 to 1969, Down and Galway won six, with the other four going to Kerry (two), Dublin (now at last with a predominantly Dublin-born selection) and Meath. In Leinster Offaly (destined to win two All-Ireland titles in the 1970s) and Longford (which, in between losing its first Leinster final in 1965 and winning its second in 1968, took its only League title in 1966) both became serious contenders for national honours. In Ulster Donegal joined Derry as rivals to Down and Cavan, although both these counties had to wait for the 1970s for real break-throughs.

The great football teams of the past twenty years — Down, Galway and more recently Dublin, one of the most evenly balanced teams ever to play Gaelic football — have shown how the game has evolved to a degree of sophistication that would have seemed impossible ninety years ago. The contrasting styles of the past three decades vindicate the founders' case for standardisation, which has not prevented different areas from retaining their own types of play. Down's successes were the result of constant physical fitness and of adaptation of modern techniques of coaching to amateur conditions. Galway introduced new concepts of forward play, which Dublin brought a stage further with the maximum use of the palmed pass. Kerry has shown that there is still merit in the old catch-and-kick style if blended with those of Galway and Dublin, although these are probably more attractive for spectators.

If proof were needed of the extraordinary resilience of hurling, suggested in recent years by the return to prominence of Clare, Wexford and Limerick and the break-through by Offaly, it is provided by the continued popularity of the game with spectators despite the powerful counter-attractions of Gaelic football since 1960. To a large extent the competition provided by the challenge to Munster's dominance by Leinster teams has been responsible. In the sixties Wexford and Kilkenny between them won five All-Ireland titles, Munster having to rely on Tipperary for four of its five titles. Probably the best hurling of the 1960s came from Tipperary and Wexford; they met in four finals, with victory going to each twice. The last final of these four, 1968, provided one of the most astonishing recoveries ever staged in a final, when Wexford's stamina turned a seemingly impregnable lead by Tipperary into a decisive if narrow win for Wexford.

If the popularity of the games is best measured by the size of the crowds attending the major events, hurling and football reached the peak of their popularity in the '50s, particularly near the end of that decade. A precise year for this peak cannot be given, mainly because of the existence of different peaks for each game. Hurling's biggest crowds came in the early '50s ; football finals continued to draw over 80,000 into the early 1960s. However, many GAA members do not agree that the size of crowds at its main games is a barometer of the Association's success. An unknown proportion of those at an All-Ireland final go to no other game in the year; a consequence of the GAA's success in recent decades is that its principal fixtures have become partly social, as well as sporting, occasions. The attendances at provincial finals, where a higher proportion of crowds represents genuine rank-and-file support, are probably a fairer reflection of public support for the GAA.

Unfortunately, at provincial level what might be called local factors tend to influence attendances. For this reason the trend revealed by All-Ireland final and semi-final crowds is not repeated. In Munster, for example, the attendances at the football final rose steadily all through the sixties, almost certainly because of the rise of Cork as a major contender for provincial and national honours. Similarly, in both Leinster and Ulster the peaks of their provincial football attendances came in the early 1960s, probably reflecting the respective rises of Offaly and Down as potential All-Ireland winners. In all three provinces figures at provincial football finals have tended to remain above the 1950 level. Part, if not most, of the explanation for this lay in the central council's policy of not permitting live television broadcasts of these fixtures.

Hurling, on the other hand, as represented by the crowds at the provincial finals of Munster and Leinster, seems at that level to have followed the pattern of attendances at All-Ireland finals. In both provinces the biggest crowds came in the 1950s, with Leinster reaching its peak somewhat earlier, presumably because of the Wexford revival. Since then Munster hurling final figures, although rather erratic, have remained well below the peak of the 1950s. In Leinster the attendance at the provincial hurling final has dropped steadily year by year. Since the standard of Leinster hurling was higher than ever in the last twenty years, it seems in retrospect that the peak of the 1950s was caused by the enormous following of the Wexford team of that period, much of it from outside the county.

It remains to point out too — as would those who do not accept All-Ireland final figures as truly reflecting the state of Gaelic games — that the number of clubs affiliated to the GAA rose annually all through the fifties, with two minor exceptions. From 2,226 in 1950 it became 2,850 in 1960, an increase of almost thirty per cent in ten years. The percentage rise each year varied from five to one, apart from 1952 and 1959, which had slight falls.

In November 1959 the GAA was seventy-five years in existence. Its two major competitions (the inter-county championships) for that year gave obvious cause for satisfaction at the state of the Association in its Diamond Jubilee year. The football successes of Derry, which got to its first All-Ireland final in 1958, and of Leitrim, which paid its first visit to Croke Park, augured well for new counties. In Munster the hurling final attracted a record 55,000; in Ulster Down's first senior Ulster title drew a record 40,000 to Clones. The crowd of 70,000 which saw Kerry beat Dublin in the All-Ireland football semi-final was a record for the event; the 77,000 that saw Waterford defeat Kilkenny in the hurling final was a record for a replayed hurling final. Almost 74,000 had attended the drawn final, compared to 35,000 on the last occasion that a hurling final was drawn — 1934, coincidentally. In the Diamond Jubilee year of 1959 the number of affiliated clubs was 2,833, an increase of nearly forty-nine per cent on the total of 1,908 for the Golden Jubilee year of 1934.

Nothing so clearly demonstrated the ideal combination of practicality and idealism in Pádraig Ó Caoimh, who that year completed thirty years as General Secretary, as the manner in which the GAA celebrated its seventy-fifth birthday. For over two years from early 1957 building contractors had been in occupation of the west side of Croke Park. Soon the familiar outlines of the old corner stand, O'Toole's prestigious Hogan Stand of 1926 and the covered terraces known as the Long Stand had disappeared for ever. By the spring of 1959 the new Hogan Stand, a magnificent double-decker affair running along the entire west side of the stadium and free of all obstructive pillars, had been completed, increasing the seating accommodation by 16,000. Costing well over a quarter of a million pounds, this new stand strengthened Croke Park's position as the finest sports stadium in Ireland and brought the capital value of Croke Park as the main physical asset of the GAA close to the half-million-pound mark.

On 11 June 1959, in the presence of President O'Kelly, himself a former player and official with the GAA, the new Hogan Stand was formally opened by the Association's president, Dr Joe Stuart, the third Clareman to head the body founded almost seventy-five years before by a Clareman. After an historical pageant devised by the Kerry writer Bryan MacMahon, in which units of the Army participated, the attendance was entertained by an interprovincial hurling match, the postponed 1959 Railway Cup final. No more appropriate event than the opening of this vast new stand could have been chosen to mark the Diamond Jubilee of the GAA, which instead of having prolonged celebrations of its seventy-fifth birthday was already looking ahead to its centenary.

For the GAA its Diamond Jubilee year of 1959, like its Golden Jubilee year, proved in many ways to be a watershed — but of a different kind from the earlier one. For, while 1934 marked roughly the beginning of the GAA's period of financial security, 1959 marked the end of an era of more or less unbroken success and the start of a period when the Association began to change course in some vital respects. Naturally none of this was apparent in 1959 to the average member, who, as he reflected with pride and satisfaction on the enormous crowds and the thrilling games of the 1950s and admired the transformation that had overtaken his favourite sports stadium in the previous couple of years, would have listened with disbelief if anyone had correctly forecast what the sixties held for Gaelic games.

The more thoughtful member of the Association would probably have observed that Irish society had in any event been changing during the whole life of the GAA. Although this is true, it was to be equally true that both the pace and the extent of change had never been as great as they proved to be in the 1960s. After forty years of struggling with economic forces which at times seemed too strong for it, the modern Irish State suddenly began to enjoy real material prosperity. This affluent state of affairs was reflected in a slowing-down of emigration, high standards of living, better working conditions and greater opportunities for leisure. Along with growing national self-confidence went a demand for the amenities of a better life that were seen to be enjoyed across the Irish Sea; a higher standard of education produced a desire to emulate wealthier countries such as Britain in our style of life.

It soon became apparent that in the new Ireland of the sixties the GAA was in danger of being adversely affected. While emigration to Britain and the United States fell, the drift from the land did not; instead, it now began to concentrate on Irish towns and cities, where the industrial boom associated with Şean Lemass led to attractive urban employment for previously badly-paid rural workers. For the GAA this trend towards greater urbanisation presented a new problem. Always a mainly rural-based body, it found that the population was on the increase in urban areas, where the GAA was weak, and that people were leaving the rural areas, where the Association had been strong. Moreover, for various historical reasons — such as the influence of the garrison society before 1922 and the rise after 1922 of a middle-class largely apathetic to Irish games — the towns had never given the GAA the same mass support it had got from the countryside.

Nor was this all. When the austerity of the war and the years just after it ended, the motor-car came to replace the bicycle and to rival the excursion-train as the principal means of travel to Gaelic games. However, many motorists, especially those owning a car for the first time, began to go elsewhere than to GAA stadia at weekends. Among this group were many GAA supporters. In some of our towns it became apparent that some new (as well as some old) forms of sport — golf, squash, and motor-sports among them — were attracting many who would otherwise have followed or participated in Gaelic games.

Nor was it merely a question of the counter-attraction of other sports which now began to affect both the income and the membership of the GAA. With a shorter working-week becoming more widespread, many young men simply did not play any outdoor games at all. In the fifties, as television gradually came to cover the eastern half of the country, we became to a large extent a nation of spectators. In addition, a substantial section of the population, especially in the younger age-groups, began to engage in organised voluntary community and social work of various kinds — all admirable, but using time previously spent playing field games. In these and other ways new demands came to be successfully made on the spare time of many young men who were potential Gaelic players. At an older age-level many potential administrators were lost to the Association for the same reasons.

Few of these problems were, of course, peculiar to the GAA. Other field games also suffered from falling attendances. The crowd at many an average soccer match played in Dublin or any of the provincial towns concerned in the '60s was often about half that at a corresponding fixture ten years before. Athletic meetings, which in the post-war decade had drawn crowds of over 25,000 in Dublin, took place in the '60s before attendances often numbered in hundreds. One may surmise also that many of those who took to such fashionable pursuits as motor sports and beagling were drawn from those who had hitherto spent Saturday afternoons in the stands of Lansdowne Road — where they now attended in large numbers on occasions of international games only. None of this was much consolation to the GAA, which because of the scale of its activities had to face similar problems on a bigger scale on its own terraces.

Pádraig Ó Caoimh was aware of these social trends of the early '60s and foresaw the problems they would pose for the GAA. Some of his annual reports at the time contain prophetic comments. Ó Caoimh was not, however, to guide the GAA much longer. For many years he had been in indifferent health, having four major operations between 1944 and 1963. Because of his ill-health the central council took steps to lighten his work-load. Extra staff, including a young Cork teacher, Seán Ó Síocháin, was taken on at Croke Park. The two premises at Croke House close to the stadium, in one of which the Secretary lived, were sold and he moved across the city to a new residence. Then in May 1964, a few months before the completion of thirty-five years as General Secretary, Pádraig Ó Caoimh died in his mid-60s.

Combining a charming personality with administrative ability of a high order, Pádraig Ó Caoimh had served the GAA in a full-time capacity for about forty-five years of his life, embracing over half the life of the Association. Nobody more accurately summed up his achievements than Ailf Ó Muirí, who as president chaired the meeting of the central council held shortly after Ó Caoimh's death. 'He gave this Association a place in the life of the country that no other national body could aspire to . . . By his outstanding virtues, he engendered an amazing goodwill which is . . . our most important asset . . . His attitude was the criterion of all our efforts . . . He was our most competent visionary . . . our most efficient businessman'. Through the positive role which Ó Muirí himself played until the appointment three months later of Ó Caoimh's successor, the office of president assumed a new dimension which he and later presidents extended to the advantage of the GAA.

On 28 August 1964 the central council met to select a successor to Ó Caoimh; forty-four delegates attended. Of seven candidates who had originally sought the post, one had withdrawn. Among the remainder were several well-known figures in the GAA, including the Dublin footballer Kevin Heffernan and Maurice Hayes of Down, later chairman of the Community Relations Commission in Northern Ireland. Seán Ó Síocháin was a clear favourite with well over half of the council;

doubtless his experience and proven ability as an assistant to Ó Caoimh for almost twenty years were assets that all his rivals lacked.

Although it was not possible for him to hold office for anything like as long a period as his two predecessors (twenty-eight years for O'Toole and thirty-five for Ó Caoimh) Ó Síocháin, by serving fifteen years before he retired in 1979, ensured that the GAA had only three chief officers in a period of almost eighty years. Each brought distinctive qualities to the office. O'Toole was a dedicated nationalist of the Sinn Féin school with a keen perception of the GAA's role in the formative years before 1922. Ó Caoimh, while adhering firmly to the line that the GAA was much more than a sports body, put the Association on firm financial foundations for the first time. Ó Síocháin for his part played a vital role in streamlining the administrative machine of the GAA, showing outstanding skill in public relations.

In marked contrast with the post of General Secretary, that of president of the GAA has, as the following Table shows, been held by no fewer than twenty-six persons in a period of ninety-five years — or twenty-five for seventy-five years if the twenty-year term of Nowlan is excluded. Since election as president has for many years been achieved only by a man who has worked his way up from being a club delegate to his county board to being a county delegate at the central council, a biographical analysis of holders of this office (such as the Table provides) gives useful information on the regional strength of the GAA and also a fair cross-section of the background of the average member. Such a study is also worthwhile because in practice, through his relationship with both the central council and the General Secretary, each president exercises a strong influence on the management of the GAA for a period of three years.

PRESIDENTIAL TABLE

NAME	NATIVE COUNTY	TERM OF OFFICE	OCCUPATION
M. Davin	Tipperary	1884–1887	farmer
E. Bennett	Clare	1887–1888	official
P. Kelly	Galway	1889–1895	farmer
F. Dineen	Limerick	1895–1898	journalist
M. Deering	Limerick	1898–1901	representative
J. Nowlan	Kilkenny	1901–1921	tradesman
D. McCarthy	Dublin	1921–1924	representative
P. Breen	Wexford	1924–1926	teacher
W. Clifford	Limerick	1926–1928	official
S. Ryan	Tipperary	1928–1932	solicitor
S. McCarthy	Cork	1932–1935	teacher
R. O'Keeffe	Kilkenny	1935–1938	teacher
P. MacNamee	Armagh	1938–1943	teacher

PRESIDENTIAL TABLE *contd.*			
NAME	NATIVE COUNTY	TERM OF OFFICE	OCCUPATION
S. Gardiner	Clare	1943–1946	teacher
D. O'Rourke	Leitrim	1946–1949	teacher
M. Kehoe	Wexford	1949–1952	teacher
V. O'Donoghue	Galway	1952–1955	teacher
S. McFerran	Antrim	1955–1958	official
J. Stuart	Clare	1958–1961	doctor
A. Ó Broin	Wicklow	1961–1964	teacher
A. Ó Muirí	Down	1964–1967	teacher
S. Ó Riain	Tipperary	1967–1970	teacher
P. Ó Fainín	Waterford	1970–1973	official
D. Keenan	Roscommon	1973–1976	doctor
C. Ó Murchú	Cork	1976–1979	official
P. MacFlynn	Derry	1979–1982	teacher
P. Ó Bogaigh	Kilkenny	1982–1985	official
M. Loftus	Mayo	1985–1988	doctor
J. Dowling	Offaly	1988–1991	official
P. Ó Cuinn	Fermanagh	1991–1994	accountant
S. Boothman	Wicklow	1994–1997	veterinary surgeon
S. Mac Donnchadha	Galway	1997–1999	teacher

Notes
(1) In column (4) 'official' covers both an employee of central government (i.e. civil servant) and of local government (e.g. county council or health board officer), and 'representative' is what was formerly called a commercial traveller.
(2) R. O'Keeffe, D. O'Rourke, V. O'Donoghue, P. MacNamee, A. Ó Muirí and P. MacFlynn had lifelong connections with the GAA in Laois, Roscommon, Waterford, Antrim, Armagh and Down.

Munster has dominated the presidency, providing twelve of the thirty-two holders of the office, with Leinster providing another seven. The thirteen teachers reflect the leading part played in the GAA by this profession almost from the start, especially by teachers from primary schools. On the other hand, despite the important role which the clergy and the male teaching orders (principally the Irish Christian Brothers) have played in the growth of the Association for some three-quarters of a century, no priest or member of a religious order has ever been president. As the presidential duties become yearly more onerous, it remains to be seen whether this position will alter. The list of presidents also shows the strong rural bias of the GAA.

Although only two have been farmers, nearly all thirteen teacher-presidents spent the greater part of their careers in small rural schools.

Some less predictable facts also emerge from the presidential Table. For a body with so strong a rural bias it is surprising to find that eleven of the thirty-two presidents have been urban-based while holding office — Dineen, Dan McCarthy, Clifford, Sean Ryan and Stuart (Dublin), Deering, Sean McCarthy and Murphy (Cork), Nowlan, MacNamee and Fanning (Kilkenny, Belfast and Waterford). Oddly, considering the central role it has played in the Association, Dublin has produced only one president, as has Leitrim although rarely to the fore in GAA affairs. Because of his business interests and family affluence Davin was not typical of the small-farmer class that has always supported the GAA; Peter Kelly of Galway remains the only genuine farmer-president in almost a century. Less surprising is the fact that the two McCarthys were both veterans of the national movement of the 1913–1922 period.

Probably the most dramatic change that occurred in the GAA in the 1960s was the progressive decline in attendances at many of its major fixtures, a phenomenon widely attributed to the establishment of Irish television. Although Telefís Éireann (now RTE) did not commence broadcasting until the start of 1961, television was being received for several years before that in many eastern counties, especially those facing the British coast. In addition, the programmes of a regional commercial station based in Northern Ireland were receivable as far west as Sligo and as far south as Wicklow. Given the prosperity of the time and the wide hire-purchase facilities available, it was not surprising that by the mid-1960s the new native station had captured an audience of hundreds of thousands. By then it had become obvious not only that this new medium of communication and entertainment would make a much deeper impact on Irish society than had been expected before its establishment, but also that its influence would be greater than that of the press.

It was ironic that one of the results of opening a national television station under Government control was to be a falling-off in the numbers going to national games, because the GAA had played an indirect part in the setting up of what is now RTE. Three years before the foundation of Telefís Éireann the Government appointed a Commission to advise it on the proposed service, and Pádraig Ó Caoimh was made a member of this body in his capacity as chief officer of the most successful native cultural body. Participating fully in the Commission's work, Ó Caoimh signed the majority recommendations issued in 1959. He was also a signatory to an important reservation which the Government effectively accepted. Only if the new service was State-controlled rather than provided by private enterprise, Ó Caoimh argued, could the national cultural interests be adequately safeguarded.

The subsequent history of Irish television saw commercial interests greatly influencing the type of service offered to the public. In particular, the treatment of native culture by RTE has satisfied hardly any interested body. In the opinion of most such bodies it has fallen short of compliance both with statutory requirements and with repeated official promises. During RTE's early years, when Eamonn Andrews played a dominant role in its affairs, Irish culture appeared to many viewers to have lost out. Moreover, despite the appointment of Mícheál O'Hehir as first head of television sports programmes in RTE, it was many years before Gaelic games got the prominence to which most GAA members felt they were entitled.

From the beginning the GAA, while appreciating the new medium's potential in the advancement of native culture, adopted a cautious and pragmatic approach to television, as if understandably fearful of the possible effects which wholesale televising of Gaelic fixtures might have on attendances. As a gesture of goodwill it accepted in the initial stages purely nominal fees for live coverage of its events (which began in the summer of 1962), while at the same time restricting this coverage annually to the two All-Ireland finals, the two football semi-finals and the St Patrick's Day games. So far as discussion programmes were concerned, congress and central council records contain abundant evidence to support the proposition that the GAA, in the early years of Irish television, had to exert continual pressure through its chief officer and central council to obtain what it regarded as its fair share of time on the screen.

The graphs compiled by the GAA Commission in 1971, when augmented by the figures for the 1970s, afford ample evidence of the downward trend in attendances at major Gaelic fixtures that has occurred since the televising of such events began in 1962. Of ten All-Ireland hurling finals between 1952 and 1970 which drew over 70,000, seven were played before 1962. The figure exceeded 65,000 only once in the 1970s, and as recently as 1979 was under 54,000. Attendances at football finals, which had once shown signs of staying well into the 80,000s, dropped (the Commission found) to a level of around 71,000 from 1965 onwards. At football finals in the '70s the average crowd was marginally under 71,000; in 1975 and 1977 it was under 67,000. For All-Ireland football semi-finals the Commission graph shows a trend-line indicating a staggering drop of forty-six per cent in attendances in the thirteen-year period between 1958 and 1970.

The impact of television is even more striking if one examines the figures at major games not televised live, the most important of which are the provincial finals. The Commission report contains graphs for five of these — the Munster and Leinster hurling and football finals from 1957 to 1970 and the Ulster football final from 1957 to 1969. For television coverage of all these since 1962 the GAA viewer has had to be satisfied with edited films often of uneven quality and often shown not earlier than six hours after the game. For three of these five events attendances rose in the periods covered. For the Munster football final the increase was as high as seventy-five per cent; for a provincial final not included in the graphs, the Connacht football final, it was six per cent per annum, an even bigger increase. A tabulated summary by the Commission shows that attendances in the sixties at all four games televised live annually fell by average annual percentages ranging from 44 to 2, compared to falls in attendances at only two of the six major events not televised live.

The figures for the 1970s show that for the hurling final the downward trend in attendances has not yet been halted. The level of 65,000 found by the Commission for the period ending in 1970 was not maintained in the '70s. For the nine years from 1971 to 1979 the average attendance was well under 62,000. In two of those years the crowd was less than 60,000 — 1973, when abnormally wet weather occurred shortly before the match, and 1979, when a CIE dispute occurred on the morning of the final.

The position regarding attendances at recent All-Ireland football finals seems to be slightly better than for hurling finals. A level of around 71,000 found by the Commission for the 1967–1970 period was followed by an average of 70,900 for the nine-year period from 1971 to 1979. If, however, the unusually small crowds of 1975 and 1977 (when only 66,000 came to the finals) are omitted, the average rises to over 72,000. Two factors, it is suggested, led to the below-average crowd in 1977 — the participation of a county that had not yet won a senior All-Ireland title and the assumption by followers that the memorable Dublin-Kerry semi-final had made the result of the final obvious in advance. The possible recurrence of such factors, to which must be added the weather factor in the Dublin area, seems not to justify the exclusion of bad years when calculating average crowds.

If further evidence is needed of the effect of live television on major Gaelic games, it is provided by the size of the crowds at the semi-finals in which the popular Dublin football team of the '70s played. As the Commission found, the combined attendance at the two football semi-finals had fallen to 68,000 by 1968. In the nine years from 1971 to 1979, however, the average rose to over 73,000. For the years when Dublin reached the semi-final stage, the average was well over 77,000; the semi-finals of 1977 and 1979 attracted a combined attendance of over 173,000 — an average of over 86,000.

Closely associated with the impact of television on Gaelic games was the effect of live television coverage by RTE in the summer of 1966 of the World Cup soccer competition. Played in England for the first time since the series began in 1930, the competition was accompanied by a crude but effective publicity campaign of a jingoistic nature. All the main games were taken live by Irish television, which used the series to boost its advertising revenue. The English players were well known to many Irish sports followers, especially in the towns where soccer has a big armchair following. In apparent breach of its statutory obligation to 'bear constantly in mind the national aim(s) of . . . developing the national culture', RTE effectively saturated the viewing public with soccer at peak viewing times for the greater part of a month.

The television coverage of the 1966 World Cup competition proved to be a shot in the arm for Irish soccer. Although attendances generally at major Irish soccer events do not seem to have risen, the game then took root in many parts of Ireland that had never known soccer, even in the days of the British garrison. Unfortunately for the GAA this happened at a time when, following the high emigration of the '50s, many rural clubs were experiencing falls in membership and difficulty in fielding teams. However, while the rise of what might be called Irish provincial soccer added one more problem to those confronting the GAA in the sixties, the healthy state of Gaelic games fifteen years later would suggest that in the long run the competition from rural soccer has done the Association little harm.

For the majority of members of the GAA with little more than a passing interest in soccer, however, it was not for the World Cup but for an event in Irish politics that 1966 was memorable. With the retirement of Sean Lemass the former Cork hurler and dual All-Ireland medallist Jack Lynch succeeded him as Taoiseach, becoming the first Corkman to lead an Irish Government since the death forty-four years before of Michael Collins. To a much greater extent than Collins, of course, Lynch owed his successful entry into public life and his continued popularity with the electorate to his remarkable achievements in the arenas of the GAA. His rise to prominence and the esteem with which he is deservedly held by all sections of the community south of the Border are a source of pride for countless members of the GAA, who see in Jack Lynch both an epitome of the place their Association has gained in Irish society and proof of its influence generally in that society.

The year 1966 was also the golden jubilee year of the Rising of 1916. The occasion was marked by elaborate year-long celebrations sponsored by the Government, as well as by many smaller events organised voluntarily at local levels. Special coins and stamps were issued by the Government. The national television service relived the events in Dublin in Easter Week, 1916 through a lavish set of documentaries screened close to the actual anniversary. Historical pageants were staged in many places, the GAA's principal one in Croke Park (where the main official one was also held) being one of the most spectacular.

The Golden Jubilee celebrations of 1966 led to a good deal of public debate on the country's current and probable future political and social attitudes. A general feeling of national self-confidence was generated by the knowledge that, despite the partitioning of the island, the Republic had surmounted major political and economic obstacles and had also gained wide acceptance internationally as a viable entity.

Holding its own in the growing community of nations necessitated a certain amount of adaptation to external conditions, a process which led to a questioning of some long-held attitudes at home. This tendency was quickened by the spread of education and was also influenced by the picture of life in the neighbouring island depicted on television. Young people in particular began to react against what they regarded as the conservative attitudes of the community. Even an organisation like the GAA soon discovered that it was not immune to this widespread questioning of traditional stances. A campaign to abolish the rules embodying the Ban began to attract wider support than before.

Most people who have the interests of the Association at heart would probably agree that the time has not yet come to assess in detail the movement in the 1960s to abolish the Ban. Until the episode recedes further into the past it would seem prudent not to risk rekindling the heat which the anti-Ban campaign occasionally caused inside the GAA. There were, in any event, so many facets to the movement that the most a person who sat through it from a side-line seat can probably do now is to record what seem to him to have been the salient facts, occasionally adding comment or interpretation that is necessarily subjective and probably far from definitive.

The first shots in the campaign to drop what had become Rule 27 of the GAA Official Guide (which imposed automatic suspension on a member playing, attending or promoting rugby, soccer, hockey or cricket) had been fired as far back as 1959 by the Dublin board, when a motion was sponsored by the Civil Service Club seeking a comprehensive investigation into the rule under the authority of the next congress. Because of a congress decision of the 1920s to limit discussion of such a rule to every third year, this motion could not get on to a congress agenda until 1962. By then the Ban had been discussed to a greater, if still limited, extent both inside and outside the GAA, and no fewer than four motions relating to it (one each from the Armagh and Carlow boards and two from Dublin) came before the 1962 congress.

Although differing widely in their terms, all four motions were decisively rejected. Lost by majorities so big that they were not even formally recorded in the minutes were the Carlow motion calling for a simple deletion of Rule 27, the Armagh motion asking for its strict enforcement and a Dublin motion requiring any proposal affecting Rule 27 to be decided by a secret ballot. On the most important motion, which embodied substantially the same call for an investigation of the rule which the Civil Service club had sponsored in 1959 at the Dublin convention, the voting was 180 for and 40 against. If any conclusion could be drawn from this treatment of the Ban by the governing body of the GAA, it is that the move to revoke Rule 27 still had little grass-roots support.

Far from being discouraged by this almost unanimous support for the Ban, some of those strongly in favour of its abolition now set about trying to ensure a more favourable reception for their ideas at the 1965 congress. The most prominent of these anti-Ban campaigners was Tom Woulfe of the Civil Service club in Dublin, who became the anti-Ban spokesman of the Dublin board. In 1964, despite a decision to exclude Rule 27 from the deliberations of a Dublin board committee charged with examining the state of the GAA in Dublin, Woulfe submitted (and gained publication of) a detailed statement of his case for the abolition of the Ban. Working closely with Woulfe but remaining in the background was the former Mayo footballer Eamonn Mongey, then a widely-read part-time columnist on Gaelic games in the *Sunday Press*.

Woulfe, a civil servant from Kerry who for many years had been an officer of the official Adoption Board set up in the early '50s , was able to establish a network of supporters through his official trips outside Dublin. Soon he and Mongey had a number of provincial associates, through whom the anti-Ban campaign was kept alive by methods such as publication of letters in the newspapers. Between them Woulfe and Mongey succeeded in creating the impression that (at a time when the average Dublin GAA supporter was apathetic on the topic) there was a widespread agitation outside Dublin to end the Ban.

The congress of 1965 produced no change on the Ban and offered little hope to the Dublin board of success in the near future. A straightforward motion sponsored by Dublin and calling for the deletion of Rule 27 was lost by 230 votes to 52. A less direct approach put forward jointly by Longford, Derry and Mayo, calling for the appointment by the central council of a special committee to ascertain if, 'having regard to the wishes of the individual members of the Association', abolition or modification of Rule 27 was advisable or desirable, was ruled out of order on a technical ground. In the light of the massive rejection of the Dublin proposal, this triple motion hardly had much chance of success. The mood of the congress on the Ban seems to have been set at the start when discussion of the new General Secretary's first report led to some sharp exchanges on the Ban.

Between the congresses of 1965 and 1968 prominent supporters of the Ban took the initiative with the publication in 1967 of a book by Brendán MacLua entitled *The Steadfast Rule*. MacLua, a member of the Croke Park staff and a talented journalist, traced the history of the Ban principle and rule from the start of the GAA in a carefully researched and trenchant, if at times partisan and even emotive, study. Although not published or sponsored by the Association, the book contained a sympathetic foreword by the president and acknowledgement of assistance from other leading supporters of Rule 27.

Although this was not generally realised at the time even by those in close touch with affairs in the GAA, the 1968 congress marked the beginning of the end of the Ban. Once again motions calling for a clearcut decision failed — one each from Dublin and Galway seeking the deletion of Rule 27 (lost by 220 votes to 88), and another from Louth which would have allowed members to attend, but not to play, the banned games. This time, however, a Mayo motion(similar to others in the names of Louth and Limerick), directing the setting up by the central council of a special committee to make the case for the retention of Rule 27, with a directive to publish a report inside three years, was passed following a well-reasoned and balanced plea from Father Leo Morahan of the sponsoring board.

As debate on the future of the Ban continued both inside and outside the GAA, the central council proceeded to carry out the assignment in the Mayo proposal. A six-member committee set up in December 1968 for this purpose included among its personnel Tom Loftus of Dublin and Peadar Kearney of Louth, presumably to put the case against the rule as their counties had indicated a desire for a change. The others were the president, Séamus Ryan, the most recent past president Ailf Ó Muirí of Armagh, Pat Fanning of Waterford (destined to succeed Ryan) and the veteran Monsignor Hamilton of Clare, all staunch advocates of the Ban. Since the monsignor died during the first quarter of the committee's life and was not replaced, opponents of Rule 27 were for most of the committee's life generously represented on this body which was to have a strong influence on the next congress.

Towards the end of 1970 this committee issued a detailed statement of over 3,000 words on the Ban. Not content with merely listing the reasons for retaining Rule 27, it also gave a brief sketch of the historical background to the Ban and then set out in detail (amounting to one-third of the document) the main arguments adduced for and against Rule 27. There followed then what the committee believed to be the principal reasons, divided into practical and idealistic, for retaining the Ban. Finally, after listing some of those changes in Irish society in the previous two decades which were generally regarded as relevant to the Ban, it ended on what might be called a cautiously neutral note by declining to recommend any change in Rule 27.

That this report effectively argued to keep the Ban is undeniable; the Mayo motion precluded it from taking an anti-Ban line. Equally undeniable is the fact that it provided, from an authoritative source inside the GAA rather than from an outside critic, the rank-and-file member with all the pros and cons of the Ban debate. By the time the report was published an important move had been made to ascertain the views on Rule 27 of the average member. At the 1970 congress (held in Galway) a Meath motion had been passed unanimously, requiring a special meeting of each club to be called to decide its attitude on the rule in time for the 1971 congress. From late autumn 1970 onwards these meetings were held all over the country; by the end of the year a substantial majority of clubs had come out in favour of ending the Ban. Nor was this all. When early in 1971 all county conventions had been held it was found that thirty counties had decided to support any congress move to delete Rule 27, with only two (Antrim and Sligo) pledged to retain the Ban.

Clearly, therefore, at the forthcoming congress in April 1971 the Ban would be lifted after sixty years. To the central council and other leading members it was also clear that the prospect of a Ban-less GAA was regarded with some alarm by many still influential members, some of them survivors of the pre-1922 period. To such members a total unqualified abolition of the Ban would be a betrayal of the ideals of the early GAA, and an admission that in future it was solely a sports body and no longer aspired to the national cultural aims it had supported for eighty-five years.

To cater for this view, now admittedly held by only a minority in the Association, while at the same time implementing the democratically reached decision of the majority of members, was the daunting task now facing the president, Pat Fanning. For this purpose he drew up a set of proposals to put to congress simultaneously with the motion for the abolition of Rule 27. So as to achieve the maximum impact at the congress information on the presidential formula was not communicated in advance to either the pro-Ban or anti-Ban group.

When on 11 April 1971 the delegates who had assembled in Queen's University, Belfast, for what was to prove a historic GAA congress began consideration of the motions on their agenda, the president skilfully but frankly unfolded his plans in a memorable speech. What they needed now was, he argued forcibly, a new charter reasserting the loyalty of the GAA, despite the ending of the Ban, to national culture, ensuring the use of the Association's resources and property for its own purposes only and clearly defining for the first time membership of the GAA. He proposed to appoint a small committee of leading members to draft this charter without delay, for submission to a special congress to be held inside two months. For himself, he promised as a matter of personal honour that no attempt would be made to frustrate the decision of members to revoke Rule 27.

Fanning's carefully constructed 'package' was at once recognised as a magnanimous gesture on the part of a man who all his life had been one of the Ban's staunchest supporters. It was unanimously accepted. It earned him a standing ovation from congress led by the anti-Ban lobby, won him the admiration of countless members of the GAA who had been fearful of the possible effects of an acrimonious division of opinion on Rule 27, and ensured a quiet and dignified death for the Ban. Fanning's realistic reaction to the club referendum on Rule 27 safely defused what might otherwise have proved an occasion for bitter recrimination between delegates. It signalled the acceptance by the older generation of the nationwide vote on the Ban, in the light of Fanning's guarantees about the continued support to be given by the GAA to native culture.

Within three days Fanning appointed a nine-man committee to draw up the new charter. In May a special congress, held in Dublin and attended by 200 delegates, took less than two hours to approve of the thirteen revised rules constituting the new charter recommended by the committee. Under the new Rule 1 the basic aim of the GAA is defined as 'the strengthening of the national identity in a 32-county Ireland through the preservation and promotion of Gaelic games and pastimes'. The property of the Association is also protected by the same rule, which stipulates that its resources are to be used solely for the previously-defined aims. Professionalism of any kind, including full-time training, is banned by the new Rule 6.

Because the Ban had been a source of controversy in the GAA for nearly half-a-century, it is easy now with hindsight to see that its deletion, as soon after 1923 as an opportunity arose, would have been wise. However, considering both its relative importance and how few of the major predictions made about the effects of ending it have proved correct, far too much time and energy were spent on the campaign of the '60s to revoke the rule. Because its opponents were initially a small group, and because its supporters regarded the Ban as a vital brick in the edifice of the GAA, a confrontation gradually developed between men who should have been united in furtherance of the aims of their Association.

As the social changes in Irish society took effect in the '60s supporters of the Ban gradually found themselves forced into a defensive position. A rule that for years had been regarded as unalterable was now, they came to realise, defensible largely (if not solely) on broad principles or idealistic grounds. Neither argument stood up as well in the 1960s as it had in the 1920s or 1930s. Moreover, much of the theoretical case for the Ban had been eroded by practice; in some places Rule 27 had become almost obsolete. Neither side to the controversy expected public opinion to turn so decisively against the Ban from 1966 onwards. This swing was probably largely caused by the younger members of the GAA.

Much discussion took place during the Ban debate on the views of the founders of the GAA on the principles embodied in the Ban. Since most of this argument was hypothetical, it was largely futile and probably played little part in swaying younger members. To many of them what probably had a greater influence on their decision to support abolition of the Ban was the knowledge that some well-known figures in the GAA itself, as well as several popular public figures unquestionably sympathetic to the Association, all favoured ending the Ban.

Fanning's presidency was notable also for other achievements. During his term the GAA held a unique youth congress; the youth hurling festival Féile na nGael was inaugurated in Thurles; the popular annual Scór competition was begun; advertising sponsorship was approved by the central council. Fanning himself would be the first to concede that much of what happened while he was president (1970–1973) was the completion of work begun by one or other of his predecessors as president in the '60s.

Rule 27 was not by any means the only topic on which, in the opinion of many members of the GAA, too much time has been spent by the Association in the past thirty years. During that period, under two General Secretaries and at least half-a-dozen presidents, almost continuous negotiations have been conducted by the central council in an effort to establish permanently harmonious relations with the GAA in the United States, which is dominated by the New York board. Yet, notwithstanding the present period of comparative calm, the only result has been a series of recurrent crises, erupting in clashes of personalities, broken agreements, cancellation of visits by teams or officials from one side or the other, and the replacement of one competition by yet another.

For the purpose of this survey the story begins with the playing in New York in 1947 of that year's All-Ireland football final, a unique experiment that was not to be repeated. It was followed by the central council's refusal to accede to the New York's board's request to stage the 1949 hurling final in that city. Mainly through the mediation of Monsignor Hamilton protracted discussions were held to try to reach agreement on regular contacts on the playing-field. In 1950 congress sanctioned an arrangement to admit the American champion state to the home National League series, the final to be played in alternate years in Dublin and New York.

Within a year difficulties had arisen. For most of the 1950s relations between New York and the parent body remained in a state of uncertainty. For a while the St Brendan Cup series inaugurated in 1954 seemed to hold promise of a new period of co-operation between the two Croke Parks. Inside two years trouble broke out again, when New York began to issue invitations to individual county teams. In 1957 the central council recommended strict adherence to the programme it had fixed; another agreement with New York was made after the 1958 congress. Pádraig Ó Caoimh in 1961 suggested that efforts be made to expand activities in other states. New York's refusal to agree led to its non-affiliation in 1962; by the mid-'60s agreement had again been reached to play some league finals in New York.

The '70s saw a new departure in the form of tours of the west coast, with the All Stars series in San Francisco replacing the earlier tours based on New York. Events in that city in 1970 marked a turning-point. After an assault on a referee during the hurling league final the central council severed all contacts with New York for a year. Most GAA officials agree that contact ought to be maintained with emigrants catering for Irish games, if such activities do not divert the GAA from its primary object of promoting the games at home. There is, however, a widespread feeling that matches against Irish-American teams do not increase support for the games in the long run and that their influence on Irish-Americans is negligible. Against the gains must be put the dislocation of home competitions and the inordinate amount of time spent by GAA officers on such tours.

The acrimony at administrative level associated with GAA trips to the United States by home teams and visits here by American selections has been absent from two other international contacts of recent years. In 1967 and 1978 teams from Australia had enjoyable contests in this country with GAA selections, despite major differences between Australian-rules football and Gaelic. On several occasions in the '70s visiting teams from Scotland belonging to the shinty code, the Scots version of hurling, have had little difficulty in adapting to the rules of the Irish game. The visits from these two countries have been returned by the GAA, notably by the successful 1968 Australian tour by the 1967 football champions Meath.

Probably the most significant change in GAA policy in modern times has been the adoption and extension of a new social role in the community since the mid-sixties. Possibly prompted by the high rates of emigration in the 1950s and the consequent loss of social amenities in many rural areas, Pádraig Ó Caoimh in the early sixties urged the Association to take a greater part in the life of the community by making the local GAA club the focal point in the social life of rural parishes. On several occasions in his last few years as General Secretary he emphasised the need for the GAA to adapt to the needs of a changing Irish society and to meet the challenge of a growing trend towards urbanisation. With characteristic accuracy he also foresaw the possibility that, as it concentrated on providing more services for players and spectators, the GAA would in the future make less spectacular advances.

In the period after Ó Caoimh's death in 1964 these ideas were developed by his successor Seán Ó Síocháin and by Ailf Ó Muirí while president. In retrospect now it seems likely that Ó Muirí's enthusiasm for the GAA community centre was crucial to its success. In the North where he lived two communities exist that never mix socially; participation in social activities by the GAA, as the best organised and most affluent nationalist voluntary body, must have seemed logical. North of the Border there has always been a greater degree of co-operation between bodies promoting native culture than has been the case in the Republic. Ó Muirí, through the success of the social centre managed by his own Lurgan club, Clann Eireann, could demonstrate a prototype of a GAA community centre that could serve as a model for others on both sides of the Border.

By 1968 the idea of the social centre was firmly established. That year the central council introduced a new system of grants, additional to those normally available for the purchase or development of grounds or the erection of dressing-rooms, of up to twenty per cent of the cost to clubs providing premises suitable for use as a centre. In 1969 a Community Centre Committee appointed by the council was given the task of advising clubs on types of centres suitable for particular areas and providing information such as plans of existing centres. In 1970, largely under the influence of Séamus Ó Riain, the present Club Development Scheme was begun to provide finance for new social centres. The board of trustees which administers this scheme considers clubs' applications for loans and raises the capital needed to fund the scheme. The scheme's initial target of £250,000 was reached in a year.

Essentially a GAA social centre is a social club directly linked to a particular GAA club, which usually controls and manages it. The centres provide amenities for players and members, their families (irrespective of age or sex) and retired players. Many also run other games such as tennis, boxing and indoor recreations. In some towns and cities the amenities provided by such centres have attracted teenage boys to Gaelic games. The Association had given a lead to other sports bodies over fifty years earlier when it established minor All-Ireland championships in both codes. As an indication of how far the GAA is prepared to go today to meet contemporary leisure demands, about half of the 140 or so social centres now in existence operate a bar.

The GAA's policy on community centres was one of several aspects of Association activities which received powerful approval in the report of the Commission on the GAA, a body whose impact on the life of the Association is likely to prove far more lasting than that of the spread of television or the ending of the Ban. This report is the result of a comprehensive in-depth investigation of every major feature of the GAA by a nineteen-member group of prominent members and supporters. Published in December 1971, it represents the most exhaustive self-analysis by a voluntary organisation ever undertaken in this country and has led to a radical over-haul of the GAA's administrative machine. A year after its publication the report was the subject of a special congress held over four days in early December 1972 and early January 1973. Attended by an average of 245 delegates, this congress authorised all the major steps recommended by the Commission to restructure the GAA, including the adoption of a new rule establishing the central council as the supreme governing body between congresses.

It was an Antrim motion at the 1969 congress that led the central council later that year to appoint a Commission to investigate the GAA's affairs under eight head-ings — structure, finance, youth, grounds, communications, hurling, discipline and sponsorship. This motion, like that from Cork at the same congress which led to the *Scór* competition, originated with an individual club; each exemplifies the potential influence on the Association of a single club. Chaired by the former president Pádraig MacNamee, the nineteen-member Commission included prominent members and supporters; Maurice Prendeville of Dublin was instrumental in draft-ing the report. So as to ensure the independence of the Commission about half of its members were from outside the GAA. It included leading figures in both the public and private sectors of industry.

Between August 1969 and autumn of 1971, when compilation of its report began, the GAA Commission met on sixty-three days. In addition 23 sub-committee meetings were held and no fewer than twenty-eight visits were paid by individual

Commission members to county board meetings. Discussions were held with twenty-six persons, including prominent members, supporters and journalists. Written submissions or information were received from eighteen persons (nine of whom gave oral evidence) and seven bodies, including three representatives of national youth organisations. Seven GAA community centres were visited and a GAA coaching workshop was attended. The Commission was also responsible for a survey of head office at Croke Park conducted by a firm of management consultants and for a pilot survey in schools on pupils' attitudes to games carried out by the Economic and Social Research Institute.

When its report appeared before Christmas 1971 the thoroughness of the Commission's investigation was immediately evident. The 60,000-word document ran to over 140 pages. There were also eight appendices covering such topics as officers' duties, committee procedure and publicity. Scattered through the report were many graphs and a mass of statistics. The report was accepted as a blueprint for the GAA of the '70s and '80s and was serialised by a national paper. Realistically it discussed various factors believed to be impeding progress, and devised a scheme for restructuring the GAA to enable it to meet the challenges it would have to face for the rest of the century. The Association's weaknesses were analysed, and the extent to which new techniques could advance the GAA's interests were considered.

The most far-reaching changes suggested by the Commission concerned the administrative structure of the GAA. Future central councils should, the report suggested, meet only quarterly and have a mainly over-seeing function. Between congresses the Association's affairs should be handled by a Management Committee answerable to the council. The programme of games and other events should be taken over by a new Activities Committee; the general development of the Association should be controlled by a Central Development Committee working to the Management Committee. To emphasise his enhanced status in a re-structured GAA the General Secretary should in future be known as the Director General. He should be supported by a management accountant (actually appointed by the time the report appeared), an Activities Officer, a Central Development Officer and a Public Relations Officer.

The longest chapter in the Commission's report dealt with the vital subject of communications. Among the topics investigated were the improvement of contacts with the press, the coverage of Gaelic games on television, the feasibility of producing films on coaching, the future of the *Our Games* annual, and the publication of year-books and of youth magazines. Surprisingly, in view of later developments in this field, sponsorship received only three pages in the entire report; it produced the only reservation. Tomás Roseingrave of Muintir na Tíre disapproved of sponsorship by cigarette manufacturers of an athletic body like the GAA, a view which has since found wide support throughout the Association.

A surprising omission from the report was an examination of Gaelic games in higher bodies of education. This was soon rectified. In 1972 the central council set up a committee under Aodh Ó Broin, a former president, which in a comprehensive report in 1973 recommended the establishment of a Higher Education Council. Since 1968 Comhairle na nOllscoil had been operating in this sphere. It had become clear that, with the increasing number of players attending new third-level institutions like regional or technological colleges, an expanded council was needed. Since 1974 the new Comhairle Árd-Oideachais has been responsible for significantly extending the range of competitions available for such students, whose support as potential leaders in the community is important to the GAA.

Since then another and equally significant extension to the range of GAA competitions has occurred. For some years before 1975 inter-factory games had been played on a largely unorganised basis. That year the president Dr Donal Keenan called a meeting of those managing such games. The result was the establishment on a formal basis of the Inter-Firms' Association, with its own constitution and holding its own annual convention. By 1980, 470 firms (some with more than one team) in twenty-five counties were taking part in a competition that has added a new dimension to GAA involvement in community activities. Not merely commercial concerns but also particular occupations, including teachers, Gardai and farmers, are now participating.

On grounds the Commission had little new to say. A comprehensive record and a valuation of each stadium, and a more effective system of control to safeguard the Association's interests, were recommended. Future expenditure should aim at improving existing grounds; every main county ground should have covered accommodation and a first-aid room. The absence of new ideas was a recognition of the soundness of GAA policy. Nowhere have the Association's long-term interests been better served by its leading officers for over fifty years than in their enlightened approach to grounds. As far back as O'Toole's period cordial relations were established with the Land Commission; at the division of estates provision was often made for a GAA pitch, which later became Association property. From the early '30s surplus funds of the central and provincial councils were given as grants to grounds, big and small. As a factor in the GAA's growth this policy of ground acquisition was not negligible.

Although in the '30s and '40s grants, even to larger grounds, were often few and far between, the balance sheets of the councils from the late '40s show that cumulatively these early grants were not insignificant. By 1947 the Leinster council had almost £27,000 invested in twelve major grounds; by the end of 1955 the figure had grown to £79,000 and by 1960 to £140,000. For the Munster council the corresponding totals for 1950 and 1960 were £26,000 and £84,000. The importance attached by the GAA to owning its own grounds is shown by the increase in the number owned from sixteen in 1929 (the year Ó Caoimh became Secretary) to 204 in 1950.

Four major grounds outside Dublin — Casement Park, Belfast, Nowlan Park, Kilkenny and the stadia at Limerick and Thurles — were selected for major development by a special Grounds Committee set up by the central council in 1963. Subsequently a further scheme, Grounds Plan 2, divided the whole country into forty units, each to be eligible for an annual grant from central council funds if it had its own grounds committee and a plan for developing the grounds in its area. By the late 1970s a global loan and grant scheme was being administered by Bórd na bPáirceanna for the benefit of club, county and provincial grounds. In 1979 clubs alone received almost £116,000 in grants, while county grounds received grants exceeding £64,000, bringing the total expenditure to the end of that year on this type of grant to almost £650,000.

As both the Association's main stadium and its headquarters, Croke Park is obviously the GAA's main physical asset. The central council balance sheet for 1979 showed that by the end of that year almost £540,000 had been spent on the ground, which sixty-four years before had been bought by the GAA for £3,500. After World War II the first major work at Croke Park, the development in 1950 and 1951 of the canal terrace, cost close on £75,000. By the mid-1950s the structures were valued at £200,000. By 1960, with the completion of the new Hogan Stand scheme at a cost of £264,000, the stadium was valued by the Association's auditors at almost £470,000.

Expenditure of such enormous proportions by a voluntary and non-commercial body like the GAA is possible only if it has financial resources which, if not actually matching the capital expenditure, at least approach it in magnitude. Fortunately, while frequently having to resort to bank overdrafts in the period, the central council's income has grown at an astonishing rate in the past twenty-five years or so. Despite being largely dependent on receipts from major games, which are sub-ject to fluctuating attendances if the weather is unkind or the standard of play regarded by potential spectators as inadequate, all the major components of the GAA's financial position have increased steadily and almost without interruption since 1950. In addition, of course, some new sources of income not dependent on the weather or the public have been found, the principal one being the fees charged for the advertisements now erected at all the major stadia.

In 1950 the assets of the central council, consisting almost entirely of its property at Croke Park, totalled £178,000. Its income for 1949–1950 was under £38,000 and it made in that year a modest surplus of £15,500 on the events under its control. Within two years the council's assets exceeded £200,000; by 1957 they had passed the £300,000 mark; in 1960 they totalled £400,000. Almost twenty years later, and after a half-decade of inflation, the assets of the central council had almost quadrupled; in the 1979 balance sheet they were valued at over £2,000,000.

In 1952–1953 the central council's income exceeded £50,000 for the first time. It was to do so in only two other years in the '50s; in five years of that decade it fell. Surplus of income over expenditure also fluctuated in the '50s. From £11,000 in 1951 it rose to £28,000 in 1956. By the end of the decade it had fallen to £20,000; the annual average surplus for the '50s was under that figure. During the 1960s central council income rose steeply. For 1960 itself it almost doubled, from £45,000 in 1959 to over £88,000. By the end of the '60s it had exceeded £100,000 on three occasions. The annual surplus fell in the '60s because of the greatly increased range and scale of activities. From £56,000 in 1960 it fell to £23,000 in 1966; it was down to £12,500 at the end of the decade.

In the 1970s annual surpluses fluctuated even more; in 1975 the central council had a deficit of over £7,000. The year 1970 itself brought a surplus of over £50,000, the highest for ten years. The exceptional year of 1975 was followed by surpluses of as much as £42,000 in 1976 but of only £13,000 in 1977. In 1979 gross income, including gate receipts of over £526,000, exceeded £645,000. Expenditure for that year totalled £548,000, leaving a surplus just short of £100,000.

The 1970s brought plenty of exciting and excellent games, with football pushing hurling somewhat into the background. After its narrow defeat by Kerry (champions again in 1970) Offaly won its first senior All-Ireland title in 1971 by defeating Galway, and joined the major football counties with a decisive win in 1972 over Kerry in a memorable replay. From then on the '70s were dominated by the popular Dublin team (winners in 1974, 1976 and 1977) and by Kerry, conqueror of Dublin in 1975, 1978 and 1979. The '70s also brought new provincial champions and two notable revivals. In Ulster Donegal won its first senior title in 1972, regaining it in 1974; Monaghan won its first senior title for thirty-eight years in 1979. In Connacht the standard of football improved through the return of Roscommon (provincial winners four times) and through Sligo's first title in forty-seven years in 1975.

In hurling the seventies saw the return to prominence of two counties that had not figured in All-Ireland finals for decades. Limerick's defeat of Cork in the Munster hurling semi-final of 1971, its first such win in thirty-one years, and its success in the National Hurling League of that year, its first in twenty-four years, showed that the county was back as a major force. The next year it lost to Clare; but in 1973, after losing the League final to Wexford, Limerick won its first Munster senior hurling title in eighteen years and its first senior All-Ireland title in thirty-three years. Although championship success had not yet attended Clare's revival, the county amply compensated in recent National Hurling Leagues.

The period from 1964 to 1970 saw the first major concerted effort on a 32-county scale since the foundation of the GAA to expand the area where hurling of a standard comparable to that of the leading counties is played. The extension of hurling to every parish in Ireland by 1984, centenary year, was the objective of the Twenty-Year Hurling Scheme prepared in 1964. Originally the scheme was divided into four five-year periods. Between 1964 and 1969 each county was to set up a hurling committee to implement the scheme. A central hurling committee would administer grants and ensure supplies of hurleys. Counties were to be graded, hurleys to be distributed in bulk, annual coaching courses to be organised and a special fund to be built up by a levy on certain matches.

The specific aim of the 1965–1969 plan, participation by 1969 of all thirty–two counties in the minor championship, was achieved. Nearly 200,000 juvenile hurleys were supplied during the life of this plan. To try to promote weak counties to the average sector and average ones to the strong sector a novel scheme of county adoption was devised, involving visits and demonstrations by counties in one group to those in a lower group. Understandably for such an ambitious project there were some failures. Progress tended to be uneven; for some years an acute shortage of adult hurleys was encountered. In general the results suggested that what the Rackard brothers had done for Wexford in the 1950s would not easily be repeated elsewhere except over a much longer period and through exceptionally persistent dedication.

In the '70s, and especially since the end of Fanning's presidency in 1973, plans for a hurling revival had to give priority to more urgent problems. The MacNamee Commission suggested a need to devise new tactics to suit the altered circumstances. Recent reports of the Central Hurling Committee reveal an apparent switch to simultaneous action on a number of fronts, including the promotion of synthetic hurleys and the use of lighter balls for juveniles. Meanwhile Féile na nGael, the annual juvenile hurling festival devised in 1971 by Séamus Ó Riain, continues to be an outstanding success. As centenary year approaches one detects evidence of a more realistic approach. In his 1978 annual report the Director General described the aim for 1984 as the restoration of hurling to 'a position of security and of acceptable standard in all four provinces'.

The political turmoil north of the Border in the past thirty years has understandably affected the GAA. The spread of civil unrest from 1968 and the subsequent violence naturally made life more difficult for the Association. Not only did it suffer from the periodic disruption of normal life; its members were among those harassed by a partisan police force, pursued by a biased legal machine and imprisoned without trial. Since the fall of Stormont in 1972 the GAA has received special attention from the British forces which, with the approval of their Government, have occupied and damaged GAA property in several places, notably the GAA grounds at Crossmaglen in Co. Armagh, recently evacuated after twenty-seven years. Repeated protests, including a meeting in London in 1971 between the GAA chief officers and a member of the British Government, have not reduced the provocation offered to a body whose only offence in British eyes can be its advocacy of a united Ireland.

When funds to relieve distress in Northern Ireland were badly needed the GAA south of the Border acted speedily and effectively. As early as 1972 the central council had collected and distributed £80,000 for this purpose. When ultimately harmony is restored between the two communities in the North the GAA may face a new problem there. With the vital necessity to build bridges between the opposing cultures, the Association may anticipate pressure for a contribution towards the strengthening of that harmony from a body with such potential for good community relations.

The GAA's achievements in the past century give ground for expecting even greater ones in the future. It arrested an important aspect of the peaceful pene-tration of Ireland by English culture and began the cultural revival which led to the political revolution of the 1913–1922 period, in which it played a major role. It saved the principal native games from extinction. It brought Irish athletics under native and democratic control. It was responsible for the Olympic successes of Irish-men in the 1906–1924 period. It changed for the good social life in rural Ireland and helped to blur divisive class distinctions, as well as teaching useful qualities like teamwork, discipline and even democratic practice. In the words of Conor Cruise O'Brien 'it organised . . . the replacement, among the young . . . of the country, of what had been a servile spirit by a spirit of manliness and freedom'.[1] Above all, it instilled a feeling of pride in things Irish and in native culture.

That the GAA has had its setbacks and still has its weaknesses is undeniable. It has so far failed to get hurling to take root outside a handful of counties. Except for a brief period in its infancy, it has not succeeded in winning Protestant support on either side of the Border. Crucial to the GAA's future is the problem of its growth in our increasingly urbanised society. While rural Ireland still gives its principal sporting loyalty to the GAA, in the towns and cities the position is different. Almost eighty years after the foundation of an Irish State partly based on the rejection of an alien culture, a substantial proportion of our urban community still spends much of its leisure time playing or following field games of that culture. As with other forms of native culture, a conscious change of community attitudes is required.

Chapter 9

1980–1999: GAMES

These final two chapters of a book first published in 1980 attempt to bring the story of the GAA to the brink of the new millennium, that is to say, to bring it up to date by covering the period of some two decades since 1980. Although it is arguable that the most important events in GAA history since then — particularly in the 1990s — have happened off the playing-field, it is on events occurring on GAA playing-fields that this chapter will concentrate. After all, since the GAA is first and foremost a sports body, it is to the Association's playing-fields that one turns first for an overview of the GAA in a period as long as twenty years. In any case, events in the history of the Association happening elsewhere are clearly connected with its games; to give an obvious example, it is unlikely that the major development of Croke Park in recent years would have been undertaken at all if attendances at big games had been falling off. What might loosely be called events in the GAA's council chambers since 1980, that is, the administrative history of the GAA, will be covered in the final chapter.

The GAA's principal competition, the All-Ireland senior football championship, continues to be by far the most popular adult spectator sport on this island, although in recent years, and especially since the new format of the hurling championship introduced in 1997, the national game of hurling is fast catching up if one is to judge from attendances at All-Ireland hurling semi-finals and finals. Indeed, a stage has now been reached when the gap between the attendances at the two finals is often less than 1,000 out of some 65,000 attending each game. The role of television, as well of course as the new format (just mentioned) of the last three stages of the hurling championship have, it will later be suggested, had a lot to do with the increased popularity of hurling reflected in the bigger crowds.

In the twenty-year period from 1980 to 1999, twenty-two football finals were played, those for 1988 and 1996 going to replays. Three salient points emerge from an analysis of the list of winners of, and contestants for, the Sam Maguire Cup. These are the continued dominance well into the 1980s of Kerry football, its eclipse in the early 1990s by Ulster football and, with the solitary exception of Galway in

1998, the failure of any Connacht county to bring the Sam Maguire trophy across the Shannon. How radically the scene has changed in Gaelic football in the past twelve years (1987 to 1999) can best perhaps be judged from two facts — that Kerry's name has been etched on the Sam Maguire Cup only once (in 1997) in that period, and similarly that the name of Dublin (Kerry's main rival in the 1970s) has also only once (in 1995) been added in the same period to the same trophy. Contrariwise, in that same twelve-year period one of three Ulster counties — Down twice and Derry and Donegal once each (with Tyrone losing to Dublin in 1995 by a single point) — has brought the Sam Maguire Cup northwards four times, while Meath (which had made a striking come-back at the end of the '80s) has won the trophy no fewer than three times. (To successes in the championship by Ulster teams must be added Derry's two recent wins in the national league, in 1995 and 1996.) Almost as remarkable as the apparent decline of Kerry and Dublin and the unmistakable rise of Ulster football has been the continued eclipse of Connacht football. Admittedly counties from the west have reached the final five times in the 1980s and 1990s — Roscommon in 1980, Galway in 1983 and 1998 and Mayo in 1989 and 1996; but Galway's popular win in 1998 has been the only time in over thirty years that a Connacht team has brought the Sam Maguire Cup to the west.

In the 1980s a striking feature of All-Ireland football finals was the dominance of Munster and Leinster, with Cork or Kerry winning six times and Meath, Offaly or Dublin winning the other four times. No Ulster county won the Sam Maguire Cup in that decade; Tyrone was the only county from that province to reach the final (in 1986) in the whole of the '80s. As for Connacht, two counties — Roscommon in 1980 and Galway in 1983 — did contest two finals of the '80s, but like Tyrone they failed at this last hurdle. How vastly different is the picture by 1999, as the Millennium approaches and the GAA enters its third century. Looking at the list of football champions for the 1990s, Leinster and Munster counties have so far in the present decade had only two more Sam Maguire victories — by Dublin in 1995 and Meath in 1996, and by Cork in 1990 and Kerry in 1997 — to bring their total in the twenty years since 1980s to eight for Munster and six for Leinster. In that same twenty-year period, however, Ulster counties (Down in 1991 and 1994, Donegal in 1992 and Derry in 1993) took the Sam Maguire Cup in four consecutive years. With Galway's victory in 1998, this means that Ulster and Connacht teams between them have won half the finals so far contested in the 1990s. Moreover, Galway's sole win in 1998 did not mean that the province failed to contest any other finals in the twenty years since 1980. Mayo reached the final three times — in 1989, 1996 and 1997 — and lost once (1996) by only one point (on a replay against Meath), and back in 1980 Roscommon lost narrowly to Kerry in the western county's first final since its defeat (by Kerry too) eighteen years earlier in 1962.

Mention of Meath's victory in 1996 serves to recall this county's formidable performance in the last twenty years. Before 1949 it had never won a senior football championship, and had indeed only twice contested a final, in 1895 and 1939. On the former occasion it had lost by a single point to Tipperary in a controversial game, and on the latter occasion by only two points to a legendary Kerry team that took the Sam Maguire Cup in 1938, 1939, 1940 and 1941. Before the twenty-year period now under review (1980—1999) Meath had contested six more finals but had won only twice — 1954 and 1967. Since 1980 it has contested five more finals; of these it won three ('87, '88 and '96) and lost two (in 1990 and 1991). Meath's performance in other football competitions in the early 1990s has also been impressive. The county took the national football leagues of 1990 and 1994, recorded two minor all Ireland wins (in 1990 and 1992) and one junior All Ireland win (in 1993). It also reached the junior finals of 1990, 1996 and 1997 and the minor final of 1993. Meath was also involved in the only two draws and replays of senior football finals since 1980. In 1988 it drew (twelve points all) with Cork, going on to win the replay by a solitary point. Much the same thing happened to Meath eight years later, but against different opponents. In 1996 it drew (twelve points all again) with Mayo, and (as in 1988) the Leinster champions won the replay by one point.

No overview of Gaelic football in the past two decades would be complete without an account of the famous Dublin-Meath saga of 1991. Rivalry between the two counties had become intense, Meath having been in three recent All-Ireland finals — 1987, 1988 and 1990. On 2 June 1991 it lined out once more against Dublin in Croke Park before 51,000 people. So well matched were the two teams and so close the marking that good football was out of the question. Meath had a poor first half and got a dubious penalty, leaving Dublin ahead by five points at the interval. However, towards the end of the seventy minutes Meath rallied, levelling the scores with ten minutes left and scoring ten points to Dublin's five in the second half to draw at 1–12 all. It is safe to say that not one of the 51,000 present anticipated how long it would take to find a winner. A week later before a crowd of 60,000 what proved to be only the first of three replays ended at 1–11 all after extra time. Again close marking prevented good football and resulted in ninety frees in 100 minutes. This time Meath led by double scores at half-time; yet the seventy-minute game ended at ten points all. In the second period of extra time each side scored 1–1, the first period having produced no scores.

A fortnight now elapsed before the third game, which had to be played on a Saturday because of an overcrowded fixture list. By now the attendance had swelled to All-Ireland final proportions — 63,000 — and at last some good open football was seen, despite both the continued tension and some erratic refereeing. Once again, with Dublin failing to score after the break, the seventy minutes ended at ten points all, and once again even extra time failed to produce a winner, the score being seventeen points all. Finally after another two weeks' preparation the third replay before 61,000 spectators on 8 July gave victory to Meath — Meath 2–10, Dublin 0–15 — a margin of a solitary point. In fact this difference was widely seen as a fair result; Dublin had dominated for sixty-five minutes, but sent a penalty wide and failed to stop a late Meath rally. Three figures give some idea of this epic series — the gross score of Meath 6–44 (sixty-two points), Dublin 3–52 (sixty-one points); the total 'gate' of £1,055,000; and the total attendance of almost 240,000!

One way to get the flavour of the last twenty years, especially the 1990s, in Gaelic football is to try to chart the fortunes of some counties which had been to the fore back in the 1970s. Kerry, which with Dublin (and to a lesser extent Galway) had been such a force in the '70s, continued in that position for much of the '80s, contesting six All-Ireland finals from 1980 to 1986, losing only one (to Offaly) in 1982. That 1982 final goes into Gaelic football records as the one in which Offaly deprived Kerry of what would have been a record-breaking five consecutive senior football titles. Yet almost incredibly, bearing in mind how (with Dublin and Meath) Offaly had for some years been actual or potential Leinster champions, this was the last final Offaly's footballers contested. Dublin also faded in the 1980s, reaching the finals of 1984 and 1985 but losing both to Kerry. But after 1986 Kerry too slumped, and it was to be eleven long years before it next got to a final, beating Mayo in 1997 by three points although failing to score a goal. Dublin too continued to remain mostly out of the finals of the 1990s, losing to Donegal in that county's first and only final in 1992 and losing again, if narrowly, to Down in 1994. Cork, which with Meath had seemed destined for a run of successes towards the end of the 1980s, has figured only twice in the 1990s — beating Meath in 1990 but losing to Derry in that county's first and only victorious appearance in a final in 1993. Nevertheless Cork's record in the present decade suggests an imposing reservoir of football talent — minor titles in 1991 and 1993, junior and All-Ireland club titles also in 1993, under-21 and club titles in 1994, together with an appearance in the 1992 junior final, as well as reaching the national league final in 1996.

In every decade of the past half-century or so a county with little or no record of having won even provincial titles suddenly rises to the top in Gaelic football. In the 1930s it was Laois, in the 1940s Roscommon and so on. Three counties performed this feat in football championships of the past twenty years — Clare in 1992, Leitrim in 1994 and Kildare in 1998. The Munster county had been close to success before 1992, but that year it won the provincial title for the first time in seventy-five years by defeating Kerry. Facing Dublin in the semi-final it was only three points down at the interval and cut this to one in the last quarter before Dublin went further ahead to win by five points (3–14 to 2–12) before an attendance of 58,000. Two years later Leitrim defeated Mayo (twelve points to ten) to take the Connacht title for the first time in sixty-seven years. Like Clare it was unlucky to be drawn against Dublin in the semi-final, going down by double scores (3–15 to 1–9) to a Dublin side that failed to break Ulster's three-year grip on the Sam Maguire Cup, Down winning by two points. Finally after several 'near misses' Kildare in 1998 won in Leinster for the first time since 1956, and although losing the final to Galway by four points seems destined to stay at or near the top in Leinster for some time yet. Three other counties which seem capable of major success in the years ahead are Louth, Offaly and Tipperary; only time (and doubtless competent management) will tell.

Three topics closely connected with the games themselves deserve at least brief mention, although it is arguable that in what purports to be principally a survey of the GAA itself none of the three is within the remit of this mainly historical record. Refereeing generally will, however, be dealt with in the final chapter since it falls under administration, but it is suggested here that most regular followers of senior football over the past twenty years would argue that the standard of refereeing in 1999 is no higher than it was in 1989. The other two topics — the standard of play and the extent of foul play — are probably so closely inter-connected that they can best be dealt with together. It is widely accepted that the standard of Gaelic football has improved considerably in the past two decades. This, if true, is surely the result of three factors — greater fitness, rule changes and more competent (indeed often professional) management. That the extent of foul play seems not to have increased greatly in the '80s and '90s in spite of the keener competition produced by greater fitness is probably a tribute more to the players than to better refereeing. Indeed, the average regular spectator or television viewer in recent years would probably be hard put to recall a second major 'scene' in addition to that at the Meath-Mayo final of 1996, and might justifiably point to the failure of the referee of the epic Dublin-Meath series of four games in 1991 (himself regarded by both sides as no model of consistency) to find only one offence that warranted a sending-off.

No account of Gaelic football in the past twenty years can be regarded as complete without including also a code of football played on a semi-professional basis at the other end of the world. The past quarter-century has seen intermittent and often inconclusive contacts between the GAA and the governing bodies of Australian rules football gradually develop into a formal if spasmodic relationship that sponsored three series of international games in the 1980s between Ireland and Australia, as well as a fourth in 1998, with yet a fifth due to be played as this book goes to press in 1999. This new dimension to Gaelic football had its origin back in November 1967, when a Meath team visited Australia. Between then and July 1983 Meath, Kerry and a Dublin colleges side toured Australia, while Australian sides (including two schoolboy teams) paid four return visits to this country — in 1967, 1968, 1981 and 1984. In 1982 the GAA congress at Killarney decided to move towards an international series and in 1983 new 'compromise rules' combining features of both codes were agreed, and a visit to Australia by the GAA's president and its Director General prepared for a first series of international games to be played in Ireland in 1984 just as the GAA's centenary year was drawing to a close.

Displaying a degree of aggression that left a bad impression on GAA spectators, the visitors won the opening game in Cork, but in the second game before a crowd of over 40,000 in Croke Park on a cold October afternoon Ireland had a narrow win. Two more series followed — in 1986 in Australia and in 1987 in Ireland. In 1986 the Irish side won two of the three games (in Melbourne and Adelaide), having lost the opening game in Perth. The 1987 series — three games again, all played at Croke Park — was won by Australia, winners of the second and third games after Ireland had won the first. A fourth series due for 1988 failed to materialise through lack of sponsorship in Australia. In 1991, however, a party of Australian schoolboys toured Ireland, winning all five games (under compromise rules) played. There had been suggestions that, although the Australian Football League (AFL) were keen to continue the novel experiment for another period, the television authorities here decided that television coverage was not worthwhile, presumably for commercial reasons. The GAA Director General in his annual report to the 1994 congress, while clearly implying that the GAA was committed to a new series under agreed rules, pointed out that the disruption which would be caused by the major building work at Croke Park made a visit by an Australian side unlikely that year. In the event it was to be ten whole years before in 1998 Croke Park patrons saw another senior Australian side in action. In two fine exhibitions under more refined compromise rules played in Croke Park in October 1998 Ireland won the series decisively, and most football supporters now look forward eagerly to the next international series in late 1999, an Irish under-seventeen team having played a three-game series in Australia in the spring of 1999.

That the new international element introduced by the Australian experiment has given an extra incentive to Irish youth to play Gaelic football cannot be denied, and it was observed that some comments by the visiting side in 1998 showed that the idea of playing for one's country (as is possible in other codes) motivated at least some of the visiting footballers. Initially the series when introduced in Ireland led to some doubts about the merits of the compromise game, due partly at least to the robust style of play engaged in by the Australians. Yet gradually it came to be realised that Australian rules, or rather some elements of it included in the compromise version, could improve aspects of Gaelic football, and experimental rules put into operation as early as the GAA's National Football League of 1989 have in the view of many opened up the game. However, it also seems probable that concern and even opposition regarding permanent links with Australian rules persisted to varying degrees into the 1990s; and it remains to be seen if the revivals of 1998 and 1999 will dissipate this feeling. Certainly the public reaction to the two games of 1998 was very positive.

In hurling the past two decades have brought a new look to the national game. This has taken the shape in the 1980s of two counties (Galway and Offaly) both in effect new to senior titles. In the 1990s it has produced a surge in popularity for the game which almost certainly is linked to the new format of the final stages of the senior and minor championships. To attempt an overview of the '80s first, this decade was dominated by Galway. This Connacht contender for the McCarthy Cup — in effect the only real contender in the province — contested six of the ten finals of the '80s and won three of them, more than any other county in the whole decade. This compares with Galway's solitary senior hurling title back in 1923, its only success before 1980 in the 96-year-old history of the GAA. The fact that the three losers to Galway in 1980, 1987 and 1988 were respectively Limerick, Kilkenny and Tipperary, all from the traditional heartland of the game, made their achievement more impressive.

Nor did Galway's hurling successes in the 1980s end with its three senior titles. In 1980 the county also won the Railway Cup, the All-Ireland club championship (Ballygar) and the Fitzgibbon Cup (UCG). In 1983 it won both the All-Ireland minor hurling title and the under-21 title. In 1987 and 1989 Galway won its fourth and fifth National Hurling League titles. These were remarkable achievements inside ten years for a county with no real opposition in Connacht, taking account of the fact that in the ninety-six years before 1980 it had clocked up only ten hurling successes — one junior All-Ireland title (1939), six Railway Cup successes and three national league wins (1931–1932, 1950–1951 and 1974–1975).

Close behind Galway in terms of hurling achievements in the 1980s came Offaly, which won two out of three finals it contested (in 1981 and 1985), but failed to maintain that same winning form against Cork in the centenary final of 1984. Like Galway, Offaly's hurling successes in the '80s extended beyond the senior grade. Near the end of the decade it won three All-Ireland minor titles in 1986, 1987 and 1989, defeating in turn three Munster counties — Cork, Tipperary and Clare. In some respects, in view of its population and the extent to which senior hurling is played in the county, Offaly's achievement in the 1980s is even greater than Galway's. For one thing, it is principally a football county and has won the highest honours in that code. Secondly, hurling is confined to a small area in south-west Offaly (almost surrounded by the neighbouring hurling county of Tipperary), so that Offaly's actual senior playing 'pool' is disproportionately small. Before 1980 Offaly had not won a Leinster senior hurling title in ninety-six years; before 1986 it had not won a Leinster minor hurling title for almost sixty years. Since 1887 (the year All-Ireland championships were inaugurated) Offaly had only two All-Ireland hurling titles to its credit in hurling — in 1923 and 1929, neither of them in the senior grade. As the 1990s were to prove conclusively, Offaly's rise in the 1980s added another county to the short list of serious contenders for the senior hurling title — the first time this has happened since the rise of Wexford in the 1950s, a revival which has also been maintained, as Wexford's success in 1996 shows.

The traditional hurling counties that had figured in so many All-Ireland finals before the rise in the 1980s of Galway and Offaly were not, however, wholly out of the running in the '80s either. Between them Cork (with wins in 1984 and 1986), Kilkenny (with wins in 1982 and 1983) and Tipperary (winners in 1989) contested all but one of the ten finals in the decade and won five of the ten. Limerick on the other hand contested only one final in the 1980s and was unlucky to meet a resurgent Galway in 1980, which had twice got to the final (and lost) in the previous five years. However, Limerick did reach four league finals in the '80s, winning two in 1983–1984 and 1984–1985. The remaining Munster hurling county, Waterford, had not figured in a final since narrowly losing to Kilkenny in 1963.

Looking at results of the nine hurling finals so far played (with that for 1999 undecided as this book goes to press), one is left with one striking impression which is confirmed by the historic pairing of Kilkenny and Offaly in the 1998 final. Munster is no longer the dominant province in terms of the senior hurling championship. With only one final left to be played in this decade, Leinster counties (Kilkenny and Offaly with two titles each; one for Wexford) have won five compared to Munster's four. No doubt Munster supporters can point to the influence on this statistic of Wexford's surprise return to the top in 1994. But equally Leinster supporters can counter by pointing out that but for Clare's historic wins in 1995 and 1997 after some eighty years the tally might well be only three for Munster. Keen students of form in senior hurling would go even further and point to the totals for each of the two provinces in the 1980s. Munster (through Cork in 1984 and 1986 and Tipperary in 1989) took the McCarthy Cup only three times out of ten, with Leinster (Kilkenny and Offaly each twice) and Connacht (Galway) being victorious in the other seven finals.

The senior hurling championships of the 1990s have been remarkable — indeed historic — for two other reasons. Firstly, for the first time in the history of the competition (now in its 102nd year) the final has twice (in 1997 and 1998) been contested by two counties from the same province — Clare versus Tipperary in 1997 and Kilkenny versus Offaly in 1998. As regular followers know, this is the result of the new format introduced in 1997, which allows the losers in both Munster and Leinster finals to return to participate in new quarter-finals. Consequently the finals of both years were contested by counties (Tipperary in 1997 and Offaly in 1998) which had already been beaten at provincial level by their ultimate opponents in the All-Ireland final, and while Tipperary lost in 1997 as it had done in the Munster final Offaly in 1998 won the national title despite having lost in its provincial final. The '90s were notable also for the 'near misses' of Limerick, which twice reached the final, only to lose unexpectedly on both occasions — to Offaly by no fewer than six points in the 1994 final (when with fifteen minutes to go Limerick seemed to be certain winners), and in 1996 to Wexford (Leinster champions again after nineteen years in the wilderness) by only two points.

The emergence of new champions in the 1990s (Clare after eighty-one years and Wexford after nearly thirty years), coupled with the absence from the winners' list of Cork since 1990, the undoubted decline of Tipperary in the past quarter-century and Limerick's failures (or sheer bad luck?) in three finals, have all naturally prompted discussion about the reasons for such dramatic changes in the hurling world. Many supporters of Munster hurling refuse to accept what the statistics seem patently to prove — that the standard in Leinster is now inherently superior to that in Munster. Similarly, hurling followers in recent years have not failed to notice that one widely expected result of the new quarter-final system, the appearance in more finals of Galway or Antrim (or both) has not so far materialised. Contrary to expectations, Galway has not won a title since 1988 and has not so far benefited from the new format, while Antrim's record has been similarly disappointing for hurling fans in Ulster. What is equally undeniable, however, is that between them these three factors — the new format, the increased number of games associated with it and the live televising of more major hurling games — have all resulted in a surge of popularity of the national game, producing not only an enormous armchair following but bigger crowds and higher 'gates' capable of being ploughed back into the development of hurling.

That hurling has experienced new levels of popularity in recent years and that the new format of both the senior and minor championships has produced new levels of thrilling play and exciting games are evident to all followers of the game. Yet behind all this apparent achievement by the GAA lies a paradox equally evident. The several revivals of hurling in the past half century or so have all failed, though the current president of the GAA is on record as claiming that it was the work of the 1960s' Coisde Iomána that triggered Galway's revival in the '80s. Today, 115 years after the founder of the GAA Michael Cusack declared the revival of the national game as one of the twin aims of the new Association, only ten of the thirty-two counties have any hope of winning the senior championship. Moreover, when to these ten — Cork, Tipperary, Clare, Limerick and Waterford (in Munster), Kilkenny, Wexford, Laois and Offaly (in Leinster),together with Galway — is added Dublin (which has not captured the McCarthy Cup for over sixty years), it will be seen that these eleven counties between them have monopolised the senior hurling championship since the competition was inaugurated 112 years ago. In short, Cusack's dream has not been realised and, as things stand at the end of 1999, is unlikely to be realised in the next 100 years.

'So what', the keen hurling follower may well ask? So long as the dozen or so counties (if one includes Antrim) that dominate the senior championship continue to serve up hurling of the kind seen in the mid and late 1990s, is not the national game in safe hands for the foreseeable future? Sadly, for those who cherish hurling and see it as part of our national culture, the answer to this question is 'No'. Before trying to substantiate that negative reply, one might well point out that, of the twelve hurling counties referred to above, one (Antrim) has only twice (in 1943 and 1989) reached the final (losing heavily on both occasions), that a second (Laois) has also only twice (in 1914 and 1949) reached the final (losing heavily once), that one of the Munster counties (Waterford) has appeared in only five finals in over 100 years (losing thrice) and that even Clare, prior to the 1995 and 1997 victories, had only made it to two finals — in 1914 and 1932. By comparison, no fewer than twenty-four of the thirty-two counties have contested All-Ireland senior football finals since 1887.

In an authoritative and comprehensive history of hurling written by a prominent Tipperary officer of the GAA, published in 1996 and revised in 1998, a final chapter entitled 'The Future of Hurling' assessed the prospects of the game in the years ahead. Using as his principal sources both a lifetime of experience in hurling and interviews with some leading officers, Séamus J. King also drew on a report of the GAA's own Hurling Revival Sub-Committee completed in November 1993 and discussed at the Association's annual congress in 1994. This sub-committee was chaired by the veteran Tipperary county secretary Tomás Baróid and included two other members from the hurling counties of Galway and Kilkenny. Appended to this sub-committee's report was a thirteen-page Appendix of statistics comprising a summary of (often inadequate) replies to a questionnaire sent to all of the thirty-two county boards, replies which reveal a state of affairs in many counties that might jolt many interested in the future of our national game.

The sub-committee made three principal findings — that in recent years (that is, before November 1993) there had been a noticeable fall in standards even in stronger counties, that few counties had shown any improvement in recent years, and that the weaker counties had major problems ensuring that the game stayed alive in those counties. A total of sixteen recommendations were made. These included the formation of a working group (with defined functions) to promote hurling, increased financial aid to weaker counties and the appointment of more coaches. There is no indication that evidence was taken from any witnesses (such as hurling officers in weaker counties), and in direct conflict with King (who in his book argued the case for a separate organisation parallel to the GAA) promotion of hurling was passed back by the sub-committee to the county boards — including, one assumes, those which had not even bothered to reply to the questionnaire. Moreover, although much emphasis was put on the expense of hurling 'gear' (mainly hurleys and helmets), it transpired that much of the financial aid available to hurling from the GAA had not been taken up. The summarised information contained in the Appendix revealed that hurling had no place in many schools or colleges; yet only one recommendation dealt with this vital aspect of the decline in hurling.

King, writing two years or so after the report, for his part painted an even gloomier picture. Insisting that 'a degree of pessimism surrounds the future of hurling', he concluded after discussion with several named experts on the game that the overall state of the game was being eroded, the skill factor (previously taught to boys of primary school age) was disappearing and the numbers playing falling. Fewer boys were taking up the game even at school because they had not indulged in the age-old habit of 'pucking about' at home, a favourite pastime of earlier generations. Far too many also, King insisted, 'dabble', that is, play several games but never acquire skills in any, often to the detriment of hurling. King also listed many of the obstacles hurling has to surmount today — the fall in the number of male primary teachers (especially Christian Brothers), the tendency for boys to drop hurling in favour of study or of soccer (the Charlton factor!), and the perceived dangers attached to hurling. He suggested that consideration be given to making the game semi-professional, and concentrating on the strong counties only — facing up to the fact that the spread of hurling in most of the ten C grade counties (listed in the report and all situated in the northern half of the island) was a waste of time and resources.

The summary of replies received to the questionnaire sent out by the Hurling Revival Sub-Committee also makes depressing reading for lovers of hurling. No fewer than seven of the thirty-two counties, including Dublin and three of the other principal centres of hurling, did not furnish any reply. One of the main hurling counties was unable to state how many under-21 clubs it had. Of the twenty-four counties which did reply, no fewer than nine supplied information which was in-complete. Several professed not to know how many schools were in their county. At least eleven of the weaker counties, most of them in Ulster, admitted to having no full-time hurling coach. One of these forecast the extinction of hurling in two years (that is, by 1995) if coaching was not introduced; another stated that its hurling board 'operated on a shoestring'. Another county admitted that 'Hurling has no profile in the county'; several indicated that 'dual players' (playing both football and hurling) presented major problems, implying that it was hurling that lost out in such a case. One western county with seventy primary schools stated that not one of them played hurling, and in another western county only 104 out of 290 primary schools played hurling.

The report of the Hurling Revival Sub-Committee was discussed at the 1994 congress, and speedy action was taken to deal with the problems it had highlighted. A high-powered Hurling Development Committee was set up which concluded that the most urgent action required was to raise the public profile of hurling. This led to the proposal by the new Committee for the new format for the minor and senior championships — the so-called 'Back-Door System', as an Antrim delegate to the 1996 congress called it. This new format, under which the defeated finalists in Leinster and Munster would return to participate in a quarter-final, was in operation experimentally for the 1997 and 1998 seasons and was widely regarded as being so successful that it was extended by a big majority at a special congress held in Wexford in the autumn of 1998. A change in the format, to run the quarter-finals on an open draw basis, thus not seeding the beaten Munster and Leinster final-ists, was agreed with a view to improving the chances of Galway and the Ulster champions. It remains to be seen, however, if the new profile of hurling will in due course lead to an improvement in the game's basic skills, which the 1993 report found to be so badly needed. Delegates to the Wexford congress were reminded by a prominent member of the Hurling Development Committee that the new format had two aims — first, to improve hurling standards in every county, and secondly to raise the profile of the game. That the second aim has been achieved cannot be doubted; but only time will tell if the first can also be achieved.

Chapter 10

1980–1999: Administration

For the GAA the most important event of the 1980s was the centenary in 1984 of the Association's foundation. To a body then (and still) largely run on an amateur basis, the unique celebration of its foundation 100 years earlier presented a formidable challenge. It required considerable advance planning, time and effort by those on the many new committees set up at all levels of the GAA. It also involved the co-operation of many outside the Association not normally involved in its activities, including officials in Government departments and semi-State bodies, as well as members of the business community.

The GAA rose magnificently in 1984 to the occasion of its own hundredth birthday. Sound long-term planning paid off when 1984 arrived; as early as 1979 a small *ad hoc* group was in existence to prepare for events not due to occur for another five years. Then in the spring of 1980 a twenty-person Centenary Committee was set up, to decide how to commemorate the centenary, to organise events at national and local level and to co-ordinate the many celebratory events planned at local levels of the Association. Over the following three years this committee carried out the groundwork necessary to make the centenary events a success. The details of the main celebrations were worked out, and guidelines were drawn up and issued on how the centenary should be marked at provincial, county and club level. The importance of the centenary was recognised by the Government in the form of a special grant of £100,000 — doubtless a small sum compared to the £20 millions received from National Lottery funds in 1998, but a welcome contribution so far as the GAA of 1984 was concerned.

Off the playing-field probably the most important centenary events were an elaborate national five-day exhibition held in the RDS headquarters at Ballsbridge, Dublin; a novel GAA Youth Congress (with nine associated workshops) held in Athlone; an historical symposium in University College, Cork, involving prominent academics; and the making of a special film by the noted producer Louis Marcus in association with RTE and the Department of Education, which depicted the place of Gaelic games in Irish life over the previous 100 years. In addition, a special Club

Day was held at many venues in July, and during a Welcome Home Week in mid-August units of the GAA from Britain, the U.S. and Australia took part.

The centenary became the occasion for many clubs to publish their own histories, a process that continued long after 1984 because many of the earliest clubs still flourishing were founded in the decade or so after 1884. In addition GAA Head Office produced a high-quality brochure outlining the centenary of service which the GAA had given to the community. Many clubs marked the centenary by purchasing outright their own grounds, by further development of grounds (including the provision of new facilities), and in some cases by opening new playing pitches. In addition, the imaginative and enterprising nature of many centenary events introduced GAA units at local levels to the benefits of commercial sponsorship.

The GAA Centenary Year was notable on the playing-fields for three main events. The All-Ireland hurling championship attracted most popular appeal, and culminated in a decisive win for Cork (in its third successive final) at Semple Stadium in Thurles, its defeated opponents being Offaly. This event was widely accepted as having been a triumph of administrative planning and co-operation between GAA Headquarters and the Tipperary county board. Secondly, the Ford motor company donated new trophies for special centenary competitions in both codes. Since these were played on an open draw basis, both supporters and critics of the conventional knock-out system got an opportunity to see the alternative type of competition actually in operation. Cork added the Ford Centenary Trophy to its All-Ireland win; in the football competition final Meath defeated Monaghan. Finally, the game of handball received a spectacular boost in 1984 with the revival, at a cost to the GAA of nearly £30,000, of the World Handball Championships, in which six countries competed.

That the celebrations of the GAA centenary extended far beyond the Association itself was seen as proof of the recognition of the GAA as a national body and of its importance in community life, especially since the establishment of an independent Irish State in 1922. The Taoiseach hosted a reception in Dublin Castle for the centenary; both the Turf Club and the Law Society hosted dinners in honour of the GAA. The National University conferred an honorary degree on the GAA's president; An Post issued two special postage stamps; RTE produced a special two-hour documentary film. The President, Dr Patrick Hillery, who fortuitously was a native of Clare like Michael Cusack, attended both the opening and closing ceremonies (held in Ennis and Croke Park respectively), as well as the historical symposium in University College, Cork.

When this unique year in GAA history was over, the Association had good reason for self-congratulation. It had ensured that, because there was no undue emphasis on the past, in the sense that it was the present and the future that were emphasised, any note of triumphalism was kept to a minimum. Indeed, most of the major policy decisions made in the years since the centenary have demonstrated that, rather than dwell on the past, the GAA has its sights firmly set on the future. In hindsight, it has become clear since 1984 that the centenary celebrations gave a new impetus to particular aspects of the Association's activities. For example, the increased club activity which began in Centenary Year has continued since then, so that the role and importance of the club has expanded greatly in the fifteen years since 1984. Yet, as the Director General remarked in his annual report to the 1994 Congress, the average club is far removed from the central council in the command chain, and his suggestion then for some sort of general club gathering every three years appears to have been overlooked since then.

Sponsorship begun in Centenary Year has not only continued but expanded enormously in the following decade-and-a-half, to the considerable advantage of the GAA, its sponsors and the community generally. The lead begun by clubs in exploiting the benefits of sponsorship in 1984 has since been followed at all levels in the GAA, and the Congress of 1991 approved the use on players' jerseys of logos and sponsors' brand names. As a result, a welcome new feature of the Association's revenue in the years since Centenary Year has been the increasing proportion of income derived from non-gate sources, such as advertising, television and other sales rights, not the least of the latter being the sale of corporate boxes in the new Cusack Stand.

Some years before 1984 and the events commemorating the GAA's centenary a major achievement of the Association in the early 1980s was the building of its new offices and headquarters, the Ceannáras block, at Croke Park. This modern three-storeyed block, which cost over £1.5 millions — a substantial expenditure at the time, if small compared to that incurred on recent building development at the stadium — was opened in 1982. Named after the GAA's co-founder Maurice Davin, it contains an assembly hall on the ground floor and offices for GAA staff on the first floor. By renting the top floor (to the Eastern Health Board) the running costs of the building are reduced. As early as 1983 over £920,000 (over sixty per cent of the cost) had been raised by the GAA, and of this total almost £250,000 had come from sponsors. Much of the credit for the funding of the new building must go to the former Director General, Seán Ó Síocháin, who had retired in 1979 and who died as recently as 1996 — the same year that saw the death of the famous radio and television commentator on Gaelic games, Mícheál O'Hehir. Similarly, most of the credit for the current Croke Park redevelopment must go to the Director General of the GAA, Liam Ó Maolmhichíl, for the vision and foresight he has displayed during his twenty years in office.

The extent to which commercial interests were prepared to come forward with financial sponsorship convinced the GAA in the 1980s of the need to exploit this new source of funding for its activities. Within a few years a number of leading Irish and multi-national firms were sponsoring some of the Association's annual and monthly events, and advertising hoardings had become common features at all major GAA grounds. Early opposition within the Association to both the principle and extent of sponsorship was overcome, but a special Work Group and the central council kept both the concept and operation of sponsorship under constant review. A central council decision of early 1986 not to accept advertisements or sponsorship from alcoholic drinks firms was later reversed by congress, and long before the end of the twenty-year period reviewed by this chapter the GAA's football and hurling champion-ships were being sponsored by Bank of Ireland and Guinness, with Church and General Assurance and AIB Bank respectively sponsoring the national leagues and the club championships. Other well known sponsors are Eircell (All Stars), Coca Cola (Féile na nGael and Féile Peil na nÓg), Irish Nationwide Building Society (jubilee awards), O'Neill's (playing gear), the National Lottery (promotion), First Active (International Services) and Aer Lingus (New Cusack Stand customer services).

Detailed guidelines on sponsorship were drawn up by the Work Group and approved by the central council, and then circulated to all units of the Association. These laid down the conditions under which sponsorship was acceptable, and a control system was then put in place. While understandably giving preference to Irish industry, the GAA has been prepared to avail itself of any assistance offered by commercial interests in order to promote the Association's activities. Fears expressed in the 1970s by opponents of sponsorship about the danger of firms intruding into the running of the Association have proved to be groundless. The GAA has also jealously guarded the amateur status of its players and as recently as November 1997 held a special delegate congress devoted to this topic.

Of considerable concern to many GAA followers of Gaelic football in the past two decades has been the state of the game itself. Several times in the early '80s this concern was reflected by the Director General in his annual reports to congress, which have come to be recognised as admirable 'state of the Union' messages from the chief executive of the Association to all units represented at congress, the ultimate decision-makers in the GAA. Among the topics to which these reports drew attention in the '80s were falling standards of play, frequent rule changes, an increase in rough play and a consequent drop in spectator interest. The Director General argued persistently for the need to have proper experiments at both inter-county and club levels before any rules were changed at national level for the major competitions, and by the same token experimental rules were in fact tried out in several national leagues in the '90s. The handpass as a tactic, so difficult to counter, was the subject of controversy and rule changes in the 1980s. Among the changes were a decision in 1980 for the retention of the handpass, its abolition as a means of scoring in 1981, then its return in a modified form in experimental rules tried out for six months in 1989–1990, and experimentally again in a restricted form in the leagues of 1995–1996.

Equally controversial for players, referees and rule-makers alike has been the tackle in football. The cynic has long since concluded that a situation has been reached (or, perhaps, was until recent rule changes) which makes it impossible for a player in possession to be dispossessed of the ball without his opponent committing some sort of foul. That this problem persists is clear from the Director-General's annual report as recently as 1997. On the other hand, it must be admitted that the new rule permitting a free kick other than a penalty to be taken from the hand or off the ground at the player's option has speeded up the game, though referees are understandably quick to ensure that a 'too speedy' hand-kick does not put the penalised team at a disadvantage. For opponents of excessive use of the handpass it has to be said that Galway's success in the 1998 All Ireland final, when the old-style direct kick appeared to get better results than Kildare's over-use of the handpass, may be seen as a defeat for the latter tactic. Associated with the state of football, of course, is the standard of refereeing, and while regular followers continue to find glaring cases of inconsistency by such officials the GAA for its part has in recent years worked hard internally on recruitment, training and monitoring of referees but is frustrated by endless television or video inquests when faults are easy to spot when it is too late.

By far the most important event in GAA history in the 1990s was the multi-million pound redevelopment of Croke Park, which will not be completed until several years after the publication of this book. While other sports bodies — and even Governments — have been content to dream of new 'green-field' sites outside Dublin, the GAA near the end of the 1980s boldly opted to remain on its 'down-town' site (only ten minutes' walk from the city centre) and to add to the existing facilities where it has had its headquarters and main stadium for the past eighty-five years. Now after only some seven years' work the result of Phase 1 of what is correctly called the Croke Park Redevelopment Programme is there for spectators, players and officials to see — a magnificent ultra-modern new Cusack Stand, visible on the city sky-line for miles around and replacing the old double-deck stand of 1937, which itself was years ahead of its time when first opened. Meanwhile, while rival organisations talk but do little else, the GAA continues to add to spectator capacity by tackling the so far uncovered portions of the stadium with the assistance of massive State funding procured on the strength of its impressive record of achievement in the 1990s. Moreover, the whole development plan for Croke Park makes an important statement about the pride, confidence and future ambitions of the Association by projecting a new image of the GAA as a modern and progressive sports body. It has also led to the other major sports organisations, in particular those catering for rugby and soccer, to consider their options regarding accommodation for spectators at major games.

With a Government grant of £5 millions obtained from National Lottery funds in 1993, work began that winter (after one whole year 'lost' in the planning process) on Phase 1 of a building programme then costed at approximately £40 millions. This envisaged not only the replacement of the existing Cusack Stand but also the provision of seating accommodation along the whole east side of the stadium other than Hill 16. To fund this development it was planned to sell some £20 millions worth of tickets to the business sector and to offer to clubs some £4 millions in term tickets. To achieve such ambitious targets an officer of the Bank of Ireland, Dermot Power, was seconded to the Croke Park staff to concentrate solely on getting mostly private sector (but also some semi-State) firms to buy forty-five self-contained boxes, giving them exclusive rights to occupy, at every game played in the stadium for ten years, these specially built private corporate boxes. A separate floor-level in the new stand would be set aside for such boxes, allowing firms to engage in their own private hospitality and in the entertainment of their own customers or clients in a restaurant exclusive to this level. The term tickets for clubs would, in addition, go far to meet the old grievance that on occasions of major matches ordinary members found themselves having to take second place to official GAA guests — many of whom were rarely seen at Croke Park for the rest of the season!

By the time the 1995 congress was held in April of that year the Director General was able to report considerable progress with the financial side of the Cusack Stand scheme. Some £15 millions worth of ticket packages had been sold and the central council had from its own resources from 1989 to 1994 made grants totalling £4 millions, with another £2 millions to be made in 1995. As a result the Association had so far been able to avoid having to resort to bank borrowing. By now £23 millions had been spent and it was estimated that further expenditure would total £20 millions. A year later the 1996 congress learned that Phase 1 — the erection of the new stand — had been completed for £35 millions without any borrowings, and that clubs had so far purchased 4,000 term tickets. Spectators who had been familiar with the old stand found that in an ingenious (if expensive) property swop the small Jesuit sports ground at the rere of the old stand had been acquired to provide an expanded entrance and forecourt to the new stand, enabling players and team officials to be driven right up to the entrance of the new stand. Allowance was also made for the laying down of a modern athletic track, and even (some twenty years down the line) the addition of a roof to cover the entire stadium.

Work on Phase 2, the development of the canal end of the stadium, commenced in 1996, and the 1997 congress was told that (sales to the corporate sector and to clubs having apparently reached saturation point) bank borrowing would be required for this work. However, when completed it would add another 21,000 seats, bringing the gross spectator capacity to 75,000. Looking further ahead to the Phase 3 period (which would involve major redevelopment of the Hogan Stand area), it was calculated that, if in the course of that work the seats in the Nally Stand (at the railway end alongside the Hogan Stand) were removed, the stadium capacity would increase to almost 80,000. In the meantime Phase 2 was estimated to cost a further £38 millions, and even allowing for borrowing it was obvious that more Government aid would by then be critical. However, by the completion of the entire project around 2002, a point would be reached when the original corporate boxes would come 'on stream' again, thus generating substantial fresh income to help defray the remaining costs.

Then in 1998 in the State's budgetary arrangements a new and substantial grant of £20 millions to the GAA was announced. For the Association's financial planners this came as an answer to their prayers, enabling them to push ahead with the remainder of Phase 2 (the canal end) in the knowledge that they could now plan Phase 3 assured of at least some funding for it. Predictably, the size of the 1998 grant drew widespread criticism; but in his annual report to the 1998 congress the Director General was able to point to some important factors ignored by the Association's critics. The grant would come, he pointed out, not from the taxpayer but from the National Lottery (as did the £5 million grant of 1994), one of the purposes of which was the assistance of sports projects. By the time all the Croke Park plans had been completed early in the next century the national exchequer (through VAT and PAYE/PRSI) will have benefited to the tune of almost £30 millions. Moreover, for most of this century the GAA has been a major player in the economic life of Dublin, and through overseas television exposure of its principal fixtures it is also a major contributor to the tourist industry. As for the frequent claim about the under-use of the stadium (since it is confined to Gaelic games), normally made in support of arguments that it be made available for other codes, the Director General pointed out that in 1997 alone no fewer than seventy-five games were played at Croke Park, including fourteen matches which had each drawn a crowd of 40,000.

With the completion in the next few years of Phase 3 (the Hogan Stand side), the GAA will have on its urban site, adjacent to all the facilities of the capital city, a modern state-of-the-art stadium years ahead of the rival sports bodies. Not only that, but since mid-1998 the GAA in this new stadium has had its own museum (at a cost of £3.5 millions), jointly designed by a world-renowned Australian designer and an Irish firm, where GAA followers of all ages may now enjoy a panoramic overview of Gaelic games in the past century displayed on two floors with the aid of the most modern museum techniques. Even before its formal opening school parties numbering several thousand had visited the new GAA Museum all through the summer of 1998. Some further distance down the road too lies a GAA Library, to cater for the increasing number of researchers at home and from overseas delving into the past of this unique sports body.

Linked to the failure of any other Irish sports body to build its own major stadium in the greater Dublin area is the recently aired question of a national stadium, to be shared by several associations and dependent to a large extent for its erection and maintenance on massive State funding. Such a major project, so far largely unthought out, would, it seems, benefit only the soccer and rugby bodies, posing the question as to what role their existing stadia at Dalymount Park and Lansdowne Road would play. In the present state of support for athletics, and given recently published plans for Santry Stadium, it seems unlikely that such a national stadium would be of much benefit to athletics, and given the GAA's ongoing need to generate income from Croke Park the possibility of staging major Gaelic games in a new national stadium seems remote. Above all, should the currently booming national economy begin to feel the draught of any incipient world recession, it can be assumed that plans for a national stadium would be put on hold — proving the wisdom of the GAA's decision to expand its present facilities on its existing site.

Along with the state of hurling (discussed in the previous chapter), another problem facing the GAA in recent years has been the state of the Association in the greater Dublin area. While both football and hurling are thriving in the city and adjoining areas, it is clear that in terms of the number of clubs the GAA is far too thinly spread over this vast area where one-third of the State's population resides. In addition, perhaps because of the pull of Croke Park on many Sundays, attendances at club games in both codes in Dublin are poor except on occasions like county finals. Furthermore, from an administrative viewpoint running the GAA in Dublin must be a nightmare for one county board, with the result that the board has been heavily in debt for many years — not far off the £1.5 millions mark, it is widely believed. At least twice in recent years the Director General has pointedly drawn attention to the recent division of Dublin county into three new administrative areas, but the Dublin board has not so far taken his hint to split up its operations similarly into four units, including one for the city.

The past quarter-century has seen many changes on the club scene in Dublin, with old clubs becoming extinct, others merging out of sheer necessity and still more (but not enough of these) being formed in newly built areas. However, there still remain thickly populated areas on the outskirts of the sprawling capital with a high proportion of school-going children which have no GAA club at all to cater for them. A century ago every village on the outskirts of a then much smaller city had its Gaelic football club; today a much bigger city has swallowed up all the villages — and the football clubs of Victorian and Edwardian Dublin that flourished in them have simply disappeared as private residential areas became centres of business. Not only that, but many of the residents of the new estates come from other counties (many in Leinster) with a strong Gaelic football tradition; yet the game has not moved with them, largely because of the lack of local clubs. To the average GAA follower from outside Dublin, who sees Dublin as a prominent football county and even twice recently reaching the Leinster hurling final, this situation is something of a mystery. It is worth remembering too that over the past quarter-century Dublin, once its footballers get beyond the Leinster final in the football championship (and even before that often), has drawn above-average attendances. It was, after all, a Dublin-Galway final that attracted 87,000 spectators as long ago as 1963, only 4,000 lower than the record 91,000 for a Down-Offaly final. The controversial 1983 final (again Dublin-Galway) was watched by over 72,000, and four other finals of the 1970s that Dublin contested had attendances of well over 70,000 each.

That this Dublin crisis is not one that can be tackled (let alone solved) by the Dublin board on its own is recognised by the GAA. As far back as the 1980s, before the satellite town of Tallaght grew to the proportion of Limerick city, a three-year development plan under a regional committee appointed a field officer charged with promoting Gaelic games and increasing the number of clubs. In the 1990s GAA Headquarters, the central council and the Leinster council have all given valuable support to the Dublin county board, with more coaches, full-time development officers and substantial grants (including £25,000 annually for three years from the provincial council), as well as a new coaching scheme from 1994 involving twenty new coaches. Much of the county board's problem at present stems from the priority that has to be given to fund-raising after the recent redevelopment of its own headquarters and main stadium at Parnell Park, at a cost of some £1.3 millions. As a result, urgent problems such as the state of hurling in second-level schools and the number of new areas with no clubs appear to be receiving less attention. Radical revision (through sub-division) of the structure of the county board and its subsidiary boards would seem to be urgently called for if Dublin is to become a unit of the GAA with the influence that its population justifies.

The centenary celebrations, the public reaction to the new international dimensions of Gaelic football and, above all, the astonishing success of the GAA in attracting support from the corporate sector for the ambitious and costly Croke Park development, all suggest that the Association is held in high esteem by the community. As it did in its first century, it has shown itself still capable of adapting to changes in Irish society. Yet some of the reaction to the recent £20 million Lottery grant might serve as a warning that the GAA cannot take Irish society for granted. In addition, the recent professionalisation of rugby is bound to put increased pressure on the amateur status of GAA players, who are already pushing for better treatment both for themselves and their coaches. Above all, the GAA must continue to earn the support and esteem of the community as a whole — not merely that major segment of it fully committed to Gaelic games.

SOURCES

General Note
The principal sources for each chapter are listed below. For the earlier chapters footnotes in the text refer either to important facts or to facts otherwise regarded as warranting footnotes. For the later chapters footnotes are almost entirely dispensed with, either because the facts are traceable from the principal sources or because the facts are easily obtainable from daily newspapers. However, a small number of facts and impressions recorded in the text will not be found in either principal sources or footnotes, because they have been obtained orally on a confidential basis from older members or supporters of the GAA, some now dead. Two random examples are Richard Blake's agnostic views (p. 65) and Dan McCarthy's close connections with the Sinn Féin leaders (p. 118).

Principal Sources
Chapter 1
Irish Sportsman, 1872–1886.

Chapter 2
Sport, 1886–1888.
Irish Sportsman, 1885.
United Ireland, 1885–1886.
Freeman's Journal, 1887.

Chapter 3
Sport, 1886–1899.
Freeman's Journal, 1891.
R. T. Blake: *How the GAA Was Grabbed* (1900).
T. F. O'Sullivan: *Story of the GAA* (Dublin, 1916).

Chapter 4
Central council minutes, 1898–1909.
Sport, 1897–1899; 1901; 1905–1910.
Freeman's Journal, 1899–1904.
Gaelic Athletic Annual, 1907–1908.

Chapter 5

Central council minutes, 1909–1921.

Sport, 1906–1921.

Gaelic Athlete, 1912–1914.

National Volunteer, 1914–1915.

Weekly Freeman's Journal, 1918–1921.

P. O'Neill: *Twenty Years of the GAA* (Kilkenny, undated).

B. Mac Giolla Choille (ed.): *Intelligence Notes 1913–1916* (Dublin, 1966).

Royal Commission on the Rebellion in Ireland (London, 1916).

Capuchin Annual, 1968: Art. by O. Snoddy.

J. Gleeson: *Bloody Sunday* (London, 1963).

Dáil Ministry & Cabinet minutes, Vol. 3.

Finance (New Duties) Act, 1916.

Chapter 6

Central council & congress minutes, 1922–1934.

Dáil Debates: Vol. 1, col. 2209; Vol. 19, cols. 2491–2494; Vol. 42, cols. 1412 & 1421; Vol. 43, cols. 153–395.

Finance Acts, 1925, 1927 & 1932.

S. Ó Ceallaigh: *Gaelic Athletic Memories* (Dublin, 1945).

Aonach Tailteann, 1924 Souvenir & Handbook.

An Camán, 1931–1934.

Cork Examiner, 1931.

Cork Weekly Examiner, 1934.

Éire: The Irish Nation, 1924.

Gaelic Athlete, 1925.

Irish Independent & Irish Press GAA Golden Jubilee Supplements, 1934.

Irish Weekly Independent, 1922–1934.

Sport, 1922–1931.

Sports Mail, 1931.

Chapter 7

Central council minutes, 1935–1949.

Annual Reports of Gen. Secretary, 1935–1950.

Report of Congress Hurling Commission, 1940.

Irish Weekly Independent, 1935–1941.

Cork Weekly Examiner, 1940–1949.

Irish Press, 1935 & 1939.

Irish Independent, 4.1.1943.

Irish Press, 26.4.1943.

Irish Times, 15.4.1941.

Kerryman, 2.3.1935.

An Ráitheachán, 1936–1937.

Tommy Doyle: *A Lifetime in Hurling* (London, 1955).

J. Carroll: *Ireland in the War Years* (London, 1975).

J. Hanly (Josephus Anelius): *National Action* (Dublin, 1942).

Chapter 8

Central council & congress minutes, 1950–1980.

Annual reports of General Secretary/Director-General, 1950–1980.

Annual financial statements to congress, 1950–1980.

Commission on GAA (report), 1971.

Our Games annuals, 1958–1978.

Gaelic Weekly, 1961–1965.

Capuchin Annual, 1960.

Chapters 9 and 10

Director-General's annual reports.

Miscellaneous

Information obtained on request from:

Richard V. Comerford (Maynooth), Liam Creavin (Meath), Fr K. Egan, PP (Portumna), Pat Fanning (Waterford), Paddy Kenny (Carrick-on-Suir), Mrs Dan McCarthy (Dublin), Eamonn Mongey (Dublin), Paddy Mulvaney (Mayo), Séamus Ryan (Tipperary), Seán O Conaill (Dublin), and Seán Ó Síocháin (Director-General, GAA, 1964–1979).

REFERENCES

CE: *Cork Examiner*
FJ: *Freeman's Journal*
Gal. A & H Soc.: *Galway Archaeological & Historical Society (Journal)*
II: *Irish Independent*
IS: *Irish Sportsman*
IT: *Irish Times*
Kerry A. & H. Soc.: *Kerry Archaeological & Historical Society (Journal)*
Louth Arch. Journal: *Louth Archaeological Journal*
Mins.: Minutes of central council (GAA)
NLI: National Library of Ireland
O'Sullivan: T. F. O'Sullivan: *Story of the GAA* (Dublin, 1916).
PRO: Public Record Office, London
RIA: Royal Irish Academy
RSAI: Royal Society of Antiquaries in Ireland
SPO: State Paper Office, Dublin

Introduction (pp. 1–4)

1. *Encyclopaedia Britannica* (1966 ed.) Vol. 3, p. 19: Vol. II, p. 569.
2. M. Marples: *A History of Football* (London, 1954), p. 21; *IS*, 2.1.1886.
3. A. O Maolfabhail: *Camán: Two Thousand Years of Hurling in Ireland* (Dundalk, 1973), p. 128.
4. *IS*, 1.4.1882; Béaloideas, Vol. 32 (1964), p. 127; T. Crofton Croker: *Fairy Legends of the South of Ireland* (London, 1825), p. 129.
5. P. W. Joyce: *Social History of Ancient Ireland* (Dublin, 1913), Vol. II, p. 474.
6. J. Dunn: *The Táin Bó Cuailgne* (London, 1914), pp. 46–55; E. O'Curry: *Manners & Customs of the Ancient Irish* (Dublin, 1873), Vol. II, p. 359.
7. Tracts Relating to Ireland (Dublin, 1843), Vol. II, No. 3, p. 23.
8. Register of Primate Swayne (Belfast, 1935), p. 12.
9. Historical Manuscripts Commission, Report 10, Appendix 5 (1885), p. 402.
10. Annual Register 1798, pp. 103–111.

11. Dublin University Magazine, Vol. 57, pp. 593–604; RSAI Journal, Vol. 39, pp. 70–74.
12. O Maolfabhail, pp. viii, ix, 101.
13. Irish Statutes Revised Edition (London, 1885), p. 319.
14. Lady Sidney Morgan's Memoirs, Vol. I, pp. 41–42.
15. Camán, 24.3.1932; R. Devereux: Carrigmenan.
16. Gormanston Papers, NLI; Camán, 5.11.1932.
17. Pue's Occurrences, 14. 8. 1756.
18. J. J. Healy, Papers, NLI; Arthur Young: Tour in Ireland (London, 1892).
19. Kilkenny Archaeological Society Transactions, Vol. II (1852–1853), p. 332.
20. P. O Maidín in CE, 30.9.1971; Young; Cork Evening Post, 4.9.1969; Camán, 29.7.1933.
21. Young.
22. Béaloideas, Vol. XIII (1943), pp. 252–253.
23. RIA Proceedings, Second Series, Vol. 2, p. 154.
24. Camán, 5.11.1932.
25. Galway A. & H. Soc. Journal, Vol. XXV, pp. 1–14.
26. Hely Dutton: Statistical Survey of Clare (Dublin, 1808), pp. 301–302; J. Boyle O'Reilly: Athletics & Manly Sports (Boston, 1880); W. S. Mason: Statistical Account of Ireland (Dublin, 1816), Vol. I, pp. 124, 157; Vol. II, p. 160; Vol. III, p. 207.
27. For examples: Studia Hibernica, Vol. 5 (1965), p. 7–29; T. De Bhaldraithe (ed.): Cinn Lae Amhlaoibhe (Dublin, 1970), pp. 10, 87, 117; T. Crofton Croker: Popular Songs of Ireland (London, 1839), p. 154; IS, 11.1.1879; Shamrock, 10.3.1883; W. N. Baptist: Short Tour Through Midland Counties of Ireland (London, 1837), pp. 140–141; Béaloideas, Vol. XI (1941), p. 136; T. Brett: Life of Dr. Patrick Duggan (Dublin, 1921), p. 7; Irish University Review, Vol. 2., No. 1, p. 66; Mr. & Mrs. Hall: Ireland, Its Scenery, Character, etc. (London, 1841), Vol. I, pp. 256–257; see also note 5 & J. J. Healy Papers, NLI.
28. Marples, p. 25; Young Ireland, 2.1.1875; Midland Tribune, 23.4.1960.
29. E. MacLysaght: Irish Life in the Seventeenth Century (Shannon, 1969), p. 354.
30. Gaelic Journal, Vol. X, pp. 549–552.
31. M. Concannon: Poems (Dublin, 1722), pp. 70–90.
32. Gaelic Journal, Vol. X, pp. 521–523; Louth Arch. Journal 1914, pp. 219–221.
33. Faulkner's Dublin Journal, 1.7.1758 & 15.4.1766; Slator's Public Gazetter, 21.4.1759; Hibernian Journal, 20.4.1766.
34. Mason, Vol. II, p. 544; E. Lysaght: Poems (Dublin, 1811), pp. 90–91; Lord Cloncurry's Personal Recollections (Dublin, 1850), p. 149; Gaelic Athlete, 9.1.1915.
35. Lord Cloncurry: Personal Recollections (Dublin, 1850), p. 177.
36. State of the County Papers (NLI), 1031/66; H. Whitney (P. Kennedy): Legends of Mount Leinster (Dublin, 1855), pp. 5 & 96; Éigse, Vol. II, p. 85; L. Daiken: Children's Games (London, 1949), pp. 27–28.
37. Our Games Annual 1964, p. 77.
38. P. Bradley: While I Remember (Dublin, 1938), pp. 76, 85, 87; Cork Daily Herald, May & June 1876; Leo Maguire in The Bell, Feb. 1943.
39. Shamrock, 10.3.1883; Béaloideas, Vol. 32 (1964), pp. 137–139 (for E. Galway).
40. Irishman, 16.10.1858; Evening Mail, 5.10.1864; IS, 4.5.1878; see Dagg, Hockey in Ireland (Tralee, 1944), p. 36.

41. *Kerry A. & H. Soc. Journal* 1970, p. 139.
42. *Cork Daily Herald*, 1876 (May & June); *Camán*, 13.1.1934.
43. *Irishman*, 2.10.1858; *Irish People*, 15.10.1864; T. Crofton Croker: *Legend of the Lakes* (London, 1825), p. 25.
43. *Irishman*, 2.10.1858.

Chapter 1 1874–1884 (pp. 5–14)

1. T. F. O'Sullivan: *Story of the G.A.A.* (Dublin, 1916), p. 4; *Blackrock College Annual* 1954, p. 75.
2. *Irishman*, 3.10.1883.
3. P. Davin: *Recollections of a Veteran Irish Athlete* (Dublin, 1939), p. 7.
4. Davin, pp. 16–17.
5. *Blackrock College Annual* 1954, p. 75.
6. *Shan Van Vocht*, 2.8.1897.
7. *Irish Football Annual* 1880, p. 96.
8. *Irishman*, 23.8.1879.
9. *United Irishman*, 4.3.1899.
10. Ní Mhuiríosa, M.: *Réamhchonraitheoirí* (Dublin, 1968), p. 24.
11. *Shamrock*, 2.2.1884; *Shan Van Vocht*, Vol. 2, p. 147.
12. Lawrence's Handbook of Cricket in Ireland, 1870–1871, p. 233.
13. See 12; also Lawrence, 1877–1878, p. 186 & *IS*, 26.10.1878.
14. *FJ*, 1.1.1883.
15. *FJ*, 13.1.1883 & 7.2.1883.
16. *FJ*, 26.1.1883; Dagg: *Hockey in Ireland* (Tralee, 1944), p. 39.
17. *Shamrock*, March 1883.
18. *UI*, 22.5.1885.
19. *Fáinne an Lae*, 3.4.1898.
20. *IT*, 6.12.1883 & 10.12.1883.
21. *IT*, 15.4.1884; *Shamrock*, 19.4.1884 & 3.5.1884; *FJ*, 10.4.1884.
22. *Shamrock*, 24.5.1884; *UI*, 24.5.1884 & 28.6.1884.
23. T. Brett: *Life of Bishop Duggan* (Tuam, 1921), pp. 7, 13, 181.
24. Statements to writer by Mrs Patricia Kelly, Killarney & P. J. Finnegan, Loughrea (grandchildren of Sweeney); Rev. P. K. Egan PP.
25. *Shamrock*, 11.10.1884.
26. Davin, p. 43.
27. Davin, p. 40.
28. Davin, p. 100; *Sport*, 26.11.1887.
29. Davin, p. 54.
30. See *FJ*, 7.1.1905.
31. *Irishman* & *UI*, 18.10.1884.
32. *Republican File*, 28.11.1933.
33. *United Irishman*, 4.3.1899; *An Camán*, 11.2.1933; *FJ*, 7.1.1905.
34. *FJ*, 3.11.1885; *Shamrock*, 15.11.1884; *Nation*, 8.11.1884; *Irish Sportsman*, 8.11.1884.

35. See 25.
36. *CE*, 3.11.1884.

Chapter 2 1884–1888 (pp. 15–33)

1. 'A Story of Great Endeavour' (P. D. Mehigan, anonymously), GAA programme for opening of new Hogan Stand, 7.6.1959, p. 6.
2. O'Sullivan, p. 20.
3. Do., p. 19.
4. *An Camán*, 15.7.1933.
5. Do.
6. O'Sullivan, p. 21.
7. *Sport*, 26.1.1895.
8. *Tipperary GAA Yearbook* 1993, art. by S. Ó Riain, p. 25.
9. *I.I.*, 30.12.1959; 6.1.1960; 11.1.1960.
10. *United Irishman*, 4.3.1899.
11. *Fáinne an Lae*, 30.4.1898.
12. *Shan Van Vocht*, 7.2.1896; *IS*, 18.12.1886.
13. *UI*, 27.12.1884; *Nation*, do.
14. Do.
15. *Irish Freedom*, Feb. 1911.
16. *Sport*, 10.7.1886.
17. *Shamrock*, 22.3.1885.
18. *Sport*, 25.8.1888.
19. See 14 & *Shamrock*, 24.3.1883.
20. *Longman's Magazine*, Feb. 1883.
21. *The Labour World*, 27.9.1890 to 1.11.1890.
22. *CE*, 29.12.1884.
23. *CE*, 18.6.1885.
24. *FJ*, 3.5.1885.
25. *IS*, 18.12.1886.
26. *UI*, 27.6.1885.
27. *FJ*, 11.4.1885.
28. *FJ*, 3.5.1885.
29. *The Republican File*, 2.1.1932.
30. *An Camán*, 22.11.1933.
31. *FJ*, 5.1.1888.
32. Irish Independent GAA Golden Jubilee Supplement 1934, pp. vii–viii (article by J. Whelan).
33. See 31.
34. *Sport*, 5.7.1890.
35. See 31.

Chapter 3 1889–1897 (pp. 34–58)

1. *FJ*, 10.11.1887.
2. PRO, London, C.O. 904/16.
3. Do.
4. Do.
5. Do.
6. SPO, Special Crimes Branch, file 2562.
7. SPO, CS Branch, files 501/296 & 2964.
8. Do.
9. SPO, CS Branch, file 2582.
10. Do.
11. SPO, CS Branch, files 2701 & 2755.
12. PRO, London, C.O. 904/16.
13. *Shan Van Vocht*, 2.8.1897.
14. *United Irishman*, 4.3.1898.
15. SPO, CS branch, files 2562 & 30618.
16. SPO, CS branch files 2964, 2562, 4467.
17. M. Bourke: *John O'Leary* (Tralee, 1967), p. 200.
18. *FJ*, 31.10.1885; *UI* 11.10.1884.
19. UI, 24.1.1885 & 6.2.1886.
20. *FJ*, 30.10.1884.
21. *UI*, 7.11.1885 & 28.11.1885.
22. *CE*, 11.5.1896.
23. *FJ*, 14.7.1896.
24. *FJ*, 3.8.1896.
25. P. Devlin: *Our Native Games* (Dublin, 1934), p. 31.

Chapter 4 1898–1909 (pp. 59–81)

1. M. Bourke: *John O'Leary* (Tralee, 1967), p. 215 et seq.
2. See note 5.
3. *CE*, 15.1.1898 & 19.2.1989.
4. See note 1.
5. *The Leader*, 15.1.1949; *CE*, 14.3.1989.
6. Dublin Co. Board official brochure, Sept. 1934, p.13.
7. For O'Donnell, see *Sport*, 24.11.1906.
8. For Cork, see *CE*, 13.6.1898.
9. 27.2.1904; *Nationalist*, 1.1.1906.
10. *CE*, 11.9.1900.
11. For Walsh, see *Gaelic Athletic Memories*, ed. S. Ó Ceallaigh (Limerick, 1945), pp. 21–23.
12. *Camán*, 31.7.1931 & 6.1.1934; O'Sullivan, p. 158.
13. *Irish Year Book*, 1908, p. 23.
14. *CE*, 11.9.1900.

15. *CE*, 16.12.1901.
16. O'Sullivan, p. 169.
17. *A History of Ireland under the Union*, by P.S. O'Hegarty (London, 1952), p. 611.
18. *The Revival of Irish Literature*, by C.Gavan Duffy & others (London, 1894), p. 129.
19. *The Gaelic League Idea*, ed. S. O Tuama (Cork, 1972), p. 34.
20. *CE*, 25.1.1893.
21. *Irish Year Book*, 1908, p. 24.
22. O'Sullivan, p. 170; *CE*, 28.3.1910; *Catholic Bulletin* 1927, pp. 300 & 302.

Chapter 5 1909–1922 (pp. 82–120)
1. Official GAA programme, 7.6.1959, pp. 5–19.
2. *CE*, 19.3.1912.
3. *Sport*, 14.1.1905.
4. *FJ* 25.2.1899 & 2.3.1899.
5. S. Ó Ceallaigh: *Gaelic Athletic Memories* (Limerick, 1945) p. 68.
6. Ó Ceallaigh, p. 16.
7. *FJ* 2.1.1901; 12.12.1903; *Cork Sportsman*, 26.12.1908.
8. Ó Ceallaigh, p. 81.
9. W. Alison Phillips: *The Revolution in Ireland 1906–1923*, pp. 56–60; *Wicklow People* 21.1.1911.
10. *Ar Aghaidh*, March 1969.
11. *CE*, 5.4.1915.
12. *Hibernian Journal*, Dec. 1914, p. 62.
13. J. J. Walsh: *Recollection of a Rebel* (Tralee, 1944), p. 18.
14. Macardle: *The Irish Republic* (Dublin, 1951), p. 226.
15. Macardle, p. 235.
16. RTE Thomas Davis talk 28.11.1971; see *IT* 30.11.1971.
17. P.S. O'Hegarty: *Ireland Under the Union* (London, 1952) p. 613.

Chapter 6 1922–1934 (pp. 121–153)
1. *Clare Champion* 1923–1925.
2. *The Irish Yearbook* 1922, pp. 197–199.
3. *The Voice of Ireland* (Dublin, 1924), art. By P. de Burca, at p. 578.
4. *CE*, 17.4.1922.

Chapter 8 1950–1980 (pp. 183–214)
1. *The Shaping of Modern Ireland* (London, 1960), pp. 15–16.

BIBLIOGRAPHY

Note: Only general books, articles, etc., covering the history of the GAA are listed below. For county and club histories and publications on Gaelic games and teams local public libraries should be consulted.

1916 *Story of the GAA*, Thomas F. O'Sullivan (Dublin).
1931 *History of the GAA 1910–30*, Phil O'Neill (*Kilkenny Journal*).
1934 *Irish Press* GAA Golden Jubilee Supplement.
1934 *Irish Independent* GAA Golden Jubilee Supplement.
1969 *The Early GAA in South Ulster*, Marcus Bourke, in Clogher Record, Vol. VII, No. 1.
1976 *Croke of Cashel*, Mark Tierney (GAA and Gill & Macmillan).
1979 *Sport as Politics: The GAA 1884–1916*, in Sport in History, ed. Cashman & McKiernan (University of Queensland Press, Australia).
1977 *Story of the GAA*, Séamus Ó Ceallaigh (Limerick).
1977 *The IRB and the Beginnings of the GAA*, W. F. Mandle, in Irish Historical Studies, Vol. XX, No. 80.
1980 *The GAA: A History*, by M. de Búrca (GAA, Dublin).
1982 *Mícheál Cíosóg*, Liam P. Ó Caithnia (B.A.C.).
1984 *The Ulster GAA Story*, Con Short (Comhairle Uladh, CLG).
1984 *Gaelic Games in Leinster 1900–1984*, M. de Búrca (Leinster Council GAA, Portlaoise).
1984 *The Glory and the Anguish*, Pádraig O'Toole (published by author).
1984 *Céad Bliain ag Fás*, M. de Búrca (B.A.C.).
1986 *Munster's GAA Story*, Jim Cronin (Comhairle na Mumhan, CLG).
1987 *The GAA and Irish Nationalist Politics 1884–1924*, W. F. Mandle (Gill & Macmillan).
1989 *Michael Cusack and the GAA*, M. de Búrca (Anvil Books).
1991 *The Story of the GAA to 1990*, M. de Búrca (Wolfhound Press for Irish Life).
1994 *Maurice Davin: First President of the GAA*, Séamus Ó Riain (Geography Publications).

INDEX